Leading
A Spiritual Life

MAULANA WAHIDUDDIN KHAN

Goodword

First published 2016
This book is copyright free

Goodword Books
A-21, Sector 4, Noida-201301, India
Tel. +91-8588822672, +91120-4314871
email: info@goodwordbooks.com
www.goodwordbooks.com

Goodword Books, Chennai
Mob. +91-9790853944, 9600105558

Goodword Books, Hyderabad
Mob. +91-7032641415, 9448651644

Printed in India

Contents

Contents

Foreword

In front of my residence there is a tree covered in green leaves and beautiful flowers. It is a source of spiritual nourishment for me. For me, it is like a spiritual partner. When I sit under this tree, I suddenly feel that there is a silent conversation going on between the two of us. Many of the articles of the present book were compiled while I sat under this tree.

The greatest lesson I have learned from this tree is: try to live on your own. Be positive in every situation. Adopt the culture of giving rather than taking, and the whole world will serve as a catchment area for you. This book encourages the reader to live like a tree in this world. According to my experience, a tree is an illustration of spiritual life. It is a model for spiritual living.

The present book is a spiritual guide for every man and woman. I hope it will give the reader a vision, facilitate clearer thinking and establish the principles of personality development. I hope it will help him defuse his stress, de-condition his conditioning and enable him to rediscover the course he should take to lead a successful life.

Life is full of unwanted experiences. There is no one who is not destined to travel through a jungle of problems. It is the destiny of every man and woman. The question is: what is the formula to deal with this?

The only successful formula is: Don't take things as an evil. Take them as a challenge. If you take things as evil, you will simply develop a negative attitude, and a negative attitude will only increase your problems. But if you take untoward situations as a challenge, this attitude will unfold the hidden capacity of your mind. You will be able to face all challenges bravely and intelligently, and sooner or later, reach your destination.

Wahiduddin Khan, New Delhi, May 3, 2016
skhan@goodwordbooks.com

I

Spirituality in Daily Life

The Tree – A Silent Speaker

~❦~

Learn the art of conversion and the whole world will become a means of spiritual food for you.

Everyone likes a house surrounded by green trees. Verdant foliage beautifies our world. It is this idea that has brought farmhouses – houses in gardens – into being.

But it is difficult to find anyone who is able to listen to the silent message of the trees or who tries to adopt the culture of the tree in his own life. The culture of planting trees is widespread but adopting the culture of the tree is seldom in evidence. Trees beautify our homes but they do not beautify the person living in that house.

A tree lives in the same world as the one in which we live. But, there is a difference. People's lives are marred by tension, malice, hate and violence, whereas all these negative features are totally missing from the tree culture. Man is like a walking tree, but he fails to follow the culture of the tree in his own life. Trees share our world. But while, for man, this world has become a source of complaint, hate and stress, this same world has a different meaning for a tree. The beauty we see in the tree has come from this very world – it has not been imported by it from outer space. How was this possible for the tree? The reason is that the tree, by nature, has adopted the art of conversion: converting things to one's own advantage.

What does the tree do? It takes minerals and water from the soil and converts them into food for itself. The tree, through the process of photosynthesis, takes light energy from the sun and converts it into chemical energy, which is then used to fuel its activities.

This is the result of the art of conversion. In doing so, every tree gives a silent message to man: Learn the art of conversion and the whole world will become a means of spiritual food for you. Make the whole world a global source of your personality development. You will be able to live in this world as a complaint-free person.

For example, if someone says something that goes against what you think, then turn it into a point for discussion. If somebody speaks ill of you, then make that a source of self-discovery. If you are discriminated against, then draw the lesson from this instance that you need to develop in yourself that missing quality on the basis of which you have been discriminated against. If someone provokes you, you should defuse the issue through unilateral avoidance. If someone makes you angry, you should calm yourself down by forgiving him. If a person differs from your point of view, then enter into a discussion with him and thus increase your own intellectual development.

There is a story which tells us that once someone hit Ram with a stone. In return Ram embraced the person and in this way he made the throwing of a stone a means to inculcate in him a positive quality, that is, love for humanity.

This story teaches us a lesson on how to adopt the culture of the tree in one's own life. If you throw a stone at a tree, it will give you a fruit in return. This is the highest kind of positive behaviour. By adopting this positive behaviour, you can make the whole world turn in your favour, just as the tree does.

Everyone is free. This free culture has filled the world with differences. It is these differences that lead to negative thoughts about others. Then what is the art of living in such a situation? It is in some way or the other to convert every difference into something positive which will be in your favour.

Garden of Spirituality

Nature is not simply a wonderful world. It is rather an amazing garden of spirituality.

Just visit a place of natural beauty, a place where there are mountains, flowing rivers, tall, lush green trees, birds on the wing, small white clouds floating in the sky, the sun shining, and so on. In such a spot, you will feel like exclaiming: "How wonderful nature is!" But nature is not simply a wonderful world. It is rather an amazing garden of spirituality. Indeed, everything in nature gives you a taste of spirituality. For example, when you see a honeybee hovering over a flower, you suddenly realize that it has a lesson to impart, for every part of nature is like a flower for you. In each part resides the nectar of spirituality. Take out this spiritual nectar and you will be motivated to turn yourself into a spiritual personality.

It should be borne in mind that spirituality is not a state of ecstasy. Ecstasy is a trance-like state, a state of bliss or a semi-conscious condition. That is, it is like a kind of drowsiness which causes blurriness in the conscious mind. But spirituality is very different from this, being marked by a high level of acute intellectual development. It is a form of intellectual awakening, rather than a semi-somnolent state of mind.

During the pre-scientific age, the notion had become current that the heart was the source of spirituality. This was taken for granted and lead to spirituality becoming a subject for meditation, that is, heart-based spirituality. Since the heart was devoid of any thinking capacity, spirituality could not, therefore, become an advanced discipline. It was reduced rather to being an array of ill-defined assumptions.

Now that we live in the age of science, it is possible to place spirituality within the framework of a mind-based discipline. Being a science just like other sciences, spirituality should be associated not with meditation but rather with contemplation. Since the domain of the physical sciences encompasses the exploration of the quantitative aspects of nature, what is discovered therein is necessarily of a material nature. The domain of spiritual science, on the other hand, encompasses the contemplation of the qualitative aspects of nature, so that, within its scope, it is things of a spiritual nature which are brought to light, just as the honeybee extracts honey from flowers.

Flowers are the greatest concern of the honeybee. For a honeybee, its whole world is a world of flowers. It never wastes its time on other things. It concentrates on flowers, takes the nectar from them and returns to its hive. The same is true of an awakened mind. For an awakened mind, the whole world is a world of spirituality. It extracts the spiritual content from everything. The awakened person thus enhances his spirituality until he grows to be a spiritual giant.

Spiritual science, in developing the mind, enables one to analyze matters in an objective manner. In complex issues, it is an aid to the making of right judgements. It helps one to view things in such a way that one's mental confusion is dispelled and one can think with total clarity. If heart-based spirituality was no more than thoughtless ecstasy, mind-based spirituality has emerged as a fine-tuned form of high thinking.

Spiritual science has evolved in the same way as the science of the solar system. In the early centuries man had given credence to the geocentric theory. As a result, no development in this science was possible. In modern times, however, man's thinking altered sufficiently for the heliocentric theory to be formulated, as a result of which solar science became a developed discipline. The same change in thinking took place in the case of spiritual science. In the pre-scientific period, people believed in heart-based spirituality, so that there could be no furtherance of the imparting of spiritual discipline. The post-scientific age being an age of mind-based spirituality, endless scope for spiritual advancement has opened up.

Our world is like a garden of all good things, and spirituality enables the individual to live in and benefit from this garden.

Applied Spirituality

Spirituality, moreover, being an inner quality, has to be applied if its external actualization is to take place.

There was once a man who left his home and all his possessions – he even sold off his precious Ferrari – and went off into the jungle to live all alone in close proximity to the trees, the flowers and the animals. His purpose was to attain to spirituality in communion with nature. He may have reached his goal, but his spirituality was only a matter of personal solace and, as such, was limited in its reach. It was not 'applied' spirituality, that is, spirituality through which others gained from one's personal spiritual experience. Practically, there is a vast difference between the spiritual person who lives within society and shares his spiritual experience with his fellow men, and one who dies in solitude without ever having benefitted others.

Spirituality fosters the development of all kinds of constructive qualities and, in so doing, makes one a complete, person. An individual endowed with such qualities is one who is wanted and needed by his society and his nation. He will be wasting his spiritual treasure if he leaves his society and goes off to some jungle to live alone in peace and tranquillity. This is, of course, a manifestation of spirituality, but in a very narrow form, and living like a hermit means a serious under-utilization of the gifts of a spiritualized person. In fact, the spiritualized person is a most desirable individual when it comes to establishing a better society, a better society being nothing but a collection of better persons. And, it is true spirituality that turns one into a better person.

To create a civilized society and keep it running on course, we need professionally trained people at the helm of affairs. Without such trained people, it is impossible to have a properly structured society. There is a similar need of spiritual individuals, for spirituality makes one a better and more mature person in terms of character and honesty, duty consciousness and mental preparedness. As such the guidance the spiritual person can give is of a superior nature and he is, therefore, the best qualified to steer the engine of social existence along the right lines.

It is such spirituality that we have called 'applied' spirituality. In the basic sense, spirituality is a personal asset, but in its expanded sense, it has many applications.

And where spirituality is an individualized matter, applied spirituality is a universalized form of it.

It is not only others who benefit from applied spirituality. The spiritual person himself also benefits. When such a person devotes himself to sharing his spiritual training with others, he adds a whole new dimension to his own spirituality. Experience can be gained only within society. Moreover, experience adds wisdom to one's spirituality. Without wisdom, spirituality is incomplete. Spirituality plus wisdom gives rise to the emergence of a superior state of being. Spirituality with wisdom is everything: spirituality without wisdom is little better than an abstraction.

Spirituality, moreover, being an inner quality, has to be applied if its external actualization is to take place. Applied spirituality means living in society as a spiritual giver. Just as the cow is the giver of milk which is good for physical health, one who has the capacity to apply his spirituality is the giver of such assistance as will be good for intellectual health.

What is applied spirituality? If you discover the value of well-wishing, and decide to live as a well-wisher for all mankind, then you are one who engages in applied spirituality. Likewise, if you have a bad experience with your neighbours, but avoid treating this as a departure from normalcy and face those neighbours with a smile, then that too is an example of applied spirituality. Spirituality comprises a set of values. And, applied spirituality means practicing these values in conjunction with your fellow men in society.

Applied spirituality is ostensibly a matter of giving. But, every instance of giving is paralleled by an instance of receiving. That is a law of nature. According to this law, the giver is not simply a giver. The giver is also the receiver of many things – appreciation, good-will, better relations and peace – from those who are the objects of his generosity.

It Requires a Prepared Mind

People see the signs, but pass them by without detecting them. One who has a prepared mind, however, is able to recognize them and then turn them into objects of contemplation.

CV Raman (1888-1970), the renowned Indian scientist, once had it pointed out to him that scientific discoveries were accidental. Raman's response was: "Yes, but such accidents occur only when the mind is prepared." The fact is that all the opportunities for scientific discovery are already present in nature. People pass by them, but fail to recognize them. A scientist, having a prepared mind, instantly recognizes and develops any such matter as could be of scientific interest the moment he comes across it. This is how scientific discovery is arrived at.

The same is true of spirituality. Tokens of spirituality

are scattered all over the world. In fact, every part of nature, great or small, is invested with spiritual content. People see the signs, but pass them by without detecting them. One who has a prepared mind, however, is able to recognize them and then turn them into objects of contemplation. It is 'discovery plus contemplation' that adds up to spirituality.

Two friends, Moti Ram and Ram Ratan Kapila, the former a jeweller and the latter an AC engineer, were in the habit of taking morning walks together in a quiet part of New Delhi. Once, along the way, they found a glittering object. Ram Ratan Kapila picked it up and pronounced it to be a piece of glass. Moti Ram, on the other hand, immediately recognized it as a diamond. His friend, although a degree holder in the science of Air Conditioning, totally failed to recognize the object for what it was. Moti Ram, being a jeweller, only took a second to recognize it. This was because, on the subject of gemstones, he had a prepared mind.

This story illustrates the importance of mental preparedness. Anyone who wants to live as a spiritual person must train himself to this end. One who has neglected to prepare himself will never be able to draw spiritual nourishment from life's experiences. In the midst of spiritual abundance, he will continue to remain spiritually starved.

What is preparation? Preparation cannot be achieved by means of taking some external course. It is an exercise in self-training. Only those who are ready to engage in self-training can enjoy spirituality. Those who do not do so, can never develop themselves as spiritual persons.

There are many aspects of self-preparation, for instance, the capacity to discern which are the relevant and which are the irrelevant aspects of any given event, so that an appropriate course of action may be taken. An acute sense of what is significant and what is not is essential, for without it, man can never experience spirituality.

To train oneself spiritually, the most important thing a person must do is to condition himself to refrain from taking offence. The moment he allows himself to be offended, he closes the door to self-training.

The process of learning always takes place within society. In social relations, a person speaks from his mind, not from another's mind. Hence it is necessary that, as regards social relations, one should be 100 per cent objective. Where there is a lack of objectivity, there is the likelihood of offence being taken. And one who takes offence shows himself to be incapable of objective thinking.

There are always two options before you – subjective thinking or spirituality. If you are desirous of spirituality, you shall have to give up thinking subjectively. If you are not ready to forego subjective thinking, spirituality will forever remain beyond your grasp.

Spirituality cannot be acquired through physical exercise. Physical exercise is quite unrelated to spirituality, the latter being a state of mind. Only with the right state of mind can spirituality be cultivated, for spirituality is a way of thinking – a function of the mind. One who has the urge to live with spirituality must train his mind for this purpose, otherwise spirituality for him will remain a distant dream.

The Power of Spirituality

The power of positive behaviour can triumph over the power of negativity, while the power of negativity cannot win anything - it can only lead to destruction.

Some people have extraordinary inherent qualities, due to which they are able to become masters of all situations. Such individuals can, when they come to a gathering, win the hearts and minds of people simply by appearing there. There is a saying about such persons: They came, they saw, they conquered.

This kind of ability to conquer is not the monopoly of extraordinary people. Any ordinary person also can win the hearts and minds of people, provided he knows the law of nature and can avail of it by the power known as the power of spirituality. According to the creation plan of God, all human beings, both men and women, have two quite different qualities - the ego and the conscience. The ego symbolizes arrogance, while the conscience symbolizes modesty.

If there is a controversy between two men, Mr. A and Mr. B, and Mr. A enters into a heated exchange and refuses to give Mr. B due respect and honour. This kind of behaviour is bound to provoke Mr. B, who will try to teach Mr. A a lesson. It is this situation which one psychologist has analyzed thus: "When one's ego is touched, it turns into super ego and the result is breakdown."

In this case Mr. A gave a challenge to Mr. B and Mr. B turned into Mr. Ego or Mr. Arrogant. This kind of behaviour will certainly go against Mr. A. Mr. A will fail to gain the upper hand over Mr. B.

Then let us take the opposite case. Suppose there is a controversy between Mr. A and Mr. B., in the course of which Mr. A avoids provoking Mr. B, having followed the principle of modesty – a unilateral compromise. This kind of behaviour on the part of Mr. A is bound to touch the conscience of Mr. B. It will cause him to engage in introspection, and he will reconsider the whole matter. He will ultimately repent having behaved in such a way as was likely to cause friction. Where previously he had considered Mr. A as Mr. Rival, he will now discover Mr. A to be his friend.

This kind of behaviour by Mr. A will change the whole scenario: a different situation is bound to emerge. It will prove that: when one's conscience is touched, it turns into super conscience and the result is complete surrender. This second formula is within the reach of every human being, and can be used quite successfully by him, however unintelligent or ordinary he may be. When you use the formula of conscience you are turning your rival against himself and it is a fact that one can fight against others but no one has the power to fight against himself. Herein lies the conquering ability of a modest person.

One can say that the second formula is a risky formula. There is every possibility that this kind of behaviour will make the other person more arrogant. He will react more aggressively. He will be more dangerous than before. But this view is completely unfounded, because it is due to an ignorance of the power of nature, or more precisely, the power of spirituality. According to nature if you challenge someone's ego, your success is doubtful but when you challenge someone's conscience, then your success is guaranteed.

People generally know the power of fighting but a wise person will tell you that the power of conscience is greater than the power of ego. At the time of a controversy, if you choose to fight, you will need arms but when you opt for the spiritual method, you don't need any arms. The power of positive behaviour can triumph over the power of negativity, while the power of negativity cannot win anything – it can only lead to destruction.

The Meaning of Love of God

❧

Love of God is not simply a philosophical issue: it is rooted in the very nature of a human being.

Love means strong affection. Love is a natural phenomenon, an elevated kind of positive response towards someone you feel is loveable. Love cannot be created in a vacuum, it requires a strong base of affection.

Love of God is this same kind of strong affection. The basis of this love is quite natural when one discovers that one was created by God and that it was God who has given mankind all such bounties as the planet earth, the life-support system, oxygen, water and food. All these things were not created by man. They are precious gifts bestowed by someone else. When one discovers this fact, one naturally becomes a lover of God. Thus, love of God is the outcome of one's discovery.

Every sincere person reaches a stage in life when he faces some basic questions such as, how did I come into existence, how is it that I find myself in a world that is extremely favourable to me? One realizes that this compatibility between man and the rest of the universe is so unique that science has observed that the universe has been custom-made for man. Love is in fact an acknowledgment of this. When we endeavour to acknowledge our super-benefactor, we call it love of God.

Although love is an inner feeling, it comes naturally to human beings to give it an external expression. It is said that man is a social animal, so it is but natural that one's inner love should also find some expression in terms of social relationships. It is this social expression of one's inner feeling that is called peace. In terms of God, love is a psychological acknowledgment of the Creator, and in terms of society, love is manifested in peaceful living among other members of society.

It is not relevant to ask how, if we cannot see God, we can express our love towards Him. This contention may have been valid in the era before nuclear science, but after the emergence of nuclear science it is totally invalid. Nuclear science has successfully established that nothing is observable in this world. For example, everyone loves his mother, but in terms of modern science, no one is able to see his mother. One's mother, as well as other things, is nothing but a combination of numerous unobservable electrons. In fact, 'mother' is an unobservable inner being whom we see with reference to her external body. Similarly, God is an unobservable being of this kind whom we see through His creation. In such a world, it is irrational to say that one cannot love God because one cannot observe Him.

Love of God is not simply a philosophical issue: it is rooted in the very nature of a human being. The fact is that if you receive some good things from anyone, you cannot do other than acknowledge his generosity. In this sense, love of God is a natural phenomenon.

25

It is also a law of nature that if you add a pinch of dye to a glass of water, all of the water becomes coloured. This principle is also applicable in the case of love. When a person has love in his heart for his Creator, at the same time he cannot resist showing his love to his neighbours. And in this electronic age, the whole world is one's neighbour.

One can say that love has two dimensions: theoretical and practical. In terms of the theoretical dimension, love means love of God and in terms of the social, love means love for all human beings.

Divine Food

While physical food gives you physical health, spiritual food maintains the health of the non-physical part of your personality.

Jesus Christ once said: 'Man cannot live by bread alone.' (Matthew 4:4) What Jesus meant was that material provision does not suffice. All bread does is sustain us physically. Further to this, one needs divine provision, or spiritual food. Without receiving such food, the individual cannot develop his or her personality.

The fact is that, in this world, everything has two distinct sides to it: the material and the spiritual. From the material things which surround you, you must be able to extract the spiritual content and, to this end, you have to develop your mind to effectively do so. Only then will you be able to garner spiritual or divine food. If material food maintains your physical health, then the divine content of material things develops your personality along spiritual lines. While physical food gives you physical health, spiritual food maintains the health of the non-physical part of your personality.

For example, let us consider water, which is a combination of two gases—hydrogen and oxygen. Although it is made up of two material elements, when it enters the human body, it becomes assimilated in it, thus giving it vital assistance in maintaining its functions. When you discover this affinity between water and your body, you provide yourself with spiritual food for thought, leading to the realization and appreciation of God's wisdom, in that He created water – a combination of chemicals – in such a way that it is completely compatible with our bodies. Discoveries of this kind, made by observing the various material objects and events around you and then extracting the spiritual content from them, will give you unlimited solace and contentment.

Extracting the spiritual content from material things will give you the spiritual food to enable you to develop yourself as a spiritual person. If your earnest desire is to live your life as a spiritual person, you must learn the art of such extraction

Miracles of Memory

When you want to express an idea, your mind instantly sets in motion a complex intellectual machine. It recalls the desired idea, extracts it from the tangled maze of facts and events in your memory, selects the appropriate words, orders them according to the rules of grammar, then activates your tongue to speak or your fingers to write. In this way, numerous actions and interactions take place within the mind at an incredibly high speed. Almost all the senses contribute to this process.

The fact is that your mind is filled with countless ideas, but if you have to express even one of them in English, you must first select the appropriate words from the jungle of the quarter million words which make up the language, after which you must put things in the correct order with unbelievable speed, and only then are you are able to utter or write down a meaningful linguistic sequence. This process is unimaginably complex, with numerous known and unknown processes going on in your mind at lightning speed. It is the interaction of these factors which results in meaningful speech or writing.

How does this all this take place? Recent research shows that there is an incredibly complex system in our mind, which is dependent upon the memory – a super-miraculous phenomenon of nature. According to Neal Barnard, an adjunct associate professor of medicine at the George Washington University School of Medicine, in Washington, D.C., "A memory is made by linking two or more of the 100 billion nerve cells in your brain, called neurons, then solidifying the connection so that you can use it later." And "your brain continues to develop neurons and build new connections to strengthen memory as you age, a phenomenon called neuroplasticity," says Brianne Bettcher, a neuropsychology fellow at the University of California, San Francisco, Memory and Aging Center. (*Nine Ways to Improve Your Memory*, Fox News, December 18, 2013).

People talk of the great miracles of the past, like the staff of Moses, the ring of Solomon and so on. But, there is a miracle even greater than these which has been bestowed by God upon every single person. This is the miracle of the mind. If you recognize this as a personal miracle, you will develop such a thrilling sense of gratitude that all complaints and protests will seem ridiculous and, moreover, superfluous. You will then live with feelings of eternal thankfulness to God.

Just a Call Away

The Creator created man in such a way that
there is no distance between the two: both are
very near to each other.

I once went on a condolence visit to two young people, a sister and a brother, whose father had died, leaving them alone in their flat in New Delhi. Naturally, both of these young people were very sad. One of the visitors, who was a family friend, spoke some words of solace. He said: "Don't worry, I am just a call away." Suddenly, a thought came to my mind. God Almighty is also just a call away from every man and woman.

The Creator created man in such a way that there is no distance between the two: both are very near to each other. It is possible for man to contact God Almighty at any moment, from wherever he may be. This concept gives every man and woman unshakable confidence. It gives every man and woman a source of help in every situation.

If you have a mobile phone in your pocket when you leave home, you will confidently believe that you are not far away from your family. You can make instant contact with your family from anywhere in the world.

The same holds true for the relationship between man and God.

I am a great believer in God. I can recall many instances when I have found myself in a state of helplessness. Then I prayed and asked God for His help and, invariably, I realized that God Almighty was with me. He solved my problem, and turned around the situation in my favour.

This belief gives me conviction and determination. In my experience, everyone is in need of such a source of conviction. In our daily lives, we frequently face situations where we feel that, with our limited resources, we cannot cope with them. We need, therefore, to believe in a supernatural source of help.

This belief energizes our minds. It gives us new courage to continue with the task in hand. This belief plays a great role in our lives in that it adds immeasurable hope to our struggle. It makes us able to tap our hidden energy.

Life is full of disadvantages. Frequently, we face areas of existence with which we are totally unfamiliar. Dealing with them takes thought and planning and, at that time, we need some pointers to a future line of action. In such a situation, belief in God serves as a lighthouse. We are like the captain of an ocean-going vessel, who finds himself in a state of loneliness and isolation. Then he spots a lighthouse on the coastline. Its light gives him new hope, and he decides to follow the path it illuminates. The result is that he is successful in reaching his destination.

Indeed, life is like sailing across a great ocean. We

need to believe that there is someone on the coast who can give us help when we are at our most helpless. This is the role of God in the life of every man and woman. One's success is fifty per cent struggle and fifty per cent hope. It is a source of great hope for everyone that God is with us. There is no distance between man and God. He is just a call away from us.

I am 91 years old, and I can say that my life has been full of challenges, full of problems, and the only thing that has saved me from succumbing in any situation is my belief in God.

Spiritual Pursuit versus Material Pursuit

It is only spiritual achievement that can give you a sense of fulfilment. Material fulfilment is seldom achievable, but spiritual fulfilment is achievable to the ultimate extent.

Disquiet is a manifestation of discontent. How does this mental state come to prevail? The reason is that all individuals are born with an unlimited desire for enjoyment, without however, having any great capacity to fulfil this desire. It is this shortcoming in human nature that makes people live their lives in a state of mental agitation.

Is it a defect in human nature which is to blame for this? Not at all. It is simply people's unawareness of themselves that creates this problem. Awareness is the key to a contented life, while unawareness is responsible for all manner of discontent and restlessness.

To properly explain this phenomenon, we have to come to grips with the scheme of things devised by the Creator. According to the creation plan, the scope for material fulfilment in this world is very limited, while the scope for spiritual fulfilment or intellectual development is so vast that only the word 'unbounded' can describe its scope.

If your aim is to achieve a state of fulfilment in the material world, you will very soon discover that here the scope for this is very limited. Food, clothes, fame, married life, entertainment – all these things are all too often eventually marred by boredom. Even going on a holiday does not necessarily give you any sense of fulfilment. A person may go on holiday with high hopes of enjoyment, yet return with a feeling of "holiday stress". This sense of a lack of fulfilment pertains to your physical being, whereas your spiritual being is untrammelled by all such constraints.

Man has a dual personality—physical and spiritual. In physical terms, a person's body most often has its limitations in terms of height, girth, health, muscularity, athleticism, and so on. Due to these limitations, a person frequently becomes dissatisfied as far as his physical prowess is concerned. On the contrary, his spiritual or intellectual being has no limits to it. The realm in which the mind travels is vast and eternal, like the space stretching throughout the cosmos. The mind travels by thinking, and there are no boundaries to the thinking process. Traversing all kinds of frontiers, it continues unhindered on its journey.

Let us consider the activities of a businessman. These are confined to the material world. Due to the narrowness of his field of action, he is very likely to become a prey to boredom. The American business magnate Bill Gates once rightly said: "Once you get beyond a million dollars, I have to tell you, it's the same hamburger."

Scientific pursuit is an example of travelling in the intellectual domain. This is why scientists seldom suffer from the businessman's ennui. For example, Newton said about himself toward the end of his life: "I was like a boy playing on the seashore, and diverting myself now and then finding a smoother pebble or a prettier shell than ordinary, whilst the great ocean of truth lay all undiscovered before me." Such was the feeling of the great scientific thinker, Albert Einstein, when he said: "The more I learn, the more I realize how much I don't know."

Greater even than scientific pursuit is the spiritual quest. The reason for this is very clear. According to Galileo Galilee, the domain of scientific pursuit is the study of the quantitative aspect of nature, while spiritual pursuit is concerned with its qualitative side. And, it is a fact that the qualitative aspect of nature is immeasurably more vast than its quantitative dimension.

One who adopts the spiritual pursuit as a matter of

intellectual activity is a spiritual scientist. A physical scientist may stop in his research at a certain point, but for the spiritual scientist, even the saying 'The sky's the limit' becomes inadequate. It is only spiritual achievement that can give you a sense of fulfilment. Material fulfilment is seldom achievable, but spiritual fulfilment is achievable to the ultimate extent.

In Search of Meaning

The criterion of having found God is that once you have found Him, you should become completely at peace

In 1946, the Austrian neurologist and psychiatrist Viktor Emil Frankl (1905 - 1997) authored a book called *Man's Search for Meaning*, and over the years, many books with similar titles have been written. During the more than three hundred years of the printing press, billions of similar books have been published in different languages and if a common title were to be given to all these books, it would, without doubt, be: *In Search of Meaning*.

A human being, by nature, is a seeker after meaning. Everyone tries to find answers to his questions, for everyone is born with an enquiring mind. And, it is this quest which has resulted in the writing of so many books on the subject, in both fictional and non-fictional genres. All, directly or indirectly, have as their central theme the quest for truth.

When an individual reaches the age of maturity, his first concern is to earn his livelihood. He takes up various kinds of jobs or engages in different types of economic activity. And when he becomes engrossed in some venture, he has a period of satisfaction. Then, gradually, a time comes when he realizes that his job is not giving him what he had been looking for. Certainly, his work puts bread on the table but, as Jesus Christ once rightly said: 'Man cannot live by bread alone.' (Matthew 4:4) To earn one's bread is everyone's first need. But, 'bread' can satisfy only one's physical requirements; it fails to give one intellectual satisfaction. This is the main cause of frustration and despair experienced by almost everyone today.

According to the Big Bang theory, the universe came into existence about 13 billion years ago. Just being in possession of this fact causes everyone to think: 'Billions of years ago, I was a non-existent entity in this vast universe. Then, I was born and nature made me part of the population of the world.' Almost every person, consciously or unconsciously, yearns to know how and why he came into existence. There are few who have not frequently reflected on existence, trying to understand the meaning of their presence in this world.

When a person is born, he immediately finds himself in a world with a life support system which he personally did not struggle to create. He then realizes that nature potentially had an entire technology already hidden within it. This technology was one of mankind's later discoveries, which was developed and refined to the point of being able to create the civilization we see around us.

Then, man questions himself: Who is behind this living drama? What is the relationship between me and that superb artist? Furthermore, there is the question of death: Why does man die and what lies in the post-death period?

If you try to explain this phenomenon, you will find a single, overarching title for it, which in religious terms is expressed as 'God'. If we accept this term, we can say that, in fact, everyone is in search of God. It is God who gives meaning to all phenomena, and, after finding God, everything falls into place.

Once I was in a crowd where I saw a little boy running around anxiously because he had been separated from his mother. He was crying and continually asking: *"Meri mummy kahan hain?"* (Where is my mother?) When he found his mother, she took him in her arms. Instantly the boy stopped crying and became calm and content.

This incident illustrates the case of man. Everyone, knowingly or unknowingly, is in search of God. And when he finds Him, he becomes calm and content. But all too often, during this search, when he runs towards various things, he very soon realizes once they come within his reach that he has not found what he was searching for. This has been true of almost every human being throughout the entire history of mankind. It is essential to re-focus his endeavours after mature consideration.

Everyone's life has two parts. The first part is a comedy, but if the seeker cannot set himself upon the right course, that is, one which will lead him to God, the second part may turn out to be a tragedy. That is because 'God' is not something which one has to be told about from outside: it is a matter of self-discovery. God can only be discovered by the individual himself. It is only the self-discovered God that can give you conviction. If you want to make your life meaningful, you have to take up this question on a priority basis. It is only your own study and your own contemplation that can give you your God. The criterion of having found God is that once you have found Him, you should become completely at peace, like the little boy in the above incident.

Jesus Christ once said: 'Seek and you will find.' (Matthew 7:7) This is not so much a religious saying as it is a law of nature. But the ultimate success of the search has an important condition to it, and that is, sincerity. One who is truly sincere in his search will certainly reach his goal.

Living with an Underdeveloped Personality

In an All India Radio interview, broadcast on November 12, 2014, a well-known actor had this question put to him by the interviewer: "You are totally different on the sets from what you are in real life. How do you succeed in performing a role which is totally different from your actual personality?" The actor replied: "When we perform, we totally detach ourselves. We cast ourselves in the mould of the character we have to play."

Our age is one of professionalism. And when an individual enters his chosen profession, he has to perform his role therein under some 'director'. While doing so, he detaches himself from himself for the time being. And sometimes he is obliged to do so on more than one occasion. But, here, there is a problem. This state of affairs is not for life. A time comes when a person has to retire from his profession and after retirement, he is faced with a new situation. Where, in the pre-retirement period he assumed the role of one positive personality after another, now, in the post-retirement period, he must return to being his own self, a self which had remained in an underdeveloped state. Now he has to live with a personality which has never been fully rounded out and leaves much to be desired.

The post-retirement period is the most precious period of any person's life, because, that is the age of maturity. Yet, the difference between the two successive periods of his life results in a feeling of desolation. In the pre-retirement period, he was acclaimed as a super-performer. Now, in the post-retirement period, he is reduced to being almost a non-performer – a nonentity. This explains why, in the second phase of their lives, almost all the so-called successful individuals live in despair and die in despair.

What is the solution to this problem? Two options present themselves. The first is to enter a profession that will last for a lifetime, and in which the careerist can have job satisfaction. The second option is to start a new life immediately after retirement – a life of his own choosing. He should then spend his time on study and healthy activities, in the course of which he should do his utmost to realize his full potential.

The Importance of the Seeking Spirit

One who does not possess the seeking spirit, is spiritually blind: he is unable to see spiritual things, even if they exist all around him.

Discovery starts with seeking. If you are a seeker, you are bound to reach your goal. This is a law of nature and, as such, is immutable. It is impossible for anyone who is imbued with the questing spirit not to achieve his goal. Indeed, this is a divine law, which was expressed thus by Jesus Christ: 'Ask and you will receive, seek and you will find, knock and the door will be opened to you.' (Matthew 7:7) Conversely, it is impossible for anyone to make a discovery without being possessed of a questing spirit.

What is seeking? Seeking means activating your mind, your eyes, your ears. When a person activates these faculties, he develops in himself the quality of perceptiveness, so conditioning himself that whenever he finds what he wants, he immediately takes possession of it.

If a blind man is thirsty and a glass of water is placed in front of him, he will not drink from it. He is incapable of perceiving it. The same is true of unseen realities. One who does not possess the seeking spirit, is spiritually blind: he is unable to see spiritual things, even if they exist all around him. Therefore, before spiritual finding comes spiritual seeking. First of all you have to make yourself a spiritual seeker, only then will you be able to discover those spiritual things, which are always in evidence around you.

The seeking spirit must be underpinned by sincerity. What is sincerity? Sincerity is freedom from deceit, falsity and hypocrisy. It is a pre-condition for the success of the seeking spirit. If you have the desire to emerge as a spiritual finder, you must develop this quality of sincerity. Anyone who wants to make himself into a spiritual person, must first of all turn himself into a sincere person, for sincerity is the price to be paid for spirituality. In this world nothing can be attained without paying its price.

A human being is like the onion which has several layers to it. Just as the core of the onion can be reached only by removing these layers, so can man's personality be reached only by removing the multiple layers that bit by bit enshroud him when he lives in society. If you are in earnest about wanting to achieve spirituality, you have no option but to rediscover your core personality by divesting yourself of these layers. Once you have done so, you will find sincerity. And, where there is sincerity, there is spirituality. Sincerity and spirituality go hand in hand. Sincerity is like the seed and spirituality its fruit.

Spirituality is the feature in all human beings that is most to be desired. It makes life meaningful in that it spurs you on to lead a purposeful life. It enables you to live with normalcy of mind even in abnormal circumstances. It saves you from wasting your time and energy on frivolous pursuits, thus ensuring that you become a healthy member of society. Spirituality is so precious that one must be prepared to pay any price for it, no matter how high. It is a goal worthy of attainment. But this can be achieved only by making sincere efforts. No one can achieve spirituality automatically.

Every person is born twice. The first birth is the physical one, in which his parents are instrumental. The second is his spiritual birth, which a person attains by his own efforts.

Explaining the Universe in Rational Terms

Because of the total freedom enjoyed by humankind, there are inevitably many problems or challenges, and it is in meeting these challenges that we develop and advance.

It is said that the entire debate over belief and disbelief boils down to one question: Does logic prevail? Those who are of a disbelieving disposition say that if there were a God, why is it that we see contradictions everywhere in the world. When we observe the universe, we come to the conclusion that throughout the material cosmos, there is a grand design. Yet, in the human world, the picture is quite different. Here, we witness misery, sorrow, suffering and all kinds of evil. According to the sceptics, this contradiction between the two scenarios—the cosmos and the human world—shows that our world is a bundle of randomness. Although in a partial sense there seems to be design in the world, when we look at the picture in totality, the design disappears. This negates the argument that if there is a design, there must be a designer.

This contradiction can, however, be explained by making a comparison. When we compare the two 'worlds', we discover that there is a fundamental dichotomy. The human world is characterized by the absence of any kind of restrictions. Man has total freedom either to tread the path of *ahimsa* (non-violence) or to engage in world wars. He can utilize nuclear energy either for constructive purposes or for the development of nuclear weapons. This kind of freedom, with its propensity to encourage chaos and conflict, has the potential to destroy all systems. The case of the cosmos is diametrically opposed to this. Despite its mind-boggling vastness and countless components, we find it entirely ordered by determinism. From the microcosm to the macrocosm, the whole universe functions under tight discipline, that is, according to natural laws. As a result, it has a highly predictable character. It is because of this predictability that we have been able to develop science and technology with precision. The absence of determinism in the human world is the reason for the social sciences not having the exactitude of the physical sciences. For example, while the solar system has but a single definition, political science has almost a dozen definitions.

This difference between our world and the rest of the universe leads us to believe that the scheme of things devised by the Creator differs from the one to the other. While the functioning of the cosmos is marked by determinism, the Creator's scheme for the human world places man in a state of complete freedom. There is deep wisdom in this difference. If we observe the physical world, we realize that the phenomenon of intellectual development is absent from it. In other words, it has remained the same for millions of years. But, in the human world, there are constant challenges, and it is this kind of challenging environment that leads to progress and development. Without experiencing challenges, there can be no creative thinking or intellectual development. When we observe the material world we find order in it, while in the human world there is seeming disorder. But, this 'disorder' is not a negative but rather a positive phenomenon. The positive explanation for this disorder in the human world is response to challenge.

Due to this difference, we have to apply two separate criteria to make a proper assessment of these arenas. The cosmos has to be judged by the yardstick of determinism, while the human world has to be judged by the yardstick of freedom of choice. Thanks to its deterministic nature, the material world offered the possibility of creating technology. Without its predictability, we would not have been able to utilize the resources of the material world for industrial development. It follows that in the human world, because of the total freedom enjoyed by humankind, there are inevitably many problems or challenges, and it is in meeting these challenges that we develop and advance. At the same time, regrettably, this total freedom also gives rise to evil.

The problem of evil is not a feature of the material world. It is a phenomenon peculiar to the human world. This ineluctable evil is the price that we of necessity pay for all those developments which have culminated in what we proudly refer to as civilization.

Learning from Nature

❦

When we discover that nature is of a friendly character, we also have no option but to adopt this friendly culture in our society.

Walter de la Mare (1873 - 1956), the English poet, once observed a lady at a dining table taking her meal. There were some eatables on the table like porridge, muffins, apples, and so on. He then had a very strange thought: outside the lady these are food items, but once the lady takes in these items, they are readily converted into a living woman, that is, Miss T. De la Mare later composed a poem on this idea. He added these lines to the poem: *It's a very odd thing, As odd as can be, That whatever Miss T eats Turns into Miss T.*

This is the miracle of Miss T's stomach. But one's mind can conceive of something that is a million times stranger than this. All these food items were produced in an external world. But, miraculously, these food items are totally in accordance with our needs. Both are complementary to each other. This complementarity between two quite different things is clear evidence that there is one Creator of both. It is a highly well-planned creation.

This phenomenon of nature leads us to believe that

there is a single force that controls the whole of nature. This in turn leads us to believe that in nature there is unity of purpose. This leads us further to believe in what may be called the oneness of God and the oneness of man. This phenomenon of nature gives us the right ideology of life – an ideology which is the basis of universal peace and brotherhood. This dispels the notion of 'we and they', it promotes oneness of thought. It saves us from all kinds of distraction.

This ideology inculcates the notion that nature is not hostile but friendly towards us. And when we discover that nature is of a friendly character, we also have no option but to adopt this friendly culture in our society.

Then the other aspect of Miss T's experience is that we try to turn all the things around us to our own advantage. We try to absorb all the things intellectually that have already been physically absorbed by our stomach. Everyone talks of spirituality. But what is spirituality? Spirituality is not anything mysterious. Spirituality can be arrived at through contemplation rather than through meditation. Spirituality is an intellectual phenomenon. In my experience, the basis of spirituality is the mind rather than the heart.

Our digestive system is a mechanism that can extract physical energy from material food. Similarly, our mind can extract spiritual energy from the same material items. Externally, these items are foodstuffs, but internally, these items are spiritual.

For example, if you think that God is constantly supplying all those natural bounties to man without asking for its price, this is a silent message to man that we too have to live as giver persons in our society without expecting that the receivers should give us anything in return. This kind of experience promotes the culture of selflessness, the culture of unilateral ethics, the spirit of living as a problem-free member of the society.

We need a model code of ethics, and nature serves as that model. Nature is a divine factory. It produces those items that are highly suitable for us. Strangely enough, this industry works without consulting us. The character of nature is a predictable one. So it is required of us that we live in our society as predictable members of it. Nature works in a predictable manner, thus it gives us this lesson: live as a predictable member of your society.

The highest quality of a human being can be summed up in these two words: predictable character.

Big Bird of the Storm

Spirituality is not something mysterious: it is a well-known discipline and can be defined as a form of positive thinking.

When there is a severe storm, birds with small wings are caught up in it, but large birds with strong wings fly upwards and save themselves from becoming victims of the storm.

On the basis of this phenomenon, there is a saying

in the English language: Big birds of the storm. This applies to people of high thinking, to those who can save themselves from the environmental storm. That is, they can live on their own without becoming affected by the external world.

Who are the 'big birds' of the storm? They are the 'big bird thinkers', who can live independently, drawing on their own mental resources.

'Big bird thinkers' are those who do not become angry even when provoked. They are those who maintain their positivity even in negative situations, who can control their thoughts in such a way that they can see all men and women as human beings, whether friends or foes, and who can keep the peace even if others turn violent. 'Big bird thinkers' are those who are so mature that nothing can distract them from their objectives, who give well-considered responses when in adverse situations, rather than simply indulging in an emotional backlash.

There is a saying in Hindi: *Kutte bhonkte rehte hain aur hathi chalta rehta hai.* (The elephant continues to walk on without being disturbed by the barking dogs). This is the best illustration of one who has the capacity for 'big bird thinking'. Life is full of storms, full of barking, full of untoward situations – these things are due to the laws of nature and no one is in a position to abolish the laws of nature. So, you have only two options: either to waste your time and energy by constantly stooping to reactionary behaviour or to ignore all undesirable situations and try to live like the elephant in the adage.

Elephant-style living is the only successful way to live in this world.

'Big bird thinking' is only another name for spiritual thinking. Spirituality is not something mysterious: it is a well-known discipline and can be defined as a form of positive thinking. All spiritual people are positive thinkers and all positive thinkers are spiritual in nature. Spirituality and positive thinking are almost synonymous with each other.

There is a beautiful story in Hindu mythology: once a man became furious and he kicked Ram in the chest. Ram's response was quite unique. He said: *'Mere lokhan seene se tumhare komal panwen ko chot to nahi lagi?'* (I hope your soft leg was not hurt by my iron chest)

It is this kind of positive response that is called spirituality. Spiritual behaviour is friendly behaviour towards every human being – to both friends and foes alike. Spiritual behaviour is like the behaviour of the flowers that can live with all their fragrance in the neighbourhood of thorns.

An Urdu poet has beautifully expressed this: *Gulshan parast hun mujhe gul hi nahi azeez, katon se bhi nibha kiye ja raha hun mein.* (I am a lover of nature, I don't only love flowers, but I can live normally with thorns as well)

Spirituality is good for the all-round development of the human personality, making one tension-free and friendly towards one's fellow men. Spirituality is the way to all kind of success.

Positive thinking makes you a 'big bird thinker' and 'big bird thinking' imbues the human character with spirituality. Although this is an inner quality, it is this inner quality that has the power to better all your external affairs.

What Parents Face Today

Parents must come to understand that their children need a double education – a professional education as well as spiritual training.

Once when I was in California, in the USA, I happened to meet a senior Indian immigrant with whom I had a conversation about education. I remarked that it was the age of education and that the greatest need of our generation was to be educated up to the highest standard. But my interlocutor said that his experience in this field had been very disappointing. He had wanted to introduce young people to higher learning, but the result had dashed his hopes. He opined that what was needed now was a re-conditioning of minds rather than learning.

I said that the fault lay with the parents. For the parents, there were only two options: either accept whatever was going to become of their children or try to understand them and address their minds in such a way that what they required of them was made clear to them. This phenomenon can be seen in every country.

Parents, having failed to understand their children's minds, go on complaining about them. It is, of course possible to change your children's way of thinking, but you must first be endowed with the intellectual ability to properly address the minds of your educated children.

The fact is that in our present society the majority of parents are traditionally minded, but they want to educate their offspring in modern educational institutions. This requires an approach which can take in a blend of the traditional and the modern. And then parents, rather than give up on their traditional thinking, should re-define it in order to make it understandable to the new generation. It is this failure that has created the problem of children's resistance to the right type of education and the problem of how to overcome this resistance. So any shortcoming in the sphere of education is the parents' fault. It is not so much a question of re-conditioning of the mind as a question of self-training. If parents want to bring about a change of attitude towards learning in their children, they must prepare themselves to be good counsellors. It is weak counselling on the part of parents that has created this problem.

Another problem is pampering. Parents have great affection for their children and this often leads to their pampering them. While affection is good, pampering is bad. Pampering fosters an easy-going nature in children and that is the worst kind of nature for any person to have in this world of harsh realities. Pampered children do not heed advice. They know nothing but their own desires. Harsh realities have no place in their dictionary.

It is for this reason that pampered children cannot meet the challenges they have to face in the external world.

Once I met two Indian boys, both graduates, who said that they found themselves in difficult circumstances. When they were at home, they were living under the protection of their parents, who were always ready to provide anything they wanted. But now that they had left their homes and wanted to find a place in the external world, they felt unloved and unwanted. Their homes had been ready to give them everything free of cost, but now they found that the external world was quite different. Here everything had its price in terms of hard work, adjustment, acceptance of reality, proving their ability and making compromises. They found that at home they had not been trained to meet such challenges.

This is what is negative about pampering. Parents' pampering is like making a product that is not wanted in the market. Parents must come to understand that their children need a double education – a professional education as well as spiritual training. The former kind of education can be had in educational institutions but the centre for the latter kind is the home. And parents are the teachers in this home institution. But parents must realize that the language of dos and don'ts will not serve the purpose. They must prepare themselves for a more sensitive and complex approach. Indeed, they must ground themselves in what may be called rational spirituality.

How to Become Beautiful

When you are a sincere person, you cannot afford to go against your conscience or moral norms, but must follow the spiritual line of conduct.

Herbert W. Armstrong (1892 - 1986), the founder of the well-known American magazine *The Plain Truth*, observed in one of his last articles that during his long professional life, he had occasion to meet hundreds and thousands of people from different denominations. But he said that if he were asked what was the quality in human beings that was the most scarce, even more scarce than radium and platinum, he would certainly say that it was sincerity. Sincerity was the noblest human quality. But very few people would measure up to this high ideal.

There are two different kinds of human behaviour in this world – the sincere and the insincere. Sincere behaviour is the result of adherence to principles, while insincere behaviour shows a lack of principle. Insincere behaviour or unprincipled behaviour is very easy to indulge in. It doesn't require much thought when one allows the situation or the circumstances to determine one's behaviour. Without applying your mind, you can follow the advice of the situation. You can easily understand what is in your interest and what is against it. So in following the dictates of the situation, you don't need any ideal yardstick to guide you. This kind of behaviour is like that of flowing water. The contours of the surface of the earth determine its path. So one who is insincere is always ready to accede to the demands of any given situation.

As compared to this, sincerity is a very difficult option. When you are a sincere person, you cannot afford to go against your conscience or moral norms, but must follow the spiritual line of conduct. It is this difference between the two that makes one a difficult option and the other a very easy option. Sincerity always invites you to ponder over the situation, to try to choose the best course of action, even if it is against your desires.

But in terms of social requirements, principled behaviour is very important. It makes you predictable to others, who can then anticipate your behaviour before dealing with you. On the other hand, insincerity makes you an unpredictable person. It becomes very difficult to understand what kind of attitude you are going to adopt in the future. Principled behaviour makes you a true human being, while unprincipled behaviour makes you an unpredictable character, one capable of inhuman behaviour.

Unprincipled behaviour can give you some benefits, but these are only of a temporary nature. Permanent benefits can be achieved only through principled behaviour. One very important aspect of sincerity is that sincere people are able to receive divine inspirations. Sincerity develops one's spirituality, while insincerity ruins one's personality. The insincere person fails to have spiritual experiences in his life. The spiritual person is only the other name for a sincere person. Moreover, sincerity makes one a self-disciplined person.

The greatest drawback of unprincipled behaviour is that it is like a form of psychological suicide. One who opts for the insincere path, first kills his conscience, for without suppressing your conscience you cannot be insincere in your behaviour. Conscience is a moral watchdog in everyone's chosen course of action. It is the finest gift bestowed by nature. One who goes against his conscience is making a self-destructive choice. One should keep his conscience alive by listening to his inner voice. One's inner voice is the voice of conscience.

Going against your conscience is not very easy. It is this behaviour that creates what is called tension or stress. If you want to live with a tension free mind, listen to the voice of your conscience and follow it without any reservation. Sincerity is not a single value. Sincerity combines all the good human values, where there is sincerity, there are all kinds of moral beauties. In contrast, insincerity is bound to wash away all kinds of moral beauties from your personality.

The Value of Forgiveness

If forgiveness is a full stop, revenge is punctuated by commas.
Forgiveness means ending an unwanted situation, while
taking revenge means endlessly extending it.

Almost every day of our lives, we meet with some
kind of bad experience, great or small, which is
inescapable. One has two options: either to ignore it or
try to take some counter measure. The first option is a
form of forgiveness, while the other amounts to seeking
revenge. Which is the better option? We must decide by
looking at the outcome, for that will be the determining
factor.

Forgiveness is certainly the better option, for it is
based on a proven formula for saving yourself from
even worse experiences. For example, forgiveness saves
you from unworthy distractions, saves your precious
time, saves you from creating even more problems. It
is an instant solution to any problem. On the contrary,
taking revenge is bound to complicate the problem, for
that means making everything go from bad to worse.
Where forgiveness can buy time, taking revenge just
wastes time without there being any benefit.

In such a situation, people are generally too prone
to place the onus for the predicament entirely upon

others. But this is an unwise reaction. The better plan is to examine one's own role in the affair. In other words, if you are having some sad experience, don't focus on the other party. Think about your own self and adopt a course of action which is better for you. At many times in our lives we are faced with two kinds of choices – anti-other thinking and pro-self thinking. Anti-other thinking makes you descend to the animal level, whereas pro-self thinking elevates you to a higher plane of human behaviour.

If forgiveness is a full stop, revenge is punctuated by commas. Forgiveness means ending an unwanted situation, while taking revenge means endlessly extending it. Forgiveness maintains your positive thinking uninterruptedly, while revenge fosters negativity. And negative thinking can lead to all kinds of evil actions.

Some would argue that forgiveness does not always work, and that it is better to adopt the tit for tat policy. But tit-for-tat is not a real solution; it does not end the problem, it only leads to a chain of action and reaction. Forgiveness puts an end to the problem once and for all, while a tit-for-tat policy only aggravates and prolongs it. There are those who will argue that the policy of forgiveness will only encourage others to indulge in further wrongdoing against us. But this is a flimsy supposition and, moreover, runs counter to the law of nature.

Psychological studies show that every human being is born with an ego and a conscience. If you follow the tit-for-tat policy, it arouses the ego of the other party, whereas if you follow the policy of forgiveness, it will activate the other person's conscience. And it is a fact that, in controversial matters, the conscience always plays a positive role.

Forgiveness and revenge are two different moral cultures. The culture of forgiveness helps in the building of a better society – a society where positive values flourish, where the spirit of co-operation prevails, where disparate groups join together and turn themselves into a peaceful society. The outcome of vengefulness is quite the reverse. The revenge culture creates an environment of mistrust, in which everyone takes others to be his or her rivals. In the last analysis, it rules out the growth of a healthy society.

Sooner or later, everyone is bound to do something wrong. But then the well known saying 'To err is human' should be borne in mind. This being so, taking revenge means making not just one mistake, but making mistake after mistake. On the contrary, forgiveness means undoing wrongs with rights. It is better to concede that, if to err is human, to forgive is even more human. Indeed, it is this concept which is expressed in the well-known saying: 'To err is human, but to forgive is divine.'

Living in Society

※

If you think you are not in a position to contribute anything to society, at least you can become a 'no-problem' person for others.

To be able to lead a respectable life in society there is a very necessary condition. And that is that you must become someone who is beneficial to others, a giver, or at least a 'no-problem person' as far as others are concerned. Other than these two options, there is no way for you to lead a respectable life in society. Those who think that there is a third way only go on to create trouble in society, and for themselves too.

Social existence is always based on the principle of give-and-take. If you are contributing positively to society, society will regard you with respect. And if you think you are not in a position to contribute anything to society, at least you can become a 'no-problem' person for others.

If you become a giver as far as others are concerned, you are helping society progress. Even if you become simply a 'no-problem' person, you are still playing a social role—by not placing any obstacle in society's progress. In the former case you are directly helping society to progress. In the latter case, you are doing this indirectly.

But people who are neither givers nor 'no problem' persons, only become a burden on society. Although according to the conventional law these people may not be criminals, this is exactly what they actually are in terms of the etiquette of human life.

The Culture of Self-Restraint

The great merit in fasting is that it trains men and women to refrain from following their desires and instead always to bow to reason. That is the spirit of *sawm*.

Fasting, in some form or the other, is part of every religion. In Islam it is called *roza*. (The Arabic equivalent of *roza* is *sawm*. *Sawm* literally means abstinence, that is, to refrain from doing something). The ninth month of the Hijri calendar, that is, Ramadan, has been especially chosen for fasting. Fasting during the month of Ramadan is obligatory for every Muslim, except when he has a genuine reason not to do so.

In every human being there are two faculties to take into consideration: one is desire and the other is reason. In all matters, the individual has to decide whether to follow his desire or his reason. The great merit in fasting is that it trains men and women to refrain from following their desires and instead always to bow to reason. That is the spirit of sawm.

According to a saying of the Prophet of Islam, one who fasts should never stoop to using abusive language; if someone abuses him, he should simply say 'I am fasting.' Islamic fasting, as far as formal practice is concerned, is to abstain from food and drink. But the actual spirit of fasting is to refrain from indulging in negative thinking and the use of negative language.

Self-control, far from being a negative or passive action, has great value in human behaviour. In life, there are more than fifty-per cent occasions when one should refrain from action, and less than fifty-per cent occasions when one should take action. This is the formula for success for both individuals and society.

Self-control is integral to social ethics. If you live alone on an island, there is no need for any control, as the absence of others leaves you free to do whatever you want to do. However, when you are living in a society, you have to give leeway to others. This is what every person on the road does when he drives a car: he either keeps to the left (or to the right depending upon which country he is in) so that he gives way to other cars and can carry on his journey without accidents. This principle is applicable to the entire life of an individual. It entails giving others the chance to live their lives while living one's own life.

Self-control is a kind of mutual adjustment. When a person adopts the way of self-control, it is far-reaching in its effects. This is because in this way he promotes the culture of self-control in society and indicates to others through his actions that they should follow the path that he is following. Thus, the way of self-control leads to a better society, while lack of self-control in individuals leads to the destruction of peace. As far as the individual is concerned, self-control serves as a means of personality development. This way of life, in turn, saves others from unnecessary problems.

There is a 'pre-control' for exercising self-control, and that is, thinking. When a person adopts a life of self-control, at all times he first thinks about what path he should tread. Only after considerable thought, does he plan out his course of action. A life lived in this way will necessarily be marked by creative thinking. In addition, self-control contributes to one's intellectual development and turns one into a man of wisdom.

In Islam, fasting is worship. And worship is for God. But fasting is the kind of worship which at one and the same time is for the sake of God and for the sake of man. Thus, if fasting is observed in the right spirit, in all sincerity, it will make an individual pious and responsible.

Making Friends out of Strangers

Develop genuine love for others in your heart and then others cannot but love you in return.

People, normally preoccupied with their family members and a small circle of friends, do not generally want to become familiar with strangers; they take strangers to be 'others'. This kind of thinking is based simply on suppositions about others – and sometimes such suppositions are unfounded. Experience shows that it is perfectly possible to make friends out of strangers.

Swami Rama Tirath (1873 - 1906) a man of considerable education, decided in the last decade of the nineteenth century to visit the USA, in spite of not having enough money to finance his stay there and in spite of there being no Indians to receive him on American soil. After a long sea voyage, he reached the American coast, where he disembarked along with the other passengers. There were many Americans who had come to receive their friends and relatives at the port, but Swami Ram Tirath eventually found himself walking all alone in a corner of the port. An American, seeing him there, approached him and asked, 'Do you have any friends in America?' Swami Ram Tirath said: 'Yes, there is one friend and that friend is here.' Saying this, he embraced the American.

This kind of behaviour was unexpected and the American was very much impressed. He said: 'Yes, I am your friend.' and then he took him along with him to his home. Swami Ram Tirath remained his guest till he left America for India.

This example has a great lesson. It is that no one is a stranger to you; everyone is your potential friend. Just behave in a friendly way and accept others as your sisters and brothers. If you can sincerely adopt this kind of friendly attitude, you will find that everyone is your friend and no one is alien to you.

The fact is that all the men and women have common ancestors, that is, Adam and Eve. This means that the whole world is a single family and everyone has that kind of attachment with others that is so noticeable in family life.

It is only distance that makes you a stranger. If you eliminate the distance, nature will prevail and all men and women will be like blood brothers and blood sisters to you. The formula for friendship is very simple. If you are truly a friend to others, then you can safely predict that they will also become your friends. Develop genuine love for others in your heart and then others cannot but love you in return.

A philosopher once rightly said that man keeps radiating certain feelings all the time. If you are a compassionate person and you are radiating compassion, then others are bound to receive those radiations of compassion from you. If you have developed love for others, then you are radiating love and others are bound to receive the radiation of love. This is the law of nature. And the law of nature works unerringly in every situation. You will therefore receive a positive response to positive radiation and a negative response to negative radiation.

The only condition in this regard is that you should be a selfless person. Positive behaviour combined with selflessness always works. It is selflessness that makes your behaviour ring true. On the contrary, if you are a selfish person, your behaviour will be like that of a salesman. And such behaviour cannot have any positive effect.

The formula for a successful life is very simple: abide by your own nature and you will be a successful person. A philosopher once aptly remarked that everyone is born like an angel but, after receiving negative impulses from his environment, he becomes otherwise. So, return to your original nature and you will be acceptable to all.

Do not Provoke Others and So be Safe from Others

Violence breeds violence and peace breeds peace. This is the simplest and best formula in life.

The white tiger has the reputation of being a large, powerful, carnivorous animal. But one such white tiger called Vijay, a resident of the Delhi zoo, had always been known to be a very gentle animal and, according to the zoo officials, had never been seen to be aggressive. However, on September 23, 2014, a group of boys went right up to the tiger's enclosure and started acting in a rowdy manner and throwing stones at it. One of the boys even jumped over the iron railing and entered the tiger's enclosure. The tiger remained motionless, watching the boy in silence for a full fifteen minutes. Then it pounced on the youth and killed him. It then dropped his dead body at the far end of its enclosure. What almost certainly provoked the tiger into attacking the boy was that the onlookers kept trying to divert its attention by pelting it with stones

This incident is not only the story of a tiger, but is rather the story of life. The tiger, or any other animal for that matter, is not innately aggressive. By nature

67

every animal is peaceful. Animals attack only when provoked or when they sense danger. Even when an animal is provoked, it attacks not out of anger but as a matter of self-defence. So long as it does not feel under any kind of threat, it remains indifferent to whatever is happening around it,

The same is true of humans. A human being is also an animal in that he possesses all those traits natural to animals. Man, too, does not attack merely for the sake of attacking. When one person hits out at another, he does so in self-defence. If a person is not provoked, he remains unruffled. Therefore, if you are in earnest about saving yourself from the violence of others, follow this principle: Provoke no one. No one at all. In other words, refrain from hurting anyone's ego. One who sedulously adheres to this principle will never have to complain of violence from others. Violence breeds violence and peace breeds peace. This is the simplest and best formula in life.

Reputation, not Honour, Will Pay Off

'Reputation is what other people know about you. Honour is what you know about yourself.'

An American author, Lois McMaster Bujold (b. 1949), once observed: 'Reputation is what other people know about you. Honour is what you know about yourself.'

Reputation is the opinion that others have about you. How is this opinion formed? It is formed on the basis of your deeds, not of your words. Reputation represents your external personality, while a sense of honour is your own inner perception of yourself. It is like self-praise, that is, believing that you are 'so and so', without taking into account what others think about you.

Your reputation is like a cheque that can be cashed at the bank. The market knows you by your reputation, and not through your self-perception. You cannot 'cash in' your self-perception or your sense of honour in the market. If you want to have a place for yourself in society, you have to create a reputation for yourself by your actual deeds. Your own sense of honour or self-praise cannot give you any status in the world.

Some people live in self-pride. They are always busy praising themselves. But, self-praise can only satisfy the person himself. Others will never pay heed to the accolades he heaps upon himself. Moreover, if you yearn to develop a quality that you do not actually possess, that will lead to some fruitless, unrealistic course of action. As a result, you will never gain the respect of others. However, everyone is born with some special quality. If you discover that quality, concentrate upon it and put it to good use, that will engender gratefulness to God in yourself and in others.

Sisters and Brothers

Spirituality begins with one who projects himself as a spiritual person. Only one who can do so will produce a spiritual result.

Swami Vivekananda, a great spiritual luminary of India, was motivated by a desire expressed by his guru, Rama Krishnan Paramhans, who once said to him: "I hope that some day you will visit the USA and introduce Indian spirituality to the American people." Swami Vivekananda took these words to heart and when, in 1893, he came to know that an international religious conference was going to be held in Chicago, he resolved to follow the advice of his guru. With the help of one of his friends, he embarked on a ship setting sail for America and after a long sea voyage, reached Chicago. There, with the help of an American he chanced to meet, he managed to receive an invitation from the conference organizers.

At the conference, he saw that everyone addressed the audience very formally as 'Ladies and gentlemen'. But when he was invited to speak, he came on to the stage and addressed them as 'Sisters and Brothers of America', then delivered his lecture. This kind of address was the first introduction to Indian spirituality that the American people had experienced. The resounding applause he received by calling his audience 'sisters and brothers' rather than 'ladies and gentlemen' – which is a very formal way of addressing people – showed that he had touched their hearts and instantly won them over.

Everyone is born the same in nature. Since all human beings have the same common ancestor, there can be no difference between an American and an Indian. It is a fact of nature that all men and women are blood brothers and sisters. So, sisterhood and brotherhood is interwoven into the very nature of every man and every woman. When you call people 'sisters and brothers', you make a profound psychological impact.

In terms of nature, or in terms of the creation plan of God, the 'we and they' concept is unrealistic; it is the obverse of the factual position. So when you address people by saying: 'ladies and gentlemen' you fail to touch people's hearts, but when you address people as 'sisters and brothers', you remove the psychological wall between yourself and them. Alienation suddenly disappears. Everyone becomes like a member of your own family.

It is a miracle; there is no doubt about it. But this miracle can be performed only when your 'sisters and brothers' is not simply a form of lip service but comes from deep down in your heart. Lip service is mere hypocrisy, while a wholehearted address is like a psychological wake-up call which has the power to rivet your listeners' attention. True spirituality comes from the heart; it has nothing to do with any mere form of address or religious rites. There is a saying: charity begins at home. The same is true of spirituality. Spirituality begins with one who projects himself as a spiritual person. Only one who can do so will produce a spiritual result.

Although spirituality is a matter of the heart, it does have certain external manifestations, which show that a spiritual person is quite different from others. If one is not truly a spiritual person, the very manner of his utterances will betray the truth about him; while if someone is truly spiritual, his speech, his tone, his way of behaving, will at once confirm his sincerity.

There are natural flowers and there are plastic flowers. Artificial flowers may look very similar to natural flowers, but they have no fragrance whatsoever; a natural flower will not only have the real flower's look but will also please you with its sweet fragrance. This is true also of spirituality: spirituality which is such only in form is like an artificial flower, while spirituality which has true spirit is like a natural flower. The former cannot bring about the required result, but true spirituality cannot only revolutionize your personality, it can produce a revolutionary change among people at large.

Love is the Best Formula

This Quranic teaching dispels the 'we and they' concept. By nature everyone is your friend. The only difference is that some are your actual friends while others are your potential friends.

There are three religions in the Semitic family – Judaism, Christianity and Islam. In historical order, Judaism comes first, Christianity second and Islam third. One teaching is common to all the three religions, that is, love.

During a visit to the US, I was invited by an American Church to deliver a lecture on Islam and peace. After my lecture a Christian scholar asked: 'In Christianity there is a moral injunction: 'Love your enemy'. Can you cite any such teaching from the Islamic scripture?'

I replied in the affirmative. In fact, all three Semitic religions have this precept in common. For example, the Old Testament, which is the sacred book of Judaism, says: 'Hatred stirs up dissension, but love overlooks all offences.' (Proverbs 10:12) It is recorded in the Bible that Jesus Christ once said: 'You have heard that it was said, "You shall love your neighbour and hate your enemy." But I say to you, love your enemies and pray for those who persecute you.' (Matthew 5:43-44)

Now let me quote what is said by Islam. In one of its chapters, the Quran says: 'Good and evil deeds are not equal. Repel evil with what is better; then you will see that one who was once your enemy has become your dearest friend.' (41:34)

This Quranic teaching dispels the 'we and they' concept. By nature everyone is your friend. The only difference is that some are your actual friends while others are your potential friends. So try to turn this potential into actuality. This is the best formula for universal brotherhood and is common to all the three religions: Judaism, Christianity and Islam.

Love is the greatest human virtue. Where there is love, everything is in harmony, and where there is hate, all that is good remains in jeopardy.

The fact is that difference is part of nature. It has rightly been said: 'Nature abhors uniformity.' This being so, it is but natural that differences will arise between individuals and groups. Then what is the solution? Love is the only answer. If a man and woman have love in their hearts, they will be able to live together harmoniously as a family. Love is a guarantee that all the differences that may arise between them will be amicably resolved.

This phenomenon is aptly illustrated by the analogy of the shock absorber, a mechanical device that lessens shock by absorbing its force.

When a car travels along a road, due to potholes or uneven surfaces, it frequently receives a series of big or small shocks. This affects the vehicle's wheels and the impact would instantly reach the traveller, were it not for the shock absorbers which guarantee that the effect of the impact will go no further than the wheels, and will not reach the traveller.

Love is just like a shock absorber within one's heart. If you have any love for others, you will have this inbuilt psychological shock absorber which will absorb any shock that comes from others. You will remain cool and level-headed in every situation.

What is the rationale behind the 'love-all' formula? It is that every other person is your benefactor. It is your lack of awareness of this fact that makes you unable to adopt this love-all culture.

We are living in a civilization. Whatever we make use of is a gift of this civilization. What is civilization? It is an advanced stage of refinement in ethical and material matters resulting from continuous effort on the part of all mankind.

For example, when man started his life on the planet earth, human existence was in a primitive state. It then took thousands of years of the joint efforts of humanity to bring civilization into existence. For example, in the beginning, man used to walk on his own two legs. Then he started traveling on horseback. After long experience, the wheel was developed, thanks to which travel by car was made possible. The uses of steam power were later discovered and travel by steamship and rail began. Man then produced airplanes which made air travel possible and further facilitated the means of contact and communication. All this was not the work of any single human being: all of humanity was involved in this process.

The discovery of this reality about history gives rise to the culture of 'love all', while unawareness of this leads to the 'hate all' culture.

The truth is that in this world the most realistic formula is that of 'love all' and the most unrealistic formula is 'hate all'. This is why all three Semitic religions teach us that we should love all others - even if they appear to be our enemies.

A World without Borders

A world without physical borders may not be achievable, but a world without psychological borders is quite attainable for anyone who so desires it.

A world without borders is one in which people should be able to live anywhere, work anywhere and contribute anywhere - for the world is one.

All thinking people have a beautiful dream — that of living in a world without borders. But for all these people, this only remains a dream, as no one has ever been able to actualize it. For my part, however, I can say that I have made it a reality. I always actually live in a world without borders. According to my experience, the concept of a world without borders is quite an achievable target.

In a single sentence, I can say that a world without physical borders may not be achievable, but a world without psychological borders is quite attainable for anyone who so desires it. There is no need for external permission for this purpose: every individual can enter into this state – by his own decision.

Let me illustrate this idea with a personal experience. Recently, on a two-week tour to America, when I reached the New York airport, I was asked to remove my shoes during the security checking process. I willingly started to remove my shoes. Once I had removed one shoe, the security officer said okay with a smile and told me to not remove the other shoe.

According to media reports, certain well-known personalities of India have had similar experiences during their visits to the US. They were offended at it and registered their complaints in the press. Why this difference? The reason was that I took the removing of my shoes as part of a discipline, while others took it as an instance of being insulted. This example shows that the goal of a world without borders is possible. It can be achieved only within a person's own mindset rather than in the external world.

If you have developed universal thinking in yourself, that is, you consider the entire mankind as brothers and sisters and take the entire world as your own, then you have already achieved the goal of living in a world without borders. You will take every incident at which people usually get offended as normal and adjust to it, just as all situations, both pleasant and unpleasant, are accepted within a family. A world without borders only requires universalization of this family culture.

Once when I went to Spain and landed at the Madrid airport, I remembered the words of an Arab tourist who, after seeing the glorious developments of Spain, recalled the days when Arabs were ruling over the country. He said with great nostalgia: 'Will the previous age ever return to us?' But when I saw the advances made in Madrid, my feelings were different. In my travelogue, I acknowledged the attainments of the people of Spain and observed that, whereas Muslims in their time had brought traditional development to Spain, the Spanish people had now brought about development according to modern scientific standards.

In the modern age, the maxim, 'everything for everyone' has been accepted as a principle. If a person takes the 'passport' and the 'visa' as parts of a normal routine, he will be able to consider every country as his own. He will happily accept these formalities.

In the modern world, nationhood is linked to the homeland. This leads to the concept of patriotism. But if a person lives by the concept of universal patriotism, he will take the whole world as his own.

A world without borders seems unachievable at the physical level, but, at the psychological level, it is quite achievable for everyone.

How to Eradicate Corruption

One aspect of spirituality is that it keeps the emotions under control and brings peace of mind.

To eradicate corruption it requires individuals who are incorruptible and, undoubtedly, what produces such individuals is spirituality. There is a saying that violence begins from the mind. This is true also of corruption: corruption begins from mind. If we can alter people's thinking, we can safely say that we shall have eradicated corruption by at least 50%. What best changes the heart and mind is spirituality: it enlightens the inner self. When an aeroplane takes off, it leaves behind everything and reaches a higher plane, at which point it is capable of flying towards its destination without any hurdles. Similarly, a spiritualized personality takes a man to a higher plane where he goes beyond all kinds of negative influences.

There are two aspects of spirituality: one is spirituality and the other is applied spirituality. Basically, spirituality is a non-materialistic approach to life's issues. There are two ways of thinking: one that is based on materialistic interest and the other which is based on a non-materialistic way of thinking. One who is spiritual gives more importance to non-material values, and it is only his non-materialistic approach that can eradicate corruption, since the root cause of corruption is the materialistic approach.

Applied spirituality enables one to infuse daily life with spiritual values and those who are spiritualized are able to distance themselves from all kinds of corrupt practices. One aspect of applied spirituality is the duty-consciousness which it induces. A rights-conscious person can see only what is in his own interest, while the duty-conscious person looks to the well-being of others and, in doing so, can never stoop to corrupt practices.

How to inculcate spirituality among people? Basically, it is a part of education, both formal and informal. Education means the training of the mind, with special emphasis on inculcating high values. To spread spiritual values in society, we need value-based education, especially during schooling, which is a preparatory period for life, and if we want to build a spiritual society, we must adopt a spirituality-oriented form of education.

One aspect of spirituality is that it makes one evaluate actions in terms of their results – a major factor in having a sense of responsibility. One who is a spiritually developed person is able to see things in terms of value. He is able to differentiate between right and wrong. There is a saying: 'A wise man is one who knows the relative value of things.' The spiritually developed person is a wise person and a wise person is one, moreover, who has a predictable character. All these qualities stem from spiritual training. It is the responsibility of reformers, therefore, to train people to become duty-conscious by enhancing their thinking capacity – for the duty-conscious person can never involve himself in any such negative activity as corruption.

One aspect of spirituality is that it keeps the emotions under control and brings peace of mind. Spiritual education is an elevated form of learning and it is the spiritually learned people who, being intellectually developed, are best able to control their emotions by applying their powers of reasoning.

The materialistic person is more concerned with material than with spiritual goals or values. Corruption is a phenomenon of the materialistic society, while spirituality is the phenomenon of spiritualized persons. It is only such persons who can build a non-corrupt society. Spirituality and corruption cannot go hand in hand. If a society is to be free of corruption, it has to be made up of spiritualized individuals. This is the only solution to the problem of corruption. This is the right beginning and only the right beginning can make it possible to reach the desired goal.

An Extended Application of Targeted Therapy

❦

The starting point must be to bring about change in the individual. The mind of the individual must be addressed in order to revolutionize his thinking.

There are about 25,000 genes in the human body. Of this total, there are a number of genes which contribute to the growth and survival of cancer. There now is a type of treatment aimed specifically at those genes, while leaving out other genes. This therapy makes use of drugs that affect the particular genes that are found only in cancer cells. It is such treatment, carried out on a selective basis, that in medical science comes under the heading of targeted therapy.

This same technique, that of targeted therapy, is invaluable when it comes to human reform. The governing factor in human behaviour being the mind, any major improvement in human conduct must start with an in-depth modification of the thinking process. This is borne out by a saying in the Bible: 'For as he thinketh in his heart, so is he.' (Proverbs 23:7) Moreover, the method of targeted therapy is useful in many other aspects of human life: it is beneficial both in the upkeep of physical health and in the development of a healthy personality.

There is much discussion about the necessity for social reform. But this has not come about, because although all the efforts made to this end have been Himalayan, they have proved infructuous. Why is this so? It is because the starting point is not the right one. The starting point must be to bring about change in the individual. The mind of the individual must be addressed in order to revolutionize his thinking. This is the right and only way to carry out social reform. Other methods have proved ineffective.

Politico-Spiritual Rendezvous

If spirituality is inner science, politics is external discipline. We need both.

The well-known English poet Rudyard Kipling once said, *East is East and West is West, and never the twain shall meet.* This maxim has been proved untrue as far as the West and the East equation is concerned, but in respect of the equation of spirituality and politics, this undoubtedly holds true.

The fact is that spirituality and politics are both full-fledged disciplines, both need total involvement. So, each can become involved in the other's discipline only at the cost of the erosion of his own. The spiritual person will lose his dedication in the realm of politics, while the politician will lose his political interest if he involves himself in spiritual matters.

But the fact remains that both the disciplines are needed to build a better society. If spirituality is inner science, politics is external discipline. We need both. How to combine both spheres? The answer lies in a single word, that is, complementarity. Each must complement the other, while maintaining its own identity. If we make an in-depth study of this subject, we will find that spirituality is inner beauty without having external *shakti* (power), while politics is external *shakti* having little inner beauty. Both are in need of each other. So the best solution is to adopt the sharing formula. The spiritual person must serve as a counsellor to the politician, and politician must serve as a booster to the spiritual person. This policy of sharing will prove beneficial to both.

A spiritual person is a self-centred person according to his nature, the politician can help him by taking him out of his individual cell, so that he may acquire more experience of human life. The same is true of the politician. Politicians are, by nature, over-ambitious and this sometimes leads them to disaster. It is at this juncture that a spiritual person can give them practical advice which will enable them to curb this over-ambitious side of their nature, thus making them more realistic.

In our ancient tradition, dharma gurus were advisers to the kings and kings were their supporters. In our present society, in terms of number, we have enough spiritual persons and we have politicians in abundance as well. But, we are not able to benefit from the two because of a lack of sharing process between them.

We need to develop a dual system of education–formal and informal. Formal education can produce educated politicians, and that is good for our society, but we also need all members of society to be spiritualized. This goal cannot be achieved through formal education. We shall have to evolve an informal type of education whose teachers are spiritual gurus, and also *ruhani murshid*. These gurus and *murshids* can teach our present day generation through interaction, discourses and the dissemination of literature.

In my experience, informal and formal education are both independent disciplines: any attempt at amalgamation cannot yield any positive result. Each discipline can try to be helpful to the other, without interfering with the other's systems. In a partial sense, I can say we need spiritualized politicians and politicized spiritual persons. Both are important: each can support the other, but only on the condition that they strictly refrain from interference.

Spiritual persons have much to share with others, and the same can be said of the politicians. But in our present society, few of them carry out this task. The reason is that people generally adopt a complaining attitude towards others and if they try to share with others, they don't know the difference between sharing and interference. If any of them want to share with the others, they must avoid complaining and must refrain from interference. Without following this course, no one can prove to be a useful member of society.

II

Learning from Nature

The Tree's Eloquent Silence

No protest, no complaint, no demand, no street activism or stage activism: simply trust your own natural abilities and work silently.

In front of my house in New Delhi there is a full-grown tree, in whose shade I am in the habit of sitting. I call it my spiritual tree. In fact, this tree is my teacher, although a silent one. The previous winter this tree, like many other trees, shed its green leaves. Gradually, it became simply like dry wood.

I was doubtful whether it would ever again turn green. But in the spring, the whole scenario changed. My spiritual tree again became a tree with lush green foliage. This rebirth of this tree was a great lesson. My spiritual tree turned into a speaking tree. It gave me a very significant message: 'O man! Don't be hopeless in any situation. After every dry season, there is a good harvest. After every spell of hopelessness, there is new hope, after every failure there is a great success, after every dark night, there is a bright morning.'

No protest, no complaint, no demand, no street activism or stage activism: simply trust your own natural abilities and work silently.

My spiritual tree never left its allotted space. It never

protested against anyone, it never demanded that others find it new living leaves. It remained at the same place and started a new process within itself. What was this process? This process was to get its food from beneath as well as from the sunlight. This strategy worked. The whole of nature came to its help and after some months it gained its lost greenery again. This is the lesson I learned from my spiritual tree.

No protest, no complaint, no demand, no street activism or stage activism: simply trust your own natural abilities and work silently. Try to re-shape your destiny. And very soon you will be glad to discover that you have regained your life.

What is a tree? A tree is an illustration from nature. Nature tells us of its scheme through trees – that after every winter a new spring will follow. What is needed is only to discover yourself, to discover your potential. Discover the opportunities around you and then avail of all these opportunities by silent planning.

My spiritual tree creates no noise, no problems, no unwanted situations. These are the secrets of a green tree. This is also the secret of human life. Adopt the tree culture and you will be a good member of your society, just like a tree which is a good 'member' of its garden.

Moreover, my spiritual tree has never asked me for anything. It has never sent any bills to my office. Yet it gives me pleasant scenery, shade, green branches, fresh oxygen, flowers, etc. It also provides a perch for chirping birds who with their beautiful songs give me a lot of pleasure. This is the culture of my spiritual tree. It silently gives me a message: 'O man! Adopt my culture and you will become a fitting ornament of the garden of the universe.'

My spiritual tree gives me the best definition of spirituality. Live as a complex free soul and you will find a complex free world to live in. Your destiny is in your hands. Never allow others to decide your destiny. Utilize your opportunities, turn your potential into actuality and very soon you will find that you have no complaints to register against others.

To my way of thinking, every tree is an embodiment of spirituality. It is a silent lexicon of spirituality. So adopt the tree as your teacher. The tree is a good teacher who is available at all times to every student. The only condition for learning from the tree is having the ability to listen to non-verbal language.

The Discovery of God

God is the greatest discovery that a person can make.

The sun is 1,200,000 times the size of our earth, and 93,004,000 miles distant from it. Despite this enormous distance, light and heat from the sun reach us in considerable amounts. By cosmic standards, the sun is a relatively small star; it only appears large to us because of its proximity. Most stars are both larger and more radiant than the sun. Vast globes of heat and light, they are scattered in huge numbers throughout the universe. They have been shining for billions upon billions of years, but their reserves of thermal energy show no signs of being exhausted. How do stars produce such vast quantities of energy? The astrophysicist Hans Bethe spent years exploring this question. Finally he discovered that the secret lies in the carbon cycle. His research in this field won him the Nobel Prize for physics in 1967.

The day that Hans Bethe made his great scientific discovery was one of great joy for him. His wife, Rose, says that she was with her husband in the New Mexico desert when it happened. It was night, and the stars shone with immense lustre down on the vast, open desert below. She looked up with astonishment at the sky. "Gosh," she exclaimed, "how brightly the stars are shining!" Her husband replied: "Do you realize, just now you are standing next to the only human being who knows why they shine at all?"

Hans Bethe's discovery only answered a minutely partial side of the real question; it did not reach the true crux of the matter. His discovery of the carbon cycle leaves another greater question unanswered: how does this carbon cycle come to operate in stars? A true believer discovers the answer to this question in the form of God, the Maker and Sustainer of the universe. It is He who has invested the stars with this magic property. Another fact which is fascinating to think about is the enormous synchronisation and harmonious existence of countless zooming stars and planets that remain in their orbits without colliding with one another – doesn't this awesome fact point to the existence of a rational being behind it all?

How ironical it is that that small discovery – of the carbon cycle – should have made a scientist lose himself in such a spontaneous outburst of feeling, when that should have happened only if he had discovered God. God is the greatest discovery that a person can make. Those who really believe in God feel jubilation at their discovery. So uncontrollable is their joy that they cannot help expressing it to others. If there are no traces of the joy of discovery, then the discovery itself has yet to be made. Nature does not remain silent on this subject. It also speaks out about its creator, that is, God.

Evidence of God

It is an obvious fact that where there is a beginning, there is a beginner. The phenomenon of beginning itself proves the existence of a beginner.

In an article titled 'A Physicist's Faith in Science and God' (The Times of India, January 31, 2015) the American Nobel-prize winning physicist Charles Townes (1915 - 2015) speaking about the universe and religion, observes:

"No one can deny that the universe is the outcome of

intelligent placing. It is unusual. We, too, are unusual. To make it possible for life to exist, special physical laws are required. So I would say that this is a very special universe. It has been intelligently planned. How can anyone confute that? So, there is indeed a spiritual world; a Creator. Most people do not realize that science, like religion, requires faith. We make so many assumptions. We believe that the laws of physics are reliable — that's a kind of faith...I do believe there is a spiritual presence in the universe. It is difficult to define God, but I can feel an Omnipresence everywhere. People ask, if God created the universe, who created God? So there's always a problem with a beginning."

Most people would admit that our universe is an intelligently designed universe. Thus, there must be a beginning of such a universe. The existence of a meaningful universe is an undeniable fact. Some people are sceptical about its beginning - how did it begin and who is the beginner? However, when looked at deeply this question seems illogical. It is an obvious fact that where there is a beginning, there is a beginner. The phenomenon of beginning itself proves the existence of a beginner. If we are compelled to believe in the beginning, then we must also, out of the same compulsion, believe in the beginner.

All our knowledge points to the fact that there is a world that exists outside of us. When we accept the existence of the world, it becomes necessary to accept that this world has had a beginning. Since a beginning without a beginner is impossible, we are compelled to believe in the existence of the beginner.

The Galaxy Speaks about its Great Creator

'The Creator is truly great! He made such a vast universe, of which our galaxy is only a tiny part!'

According to a new study, the Milky Way is at least 50% bigger than previously estimated. Research conducted by an international team at the Rensselaer Polytechnic Institute in the US has established the presence of a bulging ring of stars beyond the known plane of the Milky Way. Their findings show that the features previously identified as rings are actually part of the galactic disk, extending across the known width of the Milky Way from 100,000 light years to 150,000 light years. (*The Times of India*, March 13, 2015)

Our galaxy, the Milky Way, is a unique astronomical phenomenon of which our solar system is only a tiny part. If a person could be far away in space and have a telescope with which he could view the entire Milky Way, he would be able to see a mind-boggling spectacle. He would see that, in the vastness of space, there is a magnificent starry galaxy. On one spiral arm of this galaxy, our solar system is situated. The planet earth is part of this solar system which, along with other planets, is continually revolving around the sun.

The viewer would simply have to exclaim in wonderment: 'The Creator is truly great! He made such a vast universe, of which our galaxy is only a tiny part!'

Journey of Life, A Flowing River

If man's life is like flowing water, in which fresh water continues to be added at every moment, then it will always remain fresh and will never become stale.

Human life can be likened to a flowing river. What is a river? A river in fact is a unique phenomenon of nature. In the river fresh water is being added to the existing water at every moment. This everyday phenomenon is responsible for the freshness of the river water. In the absence of this continuous flow of newly-added water, the river will lose its freshness: it will not be able to maintain its health-giving, nay, life-giving properties.

The same method is adopted by nature with regard to man. As we know, human beings continue to be born generation after generation. Within a period of a hundred years the previous generation is replaced by

95

new men and women. If the old water is replaced with fresh water, in human beings this same occurrence takes place in the form of previous generations yielding place to new generations.

A great wisdom lies behind this system set up in human life by nature. Its aim is that the coming generation should learn its lesson from the experiences of the previous generation. By benefiting in this way, it may continue its life's journey in a far better way. This is the precious gift of the previous generation to the new generation. This is why the phrase 'old is gold' is often used with reference to the older generation.

For instance, an old father sees that his son is very intelligent but that there is one thing wrong with his temperament, and that is his over-confidence. Due to this he suffers losses in life. On seeing this, the father, in the light of his own experiences advises him thus: "My son, confidence is good, but over-confidence is bad." This advice is very useful to him.

Similarly, another old father sees that his son is impatient. He cannot wait for anything to take place in the ordinary course of events, so he gives him advice, with reference to his own experiences: "My son, life is one per cent action, and 99 per cent restraint." This advice proves very useful to his son.

Similarly, another parent finds that his son does not have the quality of perseverance. He is not able to work unflaggingly with others, therefore, in the light of his experiences he advises his son: "My son, maturity is the ability to live with things you cannot change." This advice of the father gives the son the right guidance. He reviews his actions, and re-plans his life and then achieves great success in life.

These examples show how important the previous generation is for the new generation. The previous generation bequeaths its wisdom to the new generation. It passes on such formulae as have proved right in the light of practical experiences. In this way, the older generation enables the coming generation to refrain from committing the mistakes which earlier people made, thus incurring great losses. The truth is the previous generation is a valuable gift of nature to the present generation – a gift which cannot be acquired unless granted by nature.

If man's life is like flowing water, in which fresh water continues to be added at every moment, then it will always remain fresh and will never become stale. On the contrary, water which is lying in a closed place, where fresh water is not being added, will lose its freshness. It will become unhealthy. In this matter, the flowing river is a healthy message given by nature and the experience of human history testifies to this in practice.

Noble Personality

We must extract nourishment for our development from all things and situations, including negative and unwanted ones, for we can learn much from these, too.

A tree is a physical illustration of the spiritual life. Its story is a unique one. It begins from a small seed, and then it grows and grows, until it becomes a full-fledged tree. How does this miracle take place? It is due to an inner capacity of the tree, which enables it to take food from everything: from soil, water, air, and sunlight.

A seed is quite small, less than half-an-inch perhaps, but when it grows, it becomes a large tree, sometimes over a hundred feet tall. Man, also initially a seed, has likewise great potential and when he grows up, he becomes like a giant; a superman. When he is born, he already possesses all the great human qualities, but all these are in terms not of actuality but of potential. It is for man himself to turn this potential into actuality.

But there is a difference here. A seed grows automatically, following the law of nature. Man, however, is required to develop his personality by his own efforts. This requires conscious planning. Man should, accordingly, discover himself and plan for his development

We live in a world where we face different situations, both negative and positive, wanted and unwanted. All these are like food for human beings, food for our growth. We must extract nourishment for our development from all things and situations, including negative and unwanted ones, for we can learn much from these, too.

In this world, this is the course taken by human development and, to further it, man must take food from everything. When he is angry and controls his anger, he is training himself in the art of turning negativity into positivity. When he faces a crisis situation and manages to keep his patience, he is building up his capacity for positive planning. If he faces a violent situation and refrains from reacting, he is shaping his personality in such a way that he can maintain his peace of mind, no matter in what condition he finds himself.

This gives a person the ability to conserve his energies, so that he may devote himself entirely to constructive work. When one faces a provocative situation and maintains his balance, he is building up his self-control and thus creating a mindset that will enable him to effectively manage the periodic crises besetting almost everyone in this life. It is as if he has enrolled himself in a course of intellectual improvement.

All situations, both good and untoward, are like intellectual food. If you try to face these situations with a positive attitude, you will be helping yourself grow. You will be enhancing your creativity. You will be developing your personality along positive lines. One who adopts this course will surely emerge, sooner or later, as a well-developed personality, standing tall, like a full-grown tree.

Every person is born into this world with tremendous potential, but he or she has to work hard to unfold it. This potential is bestowed on everyone by nature, but its unfolding is a task which each and every individual has to perform for himself. Nature never discriminates against anyone with regard to the blessings that it showers on one and all: in the last analysis, it is left to man himself to become a success or a failure.

The Law of Conversion

Mistakes play an important role in a man's life. If an individual does not make mistakes, he becomes intellectually stagnant.

The whole of the physical world functions by the law of conversion. Everything in this world is an example of this. Certain chemicals when combined convert into water, nutrients in the soil, plus water and sunlight, are converted into plant life and grass is converted into milk by the cow, and so on.

The same is true of human beings, for the law of conversion is also applicable to human actions. How is this so? This comes about as a consequence of following a law of nature. When one commits a bad deed, it instantly affects one's conscience. It activates a process of rethinking about one's behaviour. This rethinking leads to acknowledging one's mistake, and this in turn leads to self-correction. Thus, a bad deed is converted into something good.

Moreover, this process is not purely mechanical, but one of active re-assessment, which stirs up the entire workings of the mind, so that the faculties that were hitherto in a dormant state now come to life. This leads to creativity and further intellectual development. Ultimately, a new personality emerges.

When man is born he is like ore – in a raw state. Potentially, ore is steel, but for this raw material to be converted into steel, it has first to go through an industrial process. Only after this process has been completed does the ore emerge as steel. And, then with further processing, it takes the form of various kinds of machinery. The same is true of man. Man is born with great potential. But turning this potential into actuality likewise requires his undergoing a process – a psychological process. What activates this process is having experiences which give him a rude awakening. Some such experiences could be the committing of bad deeds, which, for an awakened mind, can be traumatic. But a bad deed is not just a bad deed. It is, in fact, like a wake-up call or a psychological challenge. For a morally aware person, his bad deeds become the kind of challenge that leads to all kinds of spiritual and intellectual development. So from being a bad person, he is converted into a good person.

Mistakes play an important role in a man's life. If an individual does not make mistakes, he becomes intellectually stagnant. Mistakes, in terms of their results, give a person a creative mind. For a human being, such a process is indispensable for intellectual development, and also for a person who is lacking in moral fibre to be converted into a worthy individual.

This law of nature gives us a great lesson. When you make a mistake, do not take it as a negative experience. Take it rather as a process of nature. Nature wants to activate your thinking, so that your state of mind, if formerly uncreative, is now blessed with creativity. In all human progress, it is this process that is the most effective. Samuel Smiles (1812 – 1904) has rightly said: 'We learn wisdom from failure much more than from success.'

Peace for the Sake of Peace

Peace cannot present a person with what he desires. It is for the person himself to reach his goal through planning and struggle.

Peace is the most discussed theme in the world. Every section of society claims that it wants to establish peace. It is difficult to find a single person who is an exception to this rule. But, why is it that peace has remained only a subject for debate, and to this day has failed to become a practical reality? This contradiction is very strange, but it is a fact that no one can deny.

The reason is that people have bracketed other ideas along with peace, which are not directly related to it. For example, people say they want 'peace with justice', or 'peace with human rights', or 'peace with equal sharing', or 'peace with a problem-free society', and so on. Such definitions of peace are unrealistic, and hence they are not practically achievable.

Peace relates to 'means' and not to 'ends'. All peace does is open up opportunities. It is then up to people to avail of these opportunities to achieve their goals. Peace cannot present a person with what he desires. It is for the person himself to reach his goal through planning and struggle.

According to the law of nature, the only right way to establish peace is to go all out to do so, without associating any other issue with it. Once peace is established, then it is everyone's own task to discover opportunities and avail of them through realistic planning.

Rain cannot of itself grow fruits and vegetables. According to the law of nature, rain is only meant for the purpose of irrigation. It is for the farmer to carry out irrigation by utilizing the rainwater and sowing the seeds in the soil. This process will then yield the required end products.

The same is true of peace. Peace is like rain. Peace

only provides you with the opportunities. It is up to people to avail of these opportunities by wise planning. That is why 'peace for the sake of peace' is the right formula. 'Peace for the sake of justice' or 'peace for the sake of anything else' is unrealistic and, therefore, unachievable.

Science and God

The study of the universe is, in an indirect way, the study of the work of the Creator.

The issue of God is the issue of the Creator of the universe. It is the very existence of a universe that necessitates thinking about the existence of its Creator, or in other words, God. The universe, or the world of nature, is the subject of scientific study. Indeed, all the branches of physical science focus upon the world of nature.

It is a generally accepted fact that the world of nature cannot be discussed as if it were a journalistic issue. This is true also of God, for God is a scientific subject. Thus, only the scientific method can be applied to the study of God, or the Creator.

Although the existence of God is not a direct area of enquiry in the field of science, it is fully related, albeit indirectly, to the subject of science. Scientific studies have only confirmed that there is a supreme factor behind all the events in our world. Science calls it the law of nature. But, this is a matter of nomenclature. If it is given religious nomenclature, another name for this supreme law of nature can be 'God'. If not directly, then indirectly, God is the greatest finding of science.

The physical universe is the subject of scientific study. But, what is the physical universe? It is the creation of a Creator. The study of the universe is, in an indirect way, the study of the work of the Creator. In this sense, modern science is modern theology. Evidence of God is spread throughout the expanding universe.

The Existence of God

Where there is a beginning there is a beginner. Without a beginner, the beginning is inconceivable.

The existence of God is a subject that has remained the prime concern of scholars in every age. When a human being ponders upon himself and the universe around him, he is naturally led to the question: who is my Creator and the Creator of the world? This subject has preoccupied man throughout history.

There have been two periods of the study of this subject. In the pre-scientific period theologians applied the argument that there is design in the universe. That is, if there is design, there must be a designer. This argument is known as the argument from design.

In the post-scientific period, many findings gave rise to new developments in the subject. In the first half of the twentieth century, the Big Bang theory was propounded, which has now gained general acceptance among scientists. The Big Bang theory states that the universe began about 13 billion years ago. This provides further evidence for the existence of God, because where there is a beginning there is a beginner. Without a beginner, the beginning is inconceivable.

Ancient philosophers believed that matter was eternal, that is, the universe had existed forever – it had neither a beginning nor an end. This concept had no place for a Creator. But the discovery of the Big Bang has proved this notion untrue.

Modern science has made another important discovery which is in favour of the existence of God. Science has discovered an invisible world apart from the visible world. This invisible world is that of the subatomic particles. This new scientific finding has shown that the demand for a visible God is unwarranted. This is because with our two eyes we cannot see anything, even the visible, as after reaching a point the 'visible' also becomes invisible. This fact has been explained in detail by Sir Arthur Eddington in his book, *Science and the Unseen World* (1929).

The Mind-Boggling Universe

The greatness of a machine is a demonstration of the great engineering mind that conceived of and constructed that machine.

According to a report published by *Time* on February 26, 2015 titled, "Scientists Find a Black Hole 12 Billion Times More Massive Than the Sun", scientists have discovered the largest black hole to date. It is not only 12 billion times bigger than the sun, but also 420 trillion times more luminous than it. The black hole's mass is 12.8 billion light years away and it is the most luminous object ever seen in such ancient space.

The greatness of a machine is a demonstration of the great engineering mind that conceived of and constructed that machine. The same is true also of the universe, which is so great that even the most sophisticated telescope cannot reveal its width and depth. This mind-boggling greatness of the universe is undeniable evidence that there is a Great Creator who created it and is sustaining it in the most perfect manner!

Such scientific discoveries impart two lessons. On the one hand, they strengthen the conviction that this universe has an all-powerful Creator. On the other hand, they highlight the fact that this all-powerful Creator is so Merciful that He did not make this massive universe harmful for man. Instead, He made it a custom-made environment for all living creatures. This realization has a humbling effect on man, which is all to the good because modesty eradicates of all kinds of evil in mankind.

Science is not a branch of religion, but certainly these discoveries are so favourable for religion that they can be called a supporting factor for it. The study of science promotes scientific thinking and a realistic approach in man which is key to his personality development.

The Ant Culture

Paradise is for those selected persons who rightfully exercise their freedom of choice and are able to maintain their positive thinking although surrounded by a jungle of negativity.

Any ant, coming upon a heap of sugar and a heap of salt, would take the sugar and ignore the salt. This is the culture of the ant and can be summed up thus: 'Ignore what is undesirable and adopt what is desirable.'

Who taught this culture to the ants? Undoubtedly, it is the Creator who instilled this instinct in the ants. It means that 'ant culture' is not merely the culture of ants; it is a divine culture. It is a part of creation. It is according to the law of nature and also a lesson that the Creator wanted to impart to man. In unspoken words, the Creator says: 'O man! Adopt the ant culture.'

The ant follows this principle by instinct. For ants, it is a natural compulsion. The ant does not know any other way. But man has freedom and he does by his own choice what animals do as a matter of instinct. Man should, of his own, follow the ant culture. What for the ant is a question of instinct, for man is a question of exercising his freedom of choice. He must exercise his intellect, realize the importance of the ant culture and adopt this culture as his own.

According to the law of nature, our world is a mixture of both negative and positive features. This culture is not accidental; it is a direct product of the divine plan. God Almighty wants to give man the credit which He never destined for the ant.

It is the right exercise of freedom that makes one a deserving candidate for paradise. Paradise is for those selected persons who rightfully exercise their freedom of choice and are able to maintain their positive thinking although surrounded by a jungle of negativity.

It would be a very easy matter for a person to adopt the ant culture. According to the law of nature, our world will always be a mixture of the negative and the positive, but by the same law of nature, negative features will always be less than one per cent and positive features will always be more than ninety-nine per cent. Discover this fact of nature and you will gain a two-fold benefit: this discovery will give you mental equilibrium and at the same time enable you to opt for the positive features and ignore those features that strike you as being negative.

We Require Intellectual Crusades

❧

The whole structuring of formal education is based on the concept of making oneself qualified in the professional market, rather than on making oneself a good member of society.

What has gone wrong with India? Before Independence, everyone had high hopes of freedom, but now they feel that something more is required to fulfil their dreams. Our most pressing need is to discover this missing element and re-plan our strategy accordingly. This is the most urgent task before our nation.

The genesis of the problem is that we failed to differentiate between pre-Independence and post-Independence India. The failure in recognising this situation is the basic cause of all our problems. We are the victims not of any kind of internal or external conspiracy but of our own misguided planning. In pre-Independence India our struggle was based on our political rights rather than on our social duties. The whole struggle was centred on rights-activism. This strategy made the whole society a rights-conscious society, while a better society is one whose members are duty-conscious.

In the pre-Independence period, the equation was between Indians and foreign occupiers. At that time, rights-based action seemed to be a valid form of activism and, therefore, it naturally worked. But, in the post-Independence period, the equation was between Indians and Indians. Now it has become essential to change our strategy from being rights-based to being duty-based. But, in this regard, we have completely failed. No single movement has produced duty-conscious people. The Constitution of India was drafted by India's best brains. When it first came into effect all its clauses were about rights: no single clause referred to duties.

There is no use in blaming others. It is better to blame ourselves. Now is the time to launch a new struggle, under the banner of 'intellectual crusades'. By intellectual crusades, I mean educational crusades, not in terms of formal education but in the sense of informal education.

Formal education is not going to help us with this, because it is totally based on professionalism. Anyone who seeks formal education knows that this is the age of professionalism and that he or she should gain a professional degree to secure a place in the job market. The whole structuring of formal education is based on the concept of making oneself qualified in the professional market, rather than on making oneself a good member of society. To build a better society in

India, we need a parallel intellectual campaign. It is this campaign that I have termed intellectual crusades.

If anyone asks me about the model of intellectual crusades, I would say that I have dedicated myself single-mindedly to this very task. We use various means of communication for this purpose, such as the print and electronic media, conferences, seminars and other places of intellectual activity.

Here, I would like to refer to an incident that illustrates my way of working. Once, when I was at the Geneva airport, I happened to meet an Indian lady. She had been working on a cultural project for the past two months and was now returning to India. While sharing her experiences of Switzerland, she immediately took to complaining. I intervened and politely said that you consider the cow a sacred animal in the ritual sense. But you have rather to follow the cow culture in your real life. The cow is a natural 'industry' which converts what is non-milk into milk. This is a demonstration by nature telling humans to adopt the cow culture by converting negativity into positivity. She instantly understood this concept and said that she would abandon the complaint culture and maintain her positive thinking in every situation.

This is what I have termed intellectual crusades. That is, giving an intellectual dose to people on every occasion, which makes them better human beings, and consequently better members of society.

The Culture of Spirituality

To save our own freedom, we have to tolerate the freedom of others. And to save our own spirituality, we have to overlook the misuse of freedom by others.

I was born in a village in Uttar Pradesh, where, at an early age, I witnessed an incident so upsetting that I have never been able to get it out of my mind. Even today I have a vivid memory of it.

Outside my village there was a mango tree, which was laden with fruit. One day I saw a village boy throwing stones at the tree till mangoes rained down on him. What shocked me was that the boy was giving the mango tree stones, while the tree was giving him fruit in return.

I did not react to this incident, but I learned a positive lesson from it. I felt at that moment that I was in the school of nature, which was teaching me this: 'If someone throws stones at you, even then you should give him fruits in return.' This would epitomise the highest of values in life. Moreover, this is the greatest way to further one's intellectual and spiritual development.

In the present world, someone or the other is bound to 'throw stones' at you. If you react, you will get nothing but anger in return. But if you curb any reaction on your part, you will have demonstrated certain very great things – the spirit of tolerance, the spirit of forgiveness and the capacity to maintain your positivity even in negative situations.

Later on in life, I discovered that in this world of problems, this is the only way to maintain one's spirituality. This is the only way of living by which you can satisfactorily develop your personality.

This was the first lesson of my life. This lesson told me what spiritual culture was, how one could maintain one's mental balance sufficiently to develop a spiritual personality. In my childhood, I understood this lesson unconsciously, but in my later life, this lesson became rooted in my conscious mind. Now it has become second nature to me. Having a nature like this has proved invaluable.

I can say that I am an even-tempered person who is not easily provoked or who allows his thinking to become negative. I live with a hate-free mind in the complete sense of the word. Having such a personality is my greatest asset, and perhaps the credit goes to the village boy who made me learn this lesson through a shocking experience.

We all love freedom. Everyone wants to live with total freedom. But this freedom culture creates a very serious problem. That is, when I exercise my freedom, say, by swinging my arms, it is very likely that I hit another person's nose. The freedom of one person can be a problem for another. Such a situation is an integral part of our lives. No one has the power to eliminate this problem.

When we react to a negative experience and start fighting with another person, we are not merely fighting with a person, but are rather infringing upon with his freedom, which is part of nature and not part of that person. Because we cannot abolish freedom, the result will be that we will be fighting all the time. Thus, we will live in frustration and negativity, and that being so, we will lose our greatest assets – spirituality and positive thinking.

To save our own freedom, we have to tolerate the freedom of others. And to save our own spirituality, we have to overlook the misuse of freedom by others. We have to ignore others' undesirable behaviour in order to ensure that our own personality development will proceed along the right lines.

This is the wise way of living in this world. It is the way of patience. It is, in the last analysis, the realistic approach to life. We must simply accept things as they are.

How to Build a Better Society

❧❧❧

Social construction, or nation building, is like growing oak trees, not cucumbers. If we set about this task in the right way, a time will come when nation building will reach a pinnacle of success.

We are living in a world of corruption. This is a distressing state of affairs, and there are few who do not long to have a corruption-free world. This, without doubt, in itself is a worthy desire, but it can be fulfilled only if the evil is rooted out in the right way. The wrong course of action will not lead us to our goal.

Many people, both political and non-political, are very much taken by the idea of raising their voices against social evils. They think this is the way to go and every day there are multiple examples of their preoccupations. Some hold forth from the stage, some protest on the streets, some organize *paidal-yatras* (journeys on foot), while others try to get results through the ballot box, and so on. The purpose of all is common, that is, to raise their voices against social and political evils. But here is the problem: such methods have been resorted to for more than half a century, without there being any appreciable outcome. It is like lavishly sowing seed to produce a splendid crop, but getting absolutely no yield in return.

Why have such sustained efforts failed to produce any positive results? The reason is very clear. Social change cannot be brought about by demonstrating on the streets. It is brought about by changing people at the intellectual level. Social change, after all, is an issue not of street activism, but of intellectual activism. The only way, therefore, to effect social change is through education, both formal and informal. This method would appear to be a very long-term one, but according to the law of nature, any result, if it is to be substantial, can be achieved only by giving the matter a great deal of forethought and then planning accordingly. Short-term planning can seldom produce any satisfactory result. And if we follow any other such self-styled method, we shall inevitably fall far short of achieving the desired outcome.

The truth of this is demonstrated by nature. In order to grow a cucumber plant, nature requires only few months. But, for it to grow a full-sized oak tree, it needs more than a century.

Social construction, or nation building, is like growing oak trees, not cucumbers. If we set about this task in the right way, a time will come when nation building will reach a pinnacle of success. However, if we do not adopt the right method, then even after putting in thousands of years of effort, we will not be able to achieve our target.

Between Pride and Modesty

If an individual acknowledges the contribution of others, it will cause him to be modest and think positively.

A successful lawyer from Uttar Pradesh decided to buy property in Unitech Golf Country Homes, in Noida. One of his friends asked him why he wanted to own property in that very expensive colony. He answered: "Because I do not want my Mercedes to be parked next to a Santro."

Why did this lawyer talk like this? It is because he considered his car a mere commercial commodity. He only knew that he had the money to buy a Mercedes and so he purchased it by paying the required amount. But, this is to seriously misconstrue the whole issue. In reality, the car, rather than being a mere commodity is a great divine gift

God created man, then He provided him with natural forms of transport such as horses, camels, mules and so on. This was the first phase of vehicles. God knew that this would not be sufficient for man. So, as a potential, He kept other forms of transport in the natural world. This potential was that of mechanical vehicles. By utilizing his God-given mind, man made many discoveries about nature, and in this way, he was able, for example, to invent the wheel. Then, after long research, he went on to invent wheeled vehicles, such as the bicycle and the car. Modern vehicles are God-given, in terms of potential. And since many countries and their citizens have been involved in turning this natural potential into actuality, these vehicles must also be seen as a gift from humanity.

If one ponders over this entire history, one will first of all be lead to acknowledgement of the Creator. In religious terms, this is known as gratitude. And when he thinks about the immense hard work on the part of humanity that went into developing these vehicles, he will thank all of humanity, as it was through its efforts that cars were first manufactured and then made into commercial commodities for common use.

Keeping this entire history in mind, one will realize that a car or a vehicle is God's great bounty, and in making it reach the commercial level, humanity as a whole has played an important role. When one thinks in this way, one will first and foremost acknowledge God and then acknowledge humanity. One will realize that the money by which one purchases a car is of indeed a very negligible value.

The above statement by the lawyer is indicative of the mindset of every person. There is no difference between people in this matter. Their case is different only in terms of degree. Every man and woman is engaged in the same kind of thinking.

However, this is not a simple matter. Those who have such a mindset will become proud and arrogant. On the contrary, one who thinks that the item he has bought from the market is from one angle a divine gift, and from another angle, a gift from humanity, and that his own contribution to it is nil, will certainly feel humbled. There is no greater virtue than modesty.

If an individual acknowledges the contribution of others, it will cause him to be modest and think positively. Such an attitude and way of thinking are the source of all kinds of social good. Failing this, arrogance and pride – which are the root cause of all social evils – will ultimately prevail.

The Power of Peace

This formula for peace is of a broad-ranging nature, that is, it is applicable at both individual and national levels. Adopt a peaceful course of action, and your success will be guaranteed.

The power of peace is greater and more effective than the power of violence. Constructive goals can be achieved only through peaceful means, while the use of violence leads nowhere except to ruination.

There is a very interesting example of this in Indian history in the not too far distant past. The freedom struggle of India started in 1857, with the leaders of that period attempting to liberate their country from British rule by resorting to violence. This trend continued up to

1919, without their goal having been achieved. That was the year that Mahatma Gandhi (1869 - 1938) entered the freedom struggle. After studying the situation, he decided to reverse the course of action. He declared that they would continue their freedom struggle, but that it would be by a strictly peaceful method. He pointed out that where the previous leaders had been using bombs, i.e. violence, against the British, they would now use the 'bomb of peace' to achieve the same end.

This declaration by Mahatma Gandhi changed the whole scenario; it paralyzed the whole machinery of the British Empire. Puzzled by this announcement, one British collector sent a telegraphic message to his secretariat, worded as follows: "Wire instruction how to kill a tiger non-violently."

The violent method gives your opponents justification for violent retaliation, but if you adopt peaceful methods, the opposite party has no grounds for using force against you. This was the logic of Gandhian peace, which ultimately led India to freedom.

This formula for peace is of a broad-ranging nature, that is, it is applicable at both individual and national levels. Adopt a peaceful course of action, and your success will be guaranteed. The violent method is a highly risky affair. That it will entail losses is almost certain, while its benefits are indeed doubtful. But in the case of the peaceful method, which entails no risk, success can be taken very much for granted.

Why is the peaceful method so effective? The reason is that the peaceful method hits a man's conscience.

And when the conscience is hit, the person concerned has no option but to surrender to you.

But the case of the violent method is quite different in that it seriously ruffles the other party's ego. It has been said, quite rightly, that when one's ego is affected, it turns into a super ego and the result is breakdown. Violence inevitably breeds violence. It thus only aggravates the problem without resolving any issues either for individuals or for nations.

The peaceful method is the method of nature. This is an immutable rule. Thanks to nature invariably treading the path of peace, we see that everywhere in nature there is perfection. Nature may be involved in disparate kinds of activities, but this creates no problems. And, undoubtedly, the reason is that it is steadfastly peaceful in its line of action.

One important aspect of the peaceful method is that it saves any wastage of time and energy. Where violence disturbs normalcy to the point of being destructive, remaining peaceful helps to normalize things and is thus constructive. Moreover, violence only breeds hatred and intolerance, while peace fosters love and compassion. Peace is the greatest social good, for it brings about positivity among people. Where there is peace there can be developmental activities. But without a peaceful atmosphere, there can be no progress whatsoever.

The stars, the planets, and all the other parts of nature are active day and night, but they never stray from the path of peace. Peace is the culture of nature; peace is the law of the universe. Rivers flow carrying the message of peace, the wind blowing day and night conveys this message: 'O man, adopt peace and be a healthy part of the world.'

Don't Be in a Hurry

In every field, one must follow this natural course; otherwise one cannot attain any worthwhile goals.

A man who was very fond of trees wanted to see a green tree in the courtyard of his home. He thought that if he planted a sapling, it would take a long time to grow into a tree. So, he went to a garden and selected a fully grown tree. He then employed several labourers to dig it up and then transport it to his courtyard where he had it planted.

The man was very happy. He thought to himself: "I have travelled a long journey in a single day. Planting a sapling or a seed would have been a lengthy business and now I have found a quick way of having a lush green tree."

But the next morning was not a happy one for him. When he looked at the tree, he found that its leaves had begun to wither, and after a few days the whole tree dried up. He was disappointed when he saw that the once green tree had become totally dried-up. When one of his friends visited him, he found him in a very sad mood. When he asked the reason, he said: "I am in a hurry, but God isn't."

This story instructs us about the law of nature, which is based on gradual development and not on sudden leaps. One who follows this law of nature will be successful, while one who fails to follow it, will be doomed to failure in this world.

This law of nature is applicable not only to trees: it is a universal law. In every field, one must follow this natural course; otherwise one cannot attain any worthwhile goals.

Why is it that when the tree was in the garden, it was green, but when the same tree was transferred to another place—the courtyard—it dried up? The reason is that when the tree was in the garden, it had its roots intact, but when it was transferred to the courtyard, it had very few of its roots left. And it is roots that give life to a tree. Without roots a tree is just wood and not a living tree.

This is a law of nature and this law of nature applies to all human activities. It is the need of every business, every profession, and every institution to have proper roots, that is, a sound basis. There is no exception to this law of nature.

For example, education is the basis for a job, reputation is the basis of a business, and infrastructure is the basis of national development. Constructing a really solid foundation requires a long period of time; you cannot have such a foundation by just taking wild leaps.

When you are in a hurry to achieve something, it means that you are denying the law of nature. You want to build a world on your own and this kind of procedure is not possible in this world. Those who engage in a gradual process will find support in nature; and without such support no achievement is possible in this world.

Why did God decree this gradual process as the course of nature? He did so for the purpose of consolidation. If you try to achieve something by leaping into things, the final result will be like an uprooted tree. But when you adopt the gradual process, you consolidate your achievement.

The Honeybee Culture

Extract what is good for you and leave what is unwanted. Do not waste your time in complaints and protests.

It is the honeybee's culture to fly out from its hive every day and reach places where flowers are available for it. The bee extracts nectar from the flower and returns to its abode. It pays no heed to anything else.

Where there are flowers, there are also other things like thorns; but the honeybee simply ignores the presence of those thorns and does not waste its time in complaining about them. It simply extracts the nectar from the flowers and returns to the hive.

This behaviour of the honeybee provides a symbolic lesson for man – 'Live like the honeybee'. That is, extract what is good for you and leave what is unwanted. Do not waste your time in complaints and protests.

People generally take offence when they are criticized. This behaviour is quite against the scheme of nature. In doing so, they pay a heavy price. They deprive themselves of the 'nectar' that is available for them in everything and every experience – that is, a good lesson, wisdom and sound advice. Every person's environment has this 'nectar' in it. Man should develop the ability to take the 'nectar' and ignore what is not 'nectar'.

Living with a focused mind is very important for every man and woman. Only a focussed mind is well developed. When you become offended or provoked, it means that you have allowed some other person to deflect your focus and disrupt your concentration.

According to the creation plan of God, every human being is like a flower. Everyone has a content of 'nectar' or a good experience to share. The only condition to extract this universal nectar is that when you enter into conversation with someone, you should neither be offended nor provoked by what is said. You should adopt the culture of the honeybee. It is only this learning process that will contribute to the development of a successful personality.

It Requires Consolidation before Expansion

~❦~

If you want to bring about any real change in society, you must first of all change individual thinking and conduct.

A tree is a unique phenomenon of nature. Its roots go deep into the soil and its trunk rises up and its branches spread out high above. This principle of nature is also applicable to the human world. That is, real change in human life can be brought about by following the natural principle: first consolidation and then expansion. Here, consolidation means to firmly establish one's base in the ground and expansion means to spread out everywhere.

If you want to bring about any real change in society, you must first of all change individual thinking and conduct. For example, if you want to successfully establish a political system, you shall have to train people's minds in such a way that they find that system acceptable. Similarly, if you want to run successful institutions, you shall first of all have to educate individual minds. Individuals are the basis of any social building. If you want to bring about change in society you have to begin your work at the level of the individual.

Building an institution without first laying a solid foundation is like building sandcastles, which soon crumble away.

The Concept of God

Scientists have only discovered the creation. But the discovery of the Creator also occurs along with the discovery of the creation.

Many people who call themselves 'secular' claim that God has no real existence. "God is a great invention of man," they say. The fact, however, is that man is a great creation of God!

Since ancient times, philosophers have been discussing the question of the existence of God, but they have been unable to arrive at any conclusive position on the matter. Galileo and Newton ushered in a new, scientific way of thinking.

God is not the subject of science. Scientists say their subject of study is 'Nature'. But what is nature? It is simply another name for the creation. In other words, science is the study of nature without reference to God.

In Newton's time, scientists believed that the universe had a 'mechanical design'. Later, Ernest Rutherford discovered that the universe had a 'meaningful design'.

And after that, in the time of Fred Hoyle it was found out that the universe had an 'intelligent design'.

In the light of these discoveries, it would be appropriate to say that God has been discovered at the intellectual level, and that the entire issue is simply one of nomenclature. In other words, it is a question of what term should be used to refer to this already-discovered Reality. Some philosophers called this Reality 'The World Spirit'. Some scientists refer to it as 'Intelligent Design'. Believers in various religions call this Reality 'God'.

Scientists have only discovered the creation. But the discovery of the Creator also occurs along with the discovery of the creation.

Spirituality and Applied Spirituality

One who believes in simple living creates problems neither for himself nor for others, and one who engages in high thinking becomes a truly selfless person.

Spirituality, the sublime character of men and women, has two facets: the internal and the external. The internal facet is positive thinking. The external facet is living in peace. Spirituality is in no way a kind of ecstasy, as is often believed. Indeed, it is a non-material culture, which means giving more importance to values which are immaterial rather than material. In essence, it promotes the philosophy of simple living and high thinking – the moral mainstay of humanity.

One who believes in simple living creates problems neither for himself nor for others, and one who engages in high thinking becomes a truly selfless person. The majority of the anti-human activities in society result from the clash between people over material interests. But if, by obeying one's spiritual proclivities, one can go beyond such interests, the result is entirely positive. One who does so will become a healthy member of society, and a society which is largely composed of such members is bound to emerge as a peaceful society.

Spirituality is a culture of nature, a demonstration of which is given to us by nature in a variety of ways. Let us take the example of a rose plant. The rose plant is a combination of two quite opposite elements: flowers and thorns. Both flowers and thorns live together on the stem of a rose plant, but there is no clash between the two. It is this feature that has made the rose plant a very beautiful and thought-provoking thing to behold, in that it is symbolic of how we should live in society without there being any friction between disparate elements.

There is spirituality of a purely internal nature and then there is spirituality which reaches out to others. Spirituality of the internal kind makes one a good human being, while 'applied' spirituality ensures harmonious interaction between the individuals, both men and women, of which society is made up. If society is a tree, the spiritual person is its flower.

Spirituality makes the individual a true human being. But this does not suffice. A person's spirituality must impinge on his environment. His elevated spiritual values must become evident in his dealings with others, and he must take the course of peaceful adjustment when a clash is imminent. At all events, he must clearly demonstrate his capacity to turn negative experiences into positive ones, and so on.

Positive men and women are like spiritual gardeners who, in their conduct towards others, turn society into a spiritual garden. 'Applied' spirituality means the bringing into play of a multiplicity of spiritual values. This is beneficial to both the spiritual person and his neighbour. It makes him a happy individual and ensures that his environs will remain free of societal problems.

Spirituality is a science, a science of the mind. It is the greatest source of positive thinking, positive taste, positive habits and positive behaviour. A positive person is a blessing for his home, for society and for his nation. In secular terms, spirituality is positive thinking and in religious terms, it is divine discipline.

III

The Problem of Stress

Stress: A Positive Phenomenon

Stress is not an evil. It is an integral part of nature and a positive activity. Our body needs movement. If there were no physical activity in the body, it would be rendered lifeless.

Nowadays stress is a common concern. Despite the use of all kinds of de-stressing techniques, it remains unrelieved. In fact, most methods of de-stressing bring on a new form of stress – like holiday stress. The reason for this failure is that people are going against nature and that is why they are unsuccessful.

Stress is not an evil. It is an integral part of nature and a positive activity. Our body needs movement. If there were no physical activity in the body, it would be rendered lifeless. The same is true of the effect that stress has on the mind. Stress is an intellectual activity. It is a sign of a healthy mind. It is only if one is intellectually awakened that one is able to treat stress as a normal phenomenon, just like physical movement. It is stress that makes one's mind alive. Without stress, intellectual processes come to a halt and this results in intellectual stagnation.

After making a detailed study of human history,

Arnold Toynbee (1889 – 1975) propounded a theory according to which, 'Man achieves civilization, not as a result of superior biological endowment, but as a response to a challenge in a situation of special difficulty which rouses him to make a hitherto unprecedented effort.' Toynbee categorized challenge as either 'crippling' or 'non-crippling'. A crippling challenge is bad, whereas a non-crippling challenge is equally good in that it stimulates nations to produce a civilization.

The same is true of stress. If man is unable to control stress, it will reach an abnormal state that is crippling; this kind of stress is fatal. But if one is able to control stress, it will remain within non-crippling limits and turn out to be a boon.

Let me give you an example. During the pre-independence era, there were two kinds of leaders: pro-Congress and pro-Muslim League. In those days, on a journey to Baharaich (Uttar Pradesh), I met a Mr. Mehmood (LLB), a pro-Muslim League leader. He introduced me to an individual who was pro-Congress. I said to Mr. Mehmood, "Both of you belong to different rival groups and yet you are keeping up your friendship. How is this?" He replied with a smile, "We have agreed to disagree." By adopting this formula, they saved themselves from stress.

During a visit to the US, I stayed for a few days with a businessman who had been living there for forty years. I found that he remained stress-free at all times. Upon undergoing an unwanted experience, he would promptly say, *"Chalo ye bhi theek hai!"* (This is also okay!)

I experienced this myself. One day, I suggested that we should go sight-seeing the following day. The next morning, he came to tell me that he was ready and had cancelled all his engagements for that day. I told him that I was not in a mood to go and would rather stay at home. Without any complaint, he instantly said, "*Chalo, ye bhi theek hai!*" I told him, "You seem to be a different kind of person. Why?" He laughed and said, "God Almighty made me and threw the mould away!"

In life, you should not try to eliminate stress. Instead you should learn the art of stress management. Most often, stress is caused due to complaints against another person. Instead of developing a complaint, we must take it easy. Taking it as a complaint would turn it into 'crippling stress.' Taking it normally would turn it into a 'non-crippling stress.' Crippling stress causes problems whereas non-crippling stress keeps the mind active. Stress is a healthy sign. The only condition is to detach it from complaints and take it as a normal phenomenon.

The Cow Culture: De-stressing is So Simple

We have to develop in our personality what may be called the capacity for conversion; we have to turn negative experiences into positive thinking.

In the 1930s, I was a student of a village madrasa in Uttar Pradesh. There I studied an Urdu Reader in which there was a poem composed by the well-known poet, Ismail Meerathi. It was titled *Hamari Gaye* (Our Cow). One of the verses went like this: *Kal jo ghas chari thi ban mein, Doodh bani woh gaay ke than mein.*

It means that the cow is a special kind of animal. It takes grass and in return gives us milk. In other words, the cow is a divine industry which is able to convert non-milk into milk. This poem became a part of my memory. It taught me a great lesson. God, the Creator, has made the cow a model for human behaviour in that it gives us a lesson in high morality. We must develop this quality of conversion in our personality, so that we may convert negative thought into positive thought.

It is said that man is a social animal. But what is society? Society is full of differences. Every day we experience some provocative situation, every day we face some unwanted behaviour from others and every day we suffer anger and tension because of conflicts arising out of differences.

Then what to do? The cow is the answer. God has created a model in the form of the cow. We have to adopt cow culture, we have to develop in our personality what may be called the capacity for conversion; we have to turn negative experiences into positive thinking.

The fact is that everyone enjoys freedom. But everyone is free to misuse his freedom. It is this misuse of freedom that creates problems. As we cannot abolish people's freedom, we have no option but to learn the art of problem management.

The present world is a testing ground. Every man and woman here is being tested. If they have freedom, it is because, without freedom, there can be no test. This freedom is God-given, and as such, no one has the license to abolish it. Thus we have no option but to follow the cow pattern, that is, to turn negativity into positivity.

The cow culture means learning the art of anger management, learning the art of converting anger into forgiveness, learning the art of converting anger into peaceability. This is the highest form of spirituality.

Leaving the society and going into the jungle or the mountains is a lower form of spirituality. The higher form of spirituality is that which is demonstrated by the cow. We have to live with people, experience all kinds of unwanted behaviour from others, but try not to react negatively. You have to imitate the cow. Just as the cow converts grass into milk, you have to convert negative thought into positive thought. This is the highest form of spirituality.

Most men and women are battling stress. They ask what is the way to de-stress themselves. I would suggest that they learn a lesson from the cow. They should adopt the cow habit in their affairs and they will be able to de-stress themselves quite successfully. The cow represents an elevated form of lifestyle. Adopt this lifestyle, and you will be able to enjoy a tension-free life.

Acceptance of Reality

You have to make an objective estimate of your strength and then attempt to adjust to the laws of nature.

I was once asked: "What is the simple formula for stress-free living?" I replied, "It is a three-word formula: Acceptance of reality." Accept the reality, and you are bound to enjoy a life that is stress and tension free.

What are stress and tension? Stress is a feeling of excessive demands being made on one's physical and mental energy and tension is a feeling of mental strain. Why are people afflicted by these evils? Perhaps, in most cases, it is because they want to live their lives according to their own way of thinking, without taking into account the existence of the external world. Its demands must necessarily be met, otherwise you will fall a prey to that form of negativity, which is generally referred to as stress.

The fact is that our life is like a cogwheel. A cogwheel is a toothed wheel that engages with another toothed wheel in order to change the speed or direction of a moving mechanism. Life runs with the help of two wheels: one is yours and the other is nature's. Your cog is weak, while nature's cog is strong. The latter has a speed of its own and you have to adjust to its pace. If you try to run your cog at a pace faster than that of nature, your cog will crack and disintegrate, while nature's will remain intact. It is this difference that inevitably creates stress. People try to run their cog according to their own will, and thus nature does not help them. Because nature's cog is stronger and man's cog weaker, it is always man who suffers.

If you plan your life as you ought, you need not suffer stress. Right planning is realistic planning. First of all, you have to make an objective estimate of your strength and then attempt to adjust to the laws of nature. Rather than place yourself in confrontation with these laws, you should fall in line with them, and, in this way, you will certainly be able to lead a stress-free life.

For example, if you get a job in a multinational organization, you will naturally not want the hire and fire rule to be applicable to you. But, to encourage a desire of this kind is unrealistic. It will lead to unpleasant complications, as this is the procedure generally followed in such companies. If you want to have a stress-free life, you have only two options: either take a multinational job and accept that the principle of hire and fire will be applicable to you, or don't take a job there at all.

Once an American professor, who had come to Delhi to deliver a lecture in a university, was approached by an Indian student who, with the aim of studying in America, asked for his help in getting admission to some university there. The professor smiled and said that admissions to universities in America were done on the basis of merit and not through recommendations. If, in such a situation, an unqualified student did go to America and did not measure up to the standards there, he would certainly start to suffer from tension. However, if he were eligible for a place in an American university, this would not be the case. There would be no tension involved.

It is important not to be over-ambitious but preferably be a realist. If you are over-ambitious, you will become a victim of tension. It is only if you set yourself achievable goals that you will be able to lead a tension-free life.

Stress is not a naturally occurring problem. It is a problem created by individuals themselves. Be ready to accept the reality. And then you will certainly be able to enjoy a stress-free life.

How to Overcome Fear

Fear is like an intellectual earthquake for our minds. It stimulates intellectual activity, which leads to creative thinking.

Fear is a common problem for every man and woman. What is fear? According to the dictionary, it is a feeling of distress, apprehension, or alarm caused by a sense of impending danger. To overcome fear, some counseling experts prescribe certain techniques which are physical in nature. Fear, however, being a problem of the mind, is unlikely to be allayed by physical solutions.

The fact is that man is a rational animal. This being so, he can readily accept only that kind of answer which addresses his reason. So, the right way to proceed is to identify the cause of fear and then eradicate it by reasoning. If one's mind can reason things out, it can surely succeed in overcoming fear.

It is a common experience to arrive at the railway station and find that your train is late. If there is some rational cause for its lateness, you will have no anxiety about it. But if the reason for the train being late is not known, you will become apprehensive. This example illustrates that the only way to solve the problem of fear is to reason it out. There is no better way to do so.

I should like to share a personal experience which

has some relevance here. I am a born perfectionist. That is why I have always wanted things to be in impeccable order. Whenever I have found things not to be in perfect order, I have become very troubled and distressed. This anxiety increased to such a great extent during my childhood that I wrote a poem on it. The following is one of its verses: *Zindagani hai ke ya khwab koi vehshatnaak* (Life seems to me to be a dreadful dream).

I have read and thought a lot about this subject. It is obvious that this is a common problem for every man and woman. But, in this world, according to the law of nature, man has to live with contradictions. That is, man is himself a perfectionist, while the world itself is far from perfect. Things will frequently be seen not to be in perfect order. After this discovery, I developed a realistic approach to life. In those days, I came across a relevant maxim: 'Maturity is the ability to live with things we cannot change.' Bearing this in mind, I was able to rationalize the issue and live with a tension-free mind.

Although fear seems to be external, in reality it is within one's own mind. Often when people enter a dark room, they think that some deadly animal is crawling across the floor. But when they switch on the light, they realize that there was nothing of the sort in the room. It had only been a figment of their imagination. Therefore, the solution to the problem of fear cannot be found outside oneself, but has to be managed at the level of one's own mind. Fear is overwhelming so long as it is considered real. If you can come to grips with the fact that fear is imaginary and not real, you will realize that your mind has suddenly been rid of fear.

Fear is apparently a negative experience, but there is also a positive aspect to it. That is, fear is like an intellectual earthquake for our minds. It stimulates intellectual activity, which leads to creative thinking. In this sense, fear has an important role to play in our lives.

Fear is an integral part of life. It keeps one's mind alive. Without fear, one risks descending into a state of intellectual stagnation. We have, therefore, only one option before us, and that is, to control our minds so that we may regard fear as a positive rather than a negative phenomenon.

Waiting for a Better Tomorrow

The Creator of this world is Himself a positive mind. He loves positivity. He loves those who follow the positive way of life.

I happened to meet a young lady who was working in a company based in Delhi. She complained that the terms and conditions of the company were not very good and that she was, as a result, suffering from stress. I asked her if she wanted a formula for de-stressing and since she seemed interested, I gave her a spiritual formula that was given by the Prophet of Islam.

According to a tradition, the Prophet said, 'Waiting for a better tomorrow is also a form of worship.'

A few months later I happened to meet the same young lady again. This time she was very happy. During our conversation, she said, "Now, I have got a job in another company which is better in every respect." This is not an isolated instance. I have tried this formula several hundred times during my own life and on each occasion, I have found it to be the best in dealing with such situations.

This formula has nothing mysterious about it. It is based on the well-established laws of nature. When you face some unwanted situation and you become negative, then you are bound to suffer some deprivation. Due to your negativity, you will hinder your intellectual development and you will become discontented with your job. You may even start underperforming and become unwanted by your company. This shortcoming in your performance will lead to a negative result in your life.

But if you adopt the above formula, you will become stress-free and full of hope. This will make thinking positively a habit. Having a positive nature will surely enhance your skills and make you a more sought-after resource.

The above formula is not a religious one. It is based on human psychology. If man's mindset turns negative, he diminishes his abilities. But if he works hard with a positive mindset, he improves his abilities. This is a law of nature. And the law of nature is irreversible.

It is an accepted fact that training enhances the scope for a man, but training is not confined to professional institutions. There is another institution of training and that is one's own mind. Positive thinking is a natural form of intellectual training. This training institution is continuously at work and progressively makes man a better personality. This is a miracle of nature and each one of us has it in his control. Everyone can have this experience.

This aspect of the mind is a great gift from nature. When we shun negativity and adopt the way of positive thinking, we initiate a process in our mind – a process of enhancement of our personality. Positivity helps to unfold our potential. As a result of this process, a positive thinker improves his prospects in life. On the contrary, negative thinking is most injurious to the process of personality development. Only positive thinking can be truly helpful in this process.

Our world is governed by well-known natural laws. The only way to progress is to discover these laws and sedulously follow them. Almost all cases of failure are a result of people failing to follow the laws of nature. Following the laws of nature is like travelling along a highway which will lead you straight to your destination. If instead you allow your vehicle to stray from this path, it will be difficult for you to reach your destination.

The Creator of this world is Himself a positive mind. He loves positivity. He loves those who follow the positive way of life. Develop positive thinking in your mind. Positive thinking will enhance your personality and a personality developed on positive lines will have every success.

Learn the Art of Ego Management

The ego problem is one's own personal affair. Others will not pay its price; one has to manage it on one's own.

The ego, an innate part of the psychology of every individual, has a crucial role to play in the personality of every human being. This is because the ego is the source of self-awareness. It is the source of conviction, confidence and determination. In this sense, it is a great strength in every human being. Thus, the ego is a healthy phenomenon. In its absence, man is reduced to futility, and as far as great achievements are concerned, they are out of the question without the ego-spirit.

This is the positive aspect of ego. But, at the same time there is also a negative aspect. It is this negative aspect that creates problems. Being a social animal, man has to live amongst people – both within the family and outside it. In other words, social living is an intrinsic requirement of every person. It is this necessity of having social relations that leads to problems. When one is alone, one's ego is in the dormant mode. But, when one is living in a society, one cannot but come into contact with other people. For this reason, there is every chance of experiencing situations which could lead to ego clashes.

Everywhere throughout nature, there is diversity – an essential part of nature's scheme. The same is true of human beings. All men and women are born with different characteristics. Society is thus a melange of different personalities. It is personal differences in tastes, ways of thinking, and modes of expression that create problems. What is called an ego-problem is actually a phenomenon arising from the simple fact of living amongst a wide variety of human beings.

It is said that when the ego is provoked, it turns into a super-ego and the result is breakdown. There is some truth in this saying, but it needs to be understood in the proper perspective. It is a phenomenon of social living rather than a phenomenon of solitary living. Society creates problems for individuals, but at the same time it has to be conceded that very few people can live alone. In social life everyone shares with others. It is this 'sharing culture' that helps individuals to develop their personality and to bring their plans to completion. Without this willingness to share, there is very little that can come within the reach of human beings.

Every person is like a rose plant, in that he has a 'flower content' and at the same time he has a 'thorn content'. This double-sidedness of all individuals should be accepted as a reality. When a person comes into contact with the 'flower content' of another, his equanimity remains undisturbed. But the moment he comes into contact with the 'thorn content' of the other person, his ego flares up. It is but natural to have this kind of contrary experience in social life. One has to accept the thorn in the same way as one accepts the flower. Failing this, one shall have to suffer irreparable loss. Sharing in social life is of benefit to everyone but, at the same time, it is accompanied by the negative experiences of ego clashes.

Then what should be done in such a situation? Learning the art of ego management is the only solution to this problem, for that is the price to be paid for enjoying the advantages of living in society. Inevitably, every commodity has its price. Without paying this price, one cannot acquire that commodity. This is very true when it comes to reaping the benefits of social living. If one wants to enjoy these benefits, one must inevitably learn the art of ego management.

The ego problem is one's own personal affair. Others will not pay its price; one has to manage it on one's own. Here there are only two choices: either manage the ego problem and prosper, or fail in its management and end in disaster.

Stress is a Good Servant but a Bad Master

When you come face to face with stress, don't take it as a negative phenomenon. Look upon it as a challenge and try to meet it. You have to activate your mind in a positive direction.

Everyone, both young and old, complains of stress or tension – a common phenomenon of our times. There are several centres established in order to enable de-stressing but these provide, at the most, only temporary relief. None of them offer any permanent solution. Tension is only the negative name of a positive phenomenon. What is generally called tension is, in fact, a sign of a healthy life. It is not an evil but a blessing in disguise.

Your mind has unlimited capacity, but this capacity, which is a gift of nature, is in the form of potential. You need to turn this potential into actuality. How should you go about doing this? Your potential can be realized only through being exposed to different kinds of stress or tension. Stress awakens our mind; stress activates the natural process which can lead to intellectual development. Stress plays a role in developing our personality.

In volleyball, there are two players: the waller and the booster. The waller has the key role in this game but he needs a booster, for without a booster, no waller can play his role properly. It is this process of boosting which is going on in the life of every human being. When you face stress of any kind, don't despair. Take it as a challenge. Take it as an intellectual booster. Stress is a positive sign, a healthy activity. It unfolds your mental potential.

All great men faced great problems. But these problems only increased their creativity, and became the source of revealing a fresh dimension to their personality. English poet, John Milton, has several major works to his credit. His masterpiece was 'Paradise Lost' and this he wrote after he had turned blind. Almost all creative people have had to surmount similar difficulties.

When you come face to face with stress, don't take it as a negative phenomenon. Look upon it as a challenge and try to meet it. You have to activate your mind in a positive direction. Don't lose your positivity; don't resort to the language of complaint.

When there is stress in your life, face it as a normal phenomenon and try to continue with your normal routine. Then, very soon, you will find that your stress has propelled you towards your betterment. If you compare your pre-stress situation and your post-stress situation, you will certainly find that your post-stress situation is an improvement on your pre-stress situation.

MK Gandhi was once subjected to humiliating treatment in South Africa. Prior to this, he was an ordinary lawyer, but as a result of this incident, he became the father of the Indian nation.

When you perceive an opportunity, and you try to avail of it, but for some reason you fail to achieve your goal; then you might suffer a feeling of tension. But you should know that there is no end to opportunities in this world. If you fail to avail of one opportunity, then don't take it as the end of everything. There are many other opportunities in life: in fact, the world is full of them. So, if you fail in the first instance, then try to avail of the second or the third opportunity, and so on. There is no full stop to opportunities – only commas! So instead of allowing yourself to be overwhelmed by tension, adopt the formula: 'Try, try, try again.'

This is the formula for de-stressing yourself. Living in worry or stopping your thinking processes is not the solution. Instead of stopping your thinking processes, enhance them, and you will soon discover that the stress you felt was acting as an intellectual booster in your life.

A Practical Formula for Peace

Man's personality is entirely in his own hands. He has total command over his own thoughts, heart and mind.

Lord Mountbatten was India's last British Viceroy. When, at midnight on August 15, 1947, he declared on All India Radio: 'Today India is free', that for India was a historic moment. But at that time the champion of the freedom struggle, Mahatma Gandhi, was not present in Delhi, as were other national leaders, to listen to this announcement.

At that crucial moment, he was in Noakhli in East Bengal trying to restore peace after bloody riots had erupted there during the pre-partition days. From Noakhli he sent a letter to one of his Gujarati friends: *Mere charon aor aag lagi hui hai, par mere man mein shanti hai.* (There is fire all around me, yet I find peace in my heart).

At that juncture, peace seemed to be a distant dream, yet Mahatma Gandhi was able to feel peace in his heart. This is the most practical formula for peace. International peace may be a long-term goal but individual peace can be achieved instantly. If you want to establish peace in the world around you, you must at the same time be sufficiently mature as to be able to achieve peace of mind, even in a highly disturbed situation.

This is the only workable formula for peaceful living and it is a duality which is quite within the capacity of every human being. Mahatma Gandhi clearly demonstrated this fact. All it requires is the art of thought management. Man's mind has enormous capabilities. It is in no way unusual for a single mind to learn two or more languages and have a command of all of them. If the bilingual formula is possible for man, then the above-stated Gandhian pattern is also possible for anyone.

Man's personality is entirely in his own hands. He has total command over his own thoughts, heart and mind. He can think as he wants to think. He can wish as he wants to wish. He can sense as he wants to sense. In a similar way, he must adopt the formula: I will live in peace whatever the cost. I will develop a peaceful mind. I will not allow anyone to disturb my mind. Thus, in the personal sphere, he can live in total peace, with complete peace of mind.

But the world outside him is not under his control. It functions quite independently. So, he must divide his intellectual activities into two parts. As far as his own mind is concerned, he can live in complete peace. But as far as the outside world is concerned, he may continue giving his advice, but must leave it to others to be instrumental (or not) in the acceptance of his advice.

You cannot change the world. Likewise, the world cannot change your mind. So, accept this arrangement and you can live with peace of mind, while at the same time offering your peaceful guidance to the world around you.

Duality is a part of life. In every field man has adopted this formula of duality – we learn two or more languages, we try to have a command of several subjects, we try to be successful in two trades, we try to engage with a number of friends, etc. So if duality is possible in other spheres, why should it not be possible in the field of peace?

It is said that every problem begins in the mind and that it can also be solved in the mind. Cultivate this mental capacity and you will be able to live with a peaceful mind, even in a situation where there is no peace in the world

Living with Courage in a Discouraging World

One should save oneself and try to live with courage in a world full of disappointments.

I once happened to meet a businessman who confided to me that formerly he had been in the habit of very generously giving his assistance to others. However, he had now stopped this practice, as he found that no one acknowledged the contribution he made, except by way of lip service. This experience had been a disappointing one for him and, as a result, he stopped helping others. I told him that there was an old saying: *Neki kar aur darya mein daal.* (Do good deeds and cast them into the river), that is, forget the good works you have performed. I explained to him that what he had experienced was not the story of just a handful of people but was rather the common experience of the majority. Therefore, the best formula is to do charity for your own inner satisfaction and not for receiving acknowledgment from others.

Charity does not just entail one's giving money to

some needy person. There are many ways to help others – being the well-wisher of others, giving good advice to others, speaking only good of others, never taking revenge, living in society as a civic-minded person – all these are ways of being of help to others. Helping others is, in reality, helping oneself. This is because activity of this kind inspires positive thinking in the one who performs it and results in the better development of one's personality. It makes one a giver-member of society. Good behaviour towards individuals helps one to behave well towards society at large.

It is a law of nature that everyone is born with his own interests at heart. But, self-interest has its minus as well as its plus points. On the plus side, it is self-interest that works as a motivating force in the human world. Without self-interest all activities would come to a halt. This is the contributing aspect of self-interest. But there is a minus point of self-interest. When a person does something purely out of self-interest, it is but natural that he would at all events very much like to take credit for whatever it is that he has done. It is this phenomenon of human nature, which is good for himself but bad for the recipient of his good deed.

The fact is that this phenomenon is due to the law of nature, and when it comes to the law of nature, one has no option but to accept it. One has to accept that this is the immutable reality. If one adopts a realistic approach to this problem, it will give an instant benefit. That is, it will make one tension-free and positive. In contrast to this, if a person reacts, he will have to pay a double price: first, in terms of the sad experience he will have of the external world and second, in terms of his own internal stress.

One should save oneself and try to live with courage in a world full of disappointments. There are few other options for anyone in this world.

How to Overcome Anxiety

Anxiety is not a physical problem. It is a way of thinking. If you are an intellectually awakened person and are able to change your thinking pattern, anxiety will not be a problem.

Anxiety is a form of distress, sometimes occasioned by the sad memories of losses suffered in the past and at other times by uncertainties regarding the future. Anxiety is a common phenomenon. Most men and women have lived in a state of anxiety at one time or another.

Anxiety is a killer. It defeats all logic. In most cases of anxiety, there is no external agent that is causing you to live with a sense of affliction. It is you yourself who induce this baneful mental state.

There are certain problems inflicted by the external world, which you are incapable of either solving or simply dismissing. However, as far as anxiety about them is concerned, this is a self-created problem. This being so, it means that the solution lies in your own hands rather than in the hands of others. So, why complain? Concentrate on doing your best, and having done so, you will be free of all kinds of anxiety.

Anxiety is not a physical problem. It is a way of thinking. If you are an intellectually awakened person and are able to change your thinking pattern, anxiety will not be a problem.

For example, if you are sad about a loss you incurred in the past, you can gain nothing by constantly thinking about something which cannot come back. The easiest way to calm your mind is to accept the fact that what you have lost is irretrievable. And, if it is the future that worries you, you can restore your mental balance by saying, 'Why do I bother about something which has not yet happened? Maybe it will never happen at all.'

Anxiety is not a real problem. It is a product of a way of thinking. Change your mental habits and adopt a positive pattern of thinking, then you will have no anxiety.

Problems are of three kinds. If a problem relates to the present, you can solve it by wise planning. If the problem relates to the past, there is always a simple solution: forget it, and the problem will instantly disappear. If the problem concerns the future, it is not a problem at all, it is simply a baseless fear. In other words, it has no valid existence. And if something is non-existent, how can it create a problem for you?

Discover the genesis of anxiety and you will easily be able to rid yourself of it. Anxiety is not a physical problem. It begins in the mind and it is only in the mind that it can be buried.

What is Patience?

A purposeful person does not take any step as an emotionally-driven reaction.

The literal meaning of *sabr*, the Arabic word for patience, is 'to stop'. A purposeful person does not take any step as an emotionally-driven reaction. When faced with any situation, he stops and thinks what response he should make that is in accordance with his principles and purpose in life, distinguishing this clearly from responses that militate against his principles and purpose. In this way, he exercises *sabr* or patience.

Patience is connected with every aspect of our lives. Suppose you feel overwhelmed by a certain desire. You choose not to set about fulfilling the desire as soon as it emerges. You control the desire and think about it and then do what wisdom demands of you in that situation. This is exercising patience.

Suppose someone has caused you trouble. You feel overwhelmed by the desire for revenge. But you stop yourself and then do what your faith wants you to do. This is exercising patience. In other words, impatience is reflected in a hasty response to a situation, while a considered, well-thought-out response is what patience is about.

Bringing Out Your Inner Diamond

❦

Like a diamond, a human being is born in the form of a potential. It is for each one of us to convert this potential into actuality.

Diamond is the most expensive mineral in the world. It is made of pure carbon. It contains the same basic elements as coal. It takes a very long time for a natural diamond to form. When a diamond is extracted from the earth, it is in the form of an ore. But after it is cut and polished, it turns into an expensive jewel. In turning a raw diamond into the final product, between 35 to 60 per cent of it is removed.

What holds true for a diamond holds true for a human being, too. Like a diamond, a human being is born in the form of a potential. It is for each one of us to convert this potential into actuality. Someone who knows this secret and works on trying to convert his potential into actuality, to transform his possibilities into a reality, alone can be called 'a diamond of a man'. If you don't try to do this, it's like dumping an unpolished diamond into the dustbin!

All of us have a potential character hidden within us. This is something that has been gifted to us by nature. This character cannot develop by itself, on its own. Instead, we need to work on developing it. It is a task that we have to do ourselves. This is our real test.

We need to discover this inner character that nature has given us. It is like an unpolished diamond. And then, with proper and wise planning, we need to work on turning this unpolished diamond into a shining jewel. If you fail in this, you will have failed in life.

What to Do in an Unfavourable Situation

Always remember that although others can create hurdles in your life, no one has the power to decide your destiny.

One of my readers says he would appreciate it very much if I could offer my guidance as to when forgiveness may not be a good idea.

Forgiveness does not mean retreating or adopting a passive attitude. It is simply doing what is possible and ignoring what is impossible. In such situations, people generally see what is right and what is wrong. But this kind of thinking is not workable. You have to see things in terms of their result. If the result of your initiatives is likely to be good, then that is a good thing, but if the result is likely to be bad, then better not embark upon them.

In this life the choice is not always between right and wrong. The choice is rather between the lesser evil and the greater evil. In every situation, things must be examined objectively. Try to discover which option is the better for you – better, not in terms of good and bad, but in terms of lesser and greater evil. When the option is between these two opposites, then no wise person will opt for a course of action that will lead to the latter.

Opting for the lesser evil is not simply avoidance. It has two very clear benefits: firstly, it saves you from further loss and secondly, you are able to economize on your time and will be able to achieve your objectives by re-planning your activities.

No situation is unfavourable in an absolute sense. It can only be so in a limited sense. And a situation being unfavourable only means that one way is closed to you while, at the same time, there are other ways open to you. You can carry on your journey simply by changing your direction. When you face such a situation, do not delay but re-assess your plans and establish your priorities along new lines. Always remember that although others can create hurdles in your life, no one has the power to decide your destiny. Your destiny is in your own hands and, by a re-examination of the situation, you can reformulate your plans and attain your objectives simply by following an alternative path. If you have to face some loss, take it as being temporary. No loss is so drastic as to be permanent.

Life is full of changes. At every moment there are changes in life. Loss and gain are also subject to change. Situations, whether positive or negative, are temporary in nature. So, when you face some unwanted situation, do not despair. Just have faith that, sooner or later, the problem will be resolved.

Situations in life are like day and night, with every dark night giving way to a bright new day. The same is true of the life of every human being. A well-known poet has rightly said: *Raat din gardish mein hain saat asman, ho rahe ga kuch na kuch ghabrayein kya.* (Seven heavens are on the move every day and night, something new will appear, then why feel frustrated?) This is the law of nature and no one has the power to change it.

History is full of such instances, both on individual and national levels. Every individual faces some unwanted situation or the other, but then, after some time, everything comes back to normal. The case of the nation is identical. Since no one can change the course of history or the facts with which it presents us, we should take a lesson from it.

An unfavourable situation, no matter what, is nothing but a new challenge. Try to meet that challenge and very soon you will find that it was truly a blessing in disguise for you. It was meant to provide you with a stepping stone to better things.

The Problem is itself a Solution

Every question or problem is a challenge to your mind. Such challenges are always taken up by the mind, which tries to meet them as its natural duty.

There is a well-known saying: 'Necessity is the mother of invention.' An equally well-known saying is: 'Where there is a will there is a way.' These sayings are based on the potential of the human mind. And every individual mind has great potential. When the mind faces some problem, it is in its nature to try to find some solution to it, unless you artificially put a stop to your thinking processes.

Once, on a visit to a city in the UK, I happened to meet a young Arab who told me that he had completed his master's degree and had registered his name for a doctorate. I was very happy to hear this and I prayed for his success. I am a great advocate of education. I always say that education is a must for all kinds of progress, both theoretical and practical. But when I visited the same city a few years later, I happened to meet this young Arab again and he told me that he had stopped working on his doctorate. I was very disturbed and asked him why. He said he had recently married an Arab lady, who had no knowledge of the English language, so he had to do all the work outside the home. I said this was not a problem and gave him my formula: Not to solve the problem is also a way of solving the problem.

On my insistence, he told his wife that his guru had ordered him to re-start his studies and leave all the household affairs to her, so that from that day onwards, she would be entirely in charge of all domestic matters, both inside and outside the home. Then a miracle happened. Within the space of just one year, his wife acquired a working knowledge of English and started managing all the domestic affairs.

If you are facing some new problem, don't just say that you don't know how to solve it. Simply involve yourself in the problem and soon you will find that your mind has embarked on a course which will enable you to resolve the issue quite rapidly.

When you feed a problem into a computer, it starts working at the incredible speed made possible by modern electronics. It explores a vast amount of data and within minutes, sometimes within seconds, it gives you the correct answer. The same is true of the mind. The mind is like a super computer, which, when you feed a problem into it, will start working and, by exploring all the relevant branches of knowledge, will provide you with a well-considered response, a well-planned solution.

Every question or problem is a challenge to your mind. Such challenges are always taken up by the mind, which tries to meet them as its natural duty. So, if you face some problem, don't lapse into a state of tension or frustration, but simply refer it to your mind. Your mind is a well-equipped problem solver and you will find that it works automatically like a machine. Indeed, it will take no rest until it has arrived at a solution.

Psychology tells us that the mind never stops. It works day and night like an automaton. And this mind is at your disposal all the time. You can use it at any time and you will find how great an aid it is to you intellectually.

A problem without the mind is a problem, but a problem combined with the mind is a solution. The mind is a powerful agent that has all the capacity needed to bridge the distance between the problem and its solution.

Psychology is the science of the mind, and this science has established that the mind has boundless capacity. It has the unlimited potential to solve any problem whatsoever. But you have to prepare your mind. You have to equip your thinking apparatus through study, observation and thinking. Initially, it is the mind which opens up opportunities and it is only you who can foster its development. Everyone is born with a mind, but it is only those who develop their minds through study and training who are able to use their minds to full capacity.

How to Lead a Successful Life

Don't complain about the problem: simply try to deal with the problem so that it should be in your favour.

Self-interest is the strongest passion of every man and woman. Everyone is full of desires. And each and every individual feels the necessity to fulfil his or her desires. It is this state of affairs that has resulted in corruption, injustice and all kinds of evil. Since, according to the creation plan, everyone is free, it is impossible to impose a complete check on social evils.

What must one do in this state of affairs? It is not possible to eliminate all social evils. The only possible option is to save oneself from the depredations of others. In other words, to live without being exploited in a world of exploitation. Exploitation is never absent, but it is always possible to save yourself from exploitation. Don't complain about the problem: simply try to deal with the problem so that it should be in your favour.

This situation, which prevails throughout the world, is not an evil. It is actually a great boon. It is what creates challenges and competition. And, challenge and competition are the only ways to human progress, nay, to all kinds of human development. In the last analysis, it is this very situation that unfolds the entire human potential.

Once I visited a zoo where I came upon a large deer park, which had been designed to be as close to nature as possible – an apparently ideal environment for wild animals. But, as a zoo official explained, the absence of predators had caused the deer to lose their fertility. It seems that when the deer were in their natural habitat, the jungle, they lived in constant danger from predators such as wolves. But, here in the zoo enclosure, their lives were devoid of such challenges and, as a result, their reproductive systems suffered from the resulting mental and physical inactivity. So, as the official explained, they introduced a wolf into the enclosure from time to time, so that the deer had to run helter-skelter from it to save their lives. Once the deer felt threatened in this way and became normally active, their fertility was revived and they became capable of reproduction.

This is a law of nature, which holds not only for animals, but also for man. All human beings are born with great potential, but to unfold this potential they need to face constant challenges. What philosophers call the 'problem of evil' is nothing but the problem of challenge. And, it is this that is responsible for maintaining the creativity of human beings.

Life is full of challenges. Every disadvantage is a challenge—poverty is a challenge, difficulty is a challenge, an unpleasant situation is a challenge, even being born with a disability is a challenge. All these challenges are blessings in disguise. These challenges are the stepping stones to progress.

Living in the Comfort Zone

❧

Your comfort zone may seem comfortable to you, but it is only a result of your way of thinking. If you change your conditioned thinking, every 'zone' will become a comfort zone for you.

One's comfort zone is a situation in which one feels safe or at ease. This phenomenon is very common. Almost every man and woman experiences this at some time or the other.

But a comfort zone is not based on reality. It is only a psychological state which may be interpreted as a comfort zone.

For example, before marriage, a boy and girl live with their respective blood relations. These gradually become comfort zones for them. But, after marriage, they have to live in a non-blood relationship. This becomes, unconsciously if not consciously, a non-comfort zone for both of them. But there is no real reason for this to be so, for it is only the result of a psychological state. If the boy and girl understand this fact, they will regard their situation as an issue of management and not of reaction.

The same is true of companies. Often when employees stay in one place over a long period of time, their place of work becomes their comfort zone and they do not feel inclined to move out of it. But again, this is purely a psychological state, and there is no real reason for them to have this feeling.

Your comfort zone may seem comfortable to you, but it is only a result of your way of thinking. If you change your conditioned thinking, every 'zone' will become a comfort zone for you.

The so-called comfort zone is a challenge-free zone. Within it, there is apparently peace, but because of the absence of challenges, you cease to have new experiences. Thus you are unable to develop intellectually or engage in creative thinking. There is the danger in this state of affairs of your becoming a victim of intellectual dwarfism.

On the contrary, if you give no importance to being in a comfort zone and are prepared to enter every new zone, the result will be that you will have new experiences every time and shall have to face different challenges at every turn. By facing these new situations, you will develop the ability to think creatively.

A comfort zone may have everything, but staying in it cannot stimulate intellectual development. Living in a comfort zone does not give you the ability to face challenges. Although this is the state of affairs at your workplace, its effects will manifest themselves even on the home front and in other domains too. Initially, you will fail to creatively solve problems at your job, but later you will also fail to creatively manage the other affairs of your life.

A comfort zone is only a beautiful name for a non-creative zone. When a bird lives in its cage, it may prove to be a comfort zone for it, but because of not putting its wings to use, it becomes lifeless.

The Scottish writer Samuel Smiles has rightly said in his book *Self-Help*: 'It is not ease but effort, not facility but difficulty, that makes man.' Difficulties make a person energetic. Where there is no difficulty, a person gradually ends up becoming dull.

It is not good, however, to jump out of your comfort zone simply out of ambition. This may prove to be a misadventure. But if circumstances require a change, do not be reluctant to accept it. Rather, admit it as a circumstantial gift. No misadventure is good, but facing changes with courage and wisdom inevitably pays off.

A comfort zone is a self-created world. You create this world under the influence of your emotions and not by applying your rational faculty. It is a fact that all the successes of history are the outcome not of emotion but of reason.

No Rose without a Thorn

One who is born in affluence and has a problem-free life, very soon finds his mind becoming dull, while one who is born into a life of problems and hardship, has an active mind.

Every man and woman wants peace of mind. But it is hard to find an individual who can say that he has attained such a state of mental equilibrium as will allow him to live a life of tranquillity. Peace of mind is a distant dream for all of us. What is the reason for this? The reason is that people hanker after ideal peace, that is, pure peace—a peace that is free from all kinds of non-peace items.

But this kind of absolute peace is not in nature's storehouse. Let us take the analogy of the rose. A rose is a very beautiful flower, but every stem has its thorns. Indeed, thorns are an integral part of the rose plant. A poet has rightly said that thorns serve as security guards for the flower. The translation of his Urdu lines is: 'The safety of the flower would become impossible if the thorns were silk-like.' So flowers have to be accompanied by thorns. There must be hard thorns along with soft flowers—that is, there must be non-peace items along with peaceful items. A peaceful mind is a very precious aspect of human nature and it too needs safety to maintain its sublime quality.

Studies in psychology show that an untroubled mind very soon becomes stagnant. It loses its creativity. For this reason, nature always leads people into challenging situations. It is a non-peace item which acts as a challenge for the mind. This guarantees that the creativity of a peaceful mind never comes to an end. A creative mind is always alive.

It is a common phenomenon that one who is born in affluence and has a problem-free life, very soon finds his mind becoming dull, while one who is born into a life of problems and hardship, has an active mind. Such a person develops creative thinking and his intellectual development continues unhindered.

Here, I would like to cite a personal experience, concerning a politician who had two sons. He loved one of his sons very much. He got this son married to someone of his choice and presented him with a farmhouse in which to live a life of comfort, just as he pleased. I met this son and conversed with him. It seemed as if I were talking to a retarded person. He did tell some jokes but could not utter a word of wisdom. I have met the other son also. He was not given a comfortable life by his father and so left the town for another place. After a few years of struggle, he emerged as a successful person. When I met him, I found that his whole conversation was full of wisdom.

The human mind, not being like a stone, needs constant challenges. In the environment of challenge, it continues to grow till it becomes a super-mind. On the other hand, in an environment where there is no challenge, the human mind becomes like a stunted plant and gradually, it shrivels away into a state of underdevelopment.

Peace is not a ready-made item. It is a self-managed item. One should be intelligent enough to develop one's mind along positive lines so that one may deal effectively with unwanted situations. A peaceful mind is only the other name of a positive mind.

The Scottish author Samuel Smiles has rightly said: 'It is not ease, but effort, not facility but difficulty that makes a man.'

It is a fact that ease and facility are constant obstacles to intellectual development, while effort and difficulties are like stepping stones to the sharpening of the intellect.

Life is a Challenge

It is also important that the moment we feel we have taken a wrong step, we must immediately take a U-turn in order to save ourselves from disaster.

The British historian Arnold Toynbee has rightly pointed out that nations must inevitably face challenges. But, there are two categories of challenges: either that which is so severely adverse as to be insuperable, or that which is – within limits – quite surmountable. The latter challenge can prove to be a stepping stone to further progress, but if the challenge is so enormous as to be of a crippling nature, it can reach unmanageable proportions and, it goes without saying, can have disastrous consequences.

As a rule, challenges fall into two categories – the tractable and the intractable. The former kind of challenge is a regular feature of nature's functioning or is part of the scheme of things as laid down by the Creator. It is the way of nature to create such situations as will result in the kind of challenges which motivate people to strive to their utmost, thus unfolding their hidden potential.

As a rule, challenges which are reasonably easy to deal with result from some natural process, but in the case of any insurmountable challenge, it is invariably the result of man's own unrealistic policies. There is a well-known saying, 'To err is human'. And it is not unusual for an individual or nation to make mistakes. But, it is also important that the moment we feel we have taken a wrong step, we must immediately take a U-turn in order to save ourselves from disaster.

There are several examples of this in the recent past. For instance, in 1965, due to internal pressure, Singapore separated from Malaysia. This event was a loss for Malaysia in terms of territory. It did present major problems, but had no devastating effect, because Malaysia adopted the realistic approach of accepting this as a challenge and dealt with it head on. It thus remained within manageable limits and led to development for both countries.

The other example is that of Germany, which, in the early years of the twentieth century, beset by political and economic problems, had initially to meet the challenge of solving serious internal issues. But when matters further deteriorated, the German leadership eventually opted for confrontation with neighbouring countries, which escalated into WWII – a challenge of such overwhelming proportions that it ultimately caused Germany to suffer a crushing defeat. However, in 1945, at the end of the second world war, the German leadership, having accepted the reality of their defeat, lost no time in taking a U-turn. That is, they set about the vigorous reconstruction of their nation, and within a very short space of time Germany emerged as the most powerful nation of Europe.

Life is a kind of trial for both individuals and nations in the sense that they are put to the test by challenges of varying degrees of tractability. At such times, every individual and nation has to opt for one of two courses: the realistic or the unrealistic course of action, or in other words, must target the achievable or the unachievable goal. This is the crucial test that confronts every individual and nation. One who opts for the realistic course of action will reach his goal, while one who strives to achieve what is in reality unattainable will certainly be doomed to failure.

The Mind: the Conscious and the Unconscious

❧

To discover the truth. The only condition is to shun distraction, to follow the well-known principle of simple living and high thinking.

Man's mind is divided into two parts: the conscious and the unconscious. These are integral parts of every individual mind, whether male or female. The conscious mind is that part of the mind which deals with everything that is within the realm of our awareness, whereas the unconscious mind deals with all those thoughts which the individual is unaware of but which nevertheless influence his behaviour.

The human body is a highly complex organism. In it, there are numerous functions in play at all times, such as seeing, hearing, digestion, respiration, different kinds of movements, etc. Almost all these functions are governed by the unconscious mind. Little effort is required on the part of the conscious mind for all these bodily activities to function smoothly.

The conscious mind, with its unlimited capacity for thinking and analyzing facts, is an exceptionally important part of our personality. But if, according to the divine plan of creation, so much is placed in the charge of the unconscious mind, what is the role of the conscious mind? It must be understood that the Creator has made the conscious mind free to involve itself largely in the great quest for truth. And to search for truth is the prime task for every man and woman.

What is truth? Truth, to define it broadly, is the reality of life. We must try to know the secret of life, the purpose of life, the real goal of life, to know what is right and what is wrong, what is good for the individual and what is good for society. In short, the deeper meaning of our lives!

The answers to these questions are not written on any mountainside. It is man's duty to discover all these things in order to gain knowledge of the truth. And the knowledge of truth is so important that the Creator has consigned our bodily affairs to the unconscious mind. Now, a man, or his conscious mind, is completely free to discover all these truths of life.

It is often seen that people live in a state of frustration. And great men are no exception. They live in frustration and die in frustration. Tension and stress are the greatest psychological diseases in our present world. What is the reason? The reason lies in people's failure to find the truth.

Everyone is a seeker by nature, but everyone lives his life without knowing its real purpose. As a result of the ensuing sense of aimlessness, people live in a state of confusion. They speak and write, but without clarity.

They live lives fraught with contradictions. They yearn to find something without knowing what it is.

A tension-free mind is one that can function positively in spite of a contradiction. People work, but find no job satisfaction. They earn money but experience no inner satisfaction. They live by the formula: 'Enjoy life!' But they don't know what life is or what real enjoyment is. It is a paradoxical situation. Everyone is living in this state of self-contradiction.

This is a self-created problem. When the Creator has given you a mind and made you free to use your mind, you should make use of this opportunity. You have to activate your thinking capacity. You have to discover the reality. You have to read what is hidden in nature in an unwritten form. This is the only way to extract yourself from this psychological chaos. The consciousness of truth is interwoven in your nature; it is very easy, therefore, to discover the truth. The only condition is to shun distraction, to follow the well-known principle of simple living and high thinking. If you want to save yourself from going astray, activate your thinking faculty. Think, think and think! You will surely reach the gates of truth.

Problems: Blessing in Disguise

~ 888 ~

If he takes the problems that arise as challenges, he will consider them in a level-headed way and, by using his powers of reasoning, will be able to solve them successfully.

The British MP Enoch Powell once said: "For a politician to complain about the media is like a ship's captain complaining about the sea." This comment by the British MP is very true. It applies not only to politicians, but to all human beings, both men and women.

The truth is that life is a challenge and everyone, regardless of their sphere of action, is faced with this problem. There is no escaping from it. If the captain of a ship takes the waves of the ocean to be a problem, he will be beset by frustration. But, when he takes the situation as a challenge, he will be able to face it with optimism.

The same is true of every individual. According to the law of nature, everyone is faced with problems, both inside and outside the home. If he takes problems as problems, he will lose hope and end in failure. However, if he takes the problems that arise as challenges, he will consider them in a level-headed way and, by using his powers of reasoning, will be able to solve them successfully.

The existence of problems in life is no evil. It is rather a blessing in disguise. In actual fact, it is problems that activate our minds. The occurrence of problems always leads to brainstorming; they save us from intellectual stagnation by stimulating intellectual awakening. The fact that problems result in creative thinking is the greatest blessing for all human beings. If you attribute problems to the instrumentality of others, you will become negative in your thinking. On the contrary, if you regard problems as integral to the law of nature, you will tackle them in a cool and calm fashion.

Problem-oriented thinking develops a negative mindset. On the other hand, challenge-oriented thinking develops a positive outlook, which is far more precious than gold or diamonds.

Make Yourself a Creative Mind

Failure in life is not final defeat. Failure means that a man has failed in achieving the first choice, but he still has the second choice.

The well-known British philosopher Bertrand Russell (1872 – 1970) says of himself in his autobiography: "When I survey my life, it seems to me to be a useless one, devoted to impossible ideals. My activities continue from force of habit, and in the company of others, I forget the despair which underlies my daily pursuits and pleasure. But when I am alone and idle, I cannot conceal from myself that my life has no purpose, and that I know of no new purpose to which to devote my remaining years."

Bertrand Russell started his life as a star personality. But when he died at the age of 97, his was a case of frustration. What was the reason behind this tragedy? An analysis of the above statement gives us the answer. One of Russell's cherished goals was the establishment of a 'single supreme world government' able to enforce peace. According to him, the only thing that would redeem mankind was co-operation, which could be achieved only through a world government. Russell devoted his life to the achievement of this goal. However, he failed utterly.

Failure in life is not final defeat. Failure means that a man has failed in achieving the first choice, but he still has the second choice. Bertrand Russell failed to discover the second choice. This was Russell's real failure.

It is said that Russell was a voracious reader. However, according to his own confession, his study was done out of habit. Habit is a recurrent, unconscious pattern of behaviour that is acquired through frequent repetition. This was Russell's weakness. He studied a lot, but he did so as a habit rather than by way of conscious planning. If you do something as a matter of conscious planning, it will make your mind creative. But, if you do something as a habit, then it will not develop creative thinking. Doing something out of habit is the same as an animal's doing things by instinct. What is instinct for an animal is habit for human beings.

Doing something as a result of conscious planning develops a person's mind and leads to creative thinking. One who so plans is capable of engaging in introspection, reassessing his work and taking a U-turn in his life. Then he can make a new choice for himself. A creative mind is an alive mind, which is in a position to take new decisions every moment.

The ideal that Bertrand Russell had set as his goal was not achievable. Had Russell been a creative mind, he would have re-examined his goal and made a new choice. This would have made his life meaningful once again.

Experience shows that people generally lack creative thinking. The reason for this is that people mostly do not consciously plan their activities. Instead they work out of habit. Even if they begin their work by conscious planning, they slowly become habitual to it and start working unconsciously. Such a person cannot take a new decision in life. He will live as a prisoner of his habits, although what is right is for him to have a living mind.

Man should do everything as a result of conscious planning. In this way man will never fall prey to frustration. Because, if his goal is right, it will lead him towards achievement. But if his goal is not right, his creative mind will take a new decision and reset his priorities.

Habit is a general term. It covers almost all human activities, from becoming addicted to wine to being part of politics – everything comes under its purview. Frustration is only for those who do things habitually. Those who do things by way of conscious planning can never become victims of frustration.

Living in a World of Profession

Make intellectual development your first priority and then try to manage all other aspects of your life.

We are living in a world of profession. In the present world, it is one's profession that defines one's identity. The profession-oriented life is the generally accepted lifestyle of every man and woman.

Having a profession means living according to the dictates of the 'money market'. And everyone tries to develop a professional skill that enables him or her to be a sharing partner in the flow of money in the market.

This culture has resulted in a new phenomenon that was absent in former times, i.e. living in accordance with external requirements and setting aside internal requirements, that is, what is required by one's inner nature. The result is that while everyone is a developed personality in terms of his profession, in terms of his own nature, everyone is an underdeveloped personality.

Take anyone at random and ask him about his profession. He will readily give you specific answers. If you speak to him about his professional subject, he will give you a detailed answer for every question. But, if you ask him about those issues which pertain to human life, that is, non-professional issues, then you will find that he is not mentally prepared to discuss this subject.

Once I was in a city in Europe, where I happened to meet a learned lady. When I asked her about her profession, I found that she was well-disposed to share information with me. I learnt a lot from her regarding her professional field. But, at the same time, she was uncomfortable with her husband and admitted that she had decided to separate from him. I asked her the reason. She replied with some confidence: "He is an adamant person and I don't like adamant people." I said that her husband was doing a very tough job and so he had to be adamant to be successful in it. But, I failed to convince her. The reason was that she knew the science of profession, but was quite ignorant of the science of life.

This is true of every man and woman. Every person is living in a culture of duality. When it comes to their profession, everyone is well-equipped. But, as far as the science of life is concerned, everyone is ill-equipped. This is so common that finding an exception is very difficult.

It is not a question of balance, it is a question of

priority. I am not saying that everyone should keep a balance between these two requirements. I am saying that everyone has to rightly set, or reset his priorities.

The problem is that when you try to reset your priorities, you fear that you are going to damage your commercial interests, because when your mind is engaged in intellectual issues, it will not be able to engage in money-related issues. You gain one thing, but at the same time you lose another. But, this is not a genuine excuse. You should not think in terms of money: you should think rather in terms of intellectual development. Intellectual development is so important that no excuse for neglecting it is acceptable. Adopt a simple formula: make intellectual development your first priority and then try to manage all other aspects of your life.

A lack of intellectual development is not a simple matter. It is the lack of intellectual development which has resulted in all those problems that are common in our present age, for example, tension, unnecessary disease, lack of peace of mind and losing that very thing that man so desperately wants – happiness.

IV

The Secret of
Super-Achievement

Save Your Nature, Save Your Time

When you follow the path set by nature, the cogs on your wheel will connect with those of nature's wheel. So you move along smoothly.

Akash Ambani, 24, the son of Mukesh Ambani, had his first media interview published in *Hello!* magazine of *The Times of India* on July 20, 2014. During this interview, Akash Ambani spoke of some of the healthy traditions of his family. For instance, during his school days, his mother gave him very little pocket money, a pittance compared to what his friends got. Second, there was the advice given to him by his grandfather, Dhirubhai Ambani: "Money lost can be earned again, but lost time is lost forever. So use your time judiciously." These two items are basic to a successful life.

A small amount of pocket money means a simple life. It serves as a regulator in that it restrains you from going astray and indulging in unwanted activities. It becomes a compulsory check that saves you from developing bad habits, engaging in distractions, having an easy-going life and ending up with an unhealthy character.

It prevents you from following that pattern of life in which you pursue only your own self-interest.

Thus, less pocket money saves a person's nature. It saves a person from ruining his natural qualities. It makes one Mr. Nature rather than Mr. Artificial. There is no doubt that being true to one's nature is the source of all good and turning away from one's nature is the source of all evil. Less pocket money prevents you from leading an unnatural life, for the simple reason that you are unable to pay its price. The truth is that adhering to one's nature develops good character, while turning away from it develops bad character.

Nature, as described by the Creator Himself, is the right framework for any individual. For any human being the secret of life is following one's nature. Doing so leads to right development. A person who departs from his true nature cannot develop his personality in the correct way.

The second important principle is: "Money lost can be earned again, but lost time is lost forever." After his own nature, the greatest asset of a person is time. Success comes to one who utilizes his time. One who wastes his time will fail in life.

But, adopting this way of life is not very simple. It requires a wise teacher to instruct one. Akash Ambani found that teacher in his mother. His mother serves as a role model for other women. Everyone is born with two great assets. Internally, it is his God-given nature and externally, it is that precious thing called time. One who recognizes these two divine gifts can ensure success.

When you follow the path set by nature, the cogs on your wheel will connect with those of nature's wheel. So you move along smoothly. If you deviate from the course of nature, you will fail to connect your cogs with the cogs on nature's wheel. Such a person is left unsupported and can never be successful. The same is true of time. Time is the prime asset that is required for successful planning. If you fail to make good use of your time, you will be deprived of that sole basis after which there is no other basis for success.

Success is the outcome of right planning. There are two basic factors in right planning: internally, it is the nature with which you are born, and externally, it is that span of time in which you organize all your activities. If you are lacking in either of these, it will lead to disaster.

Success comes from planning, and planning is the wise utilization of these two gifts – natural wisdom and time.

Here is Good News for Everyone!

❧

No failure can stop you on your journey, provided you maintain your positivity. It is your positive thinking that matters and not the negative experience.

Jamsetji Nusserwanji Tata (1839 – 1904) was an Indian pioneer industrialist, best known as the founder of the Tata Group, India's biggest conglomerate company. His story gives us a great lesson. Once he wanted to book a room in the Watson's Hotel in Bombay. At that time, the hotel did not permit Indians, who were non-white. In British India, hotels accepted only European guests.

Apparently, this was a sad experience for Jamsetji Tata. But he did not become negative about it. He decided rather to open up his own grand hotel, greater than the Watson's Hotel. For this he drew up a unique plan. He travelled to London, Paris, Berlin and Düsseldorf to take ideas and arrange for materials and pieces of art, furniture and interior artefacts for his hotel. Jamsetji Tata was denied entry in a Bombay hotel, but his vision gave him a greater entry into the whole world. The result was that after a long effort, he opened the greater grand luxury hotel Taj Mahal Palace & Tower on December

16, 1903. This was the first Taj property and the first Taj hotel. The building overlooks the Arabian Sea.

This is a historical example that tells us a great secret of life. If you have a sad experience, don't become negative or react, and don't complain against anyone. Rather re-plan your course of action on positive lines. Expend all your energy on constructive activities rather than complain or protest. And the result will be miraculous: maybe you will gain in the future more than what you had lost in the past.

The story of Jamsetji Tata is not a story of luck. It is the story of positive thinking. It was not accidental luck that helped Tata. It was his own creative planning that led to the above result. Tata's success was not a personal event. It was an example of how one's mind can unfold its hidden potential at the time of crisis.

It is a law of nature that the quantum of scope is more than the quantum of failure. No failure can stop you on your journey, provided you maintain your positivity. It is your positive thinking that matters and not the negative experience. If your first plan fails, that is good news for you. According to the law of nature, your experience of failure will activate your mind. It will open up new windows that were until now closed. Your failure enables you to work in a better way and attain greater success. Thus, it is a blessing in disguise.

History tells us of many individuals who emerged as heroes after their failure. Failure simply enabled them to re-plan their lives, and then to touch new heights of success. Almost all super-achievers were super-losers in the beginning. The journey of great achievement begins from great failure. In its final stage, success is an external phenomenon. But in its primary stage, it is the result of an internal decision.

It is said that no one can reach the heights of success if he hasn't experienced failure. If you maintain your positivity, then failure gives you a good vision, new ideas for planning, and new ways to proceed on your journey. This is the lesson of the whole of human history.

Super-achievement is everyone's dream, but super-achievement does not suddenly knock at your door. It requires hard labour, continuous effort, well-considered planning, the utilization of full energy on a single focus, and, most importantly, unshakable positive planning. Success always comes to those who are true seekers of success. Make yourself a true seeker of success and you will certainly reach your destination.

The Role of Difficulty

Never complain to others. Try to utilize your own mind, and you will certainly achieve anything you want to in life.

In his book, *Self-Help*, published in 1859, the Scottish author and reformer Samuel Smiles rightly observes: 'It is not ease but effort, not facility but difficulty that makes man.' This statement is based on a natural fact and history has proved its veracity. All those men who attained greatness, regardless of which walks of life they came from, were the products of difficulty and not of facility. They faced challenges and emerged as super-achievers.

But the question is why difficulty has a greater role to play in the building of a personality than facility. The reason is traceable to one of the laws of nature. It is this law of nature that is responsible for bringing about this result.

The fact is that all of our actions, big or small, are directly related to our minds. It is the mind that directs all the activities of our personality. The human mind is greater than all the great things of the universe: it has mind-boggling qualities. It is the mind that is the master of the human personality, as it controls all of our activities. Studies show that all our performances depend totally on our minds. The mind has unlimited reserves of energy. When we decide to do anything, the mind at once releases energy and we perform with the aid of this energy. The mind is the prime source of energy and whatever we do can only be done with the help of this energy. If we choose to do some easy task, then the mind will release a lesser amount of energy. And, if we decide to do some difficult or great task, then the mind will release a greater amount of energy.

The building of a personality depends on one's own efforts. If one is an easy-going person then he is bound to receive lesser energy from his mind and the result will be that his personality will become a weak personality. If one is ambitious and chooses to embark on a great task, then certainly his mind will release a greater amount of energy, the result of which will be that he will develop a strong personality.

Everyone is born with the same mind that is full of energy. But some people fail to utilize their energy and die without developing their personalities. The other kind of people are those who set a great task as their goal. Thus, their minds release a greater amount of energy for the performance of this task, and so they become super-achievers.

Man himself is the master of his destiny. This saying is true, but not in the mysterious sense. It all depends on how much a person has unfolded his mind and how much energy the mind has released. One achieves greater or smaller successes in life depending on how much energy one's mind releases. Every man is a self-made man. But the quantum of success depends on one's own planning. Wise planning makes one a superman, while unwise planning makes one lag behind in life.

The mind of a man is like a great water reservoir. Opening the gate of this reservoir depends on one's target. If one's target is an ordinary target then the mind will open the door of energy on a lesser scale. But, if the target is a high one, the mind will open the gate of energy on a higher scale. It is this difference that decides the level of one's achievement.

Never complain to others. Try to utilize your own mind, and you will certainly achieve anything you want to in life.

How to Become a Super-Achiever

~§§§~

Everyone is born with some unique quality, and success depends upon discovering it and then utilizing it with sound planning.

A Muslim youth of my acquaintance, born in a village and madrasa-educated, can speak two foreign languages fluently – Arabic and English, without ever having studied for a university degree. I asked him once to tell me the secret of his unusual success. He uttered a single word: *Junoon* (madness). This means that if you have unflagging determination to achieve your target, you will certainly do so.

That youth was a common man. But this formula is also true of those who are known as great minds. One such case is that of Albert Einstein, who, although started his life from very lowly beginnings, made such discoveries as ultimately changed the course of scientific history.

Albert Einstein was born in 1879 to a poor family. He started out with no means whatsoever, living in destitution and misery. But, from the very outset, he was an ambitious person and was blessed with a very special sagacity – the determination to pursue his goal to the very end. This determination became his greatest asset, and finally he emerged as the greatest scientific mind of the world.

This is no mystery. It is a formula of nature, and applies to every man and woman. Everyone is born with great qualities. Potentially, every man is a superman and every woman is a superwoman. What is required is an insatiable desire to turn this potential into actuality.

Success is not a gift. It is the result of your own striving. If you want to be a super-achiever, first of all you have to recognize your own capabilities. Everyone is born with some unique quality, and success depends upon discovering it and then utilizing it with sound planning.

But always remember that you are a creature, you are not a creator. You have to know your limitations. You have to know what the external compulsions are. You have to know the law of nature. Missing out on any one of these two aspects of life will lead only to disaster.

Be ambitious, but not an adventurist. Be confident, but never lose your modesty. Be very clear about your target, but never try to achieve it at the cost of another person's success or peace of mind. You have to be a good planner, but keep away from any kind of corrupt practice. It is good to be a self-made person but not by usurping others' rights. In short, never succumb to a negative experience: try to turn negativity into positivity.

Always remember that it is not your intention or your desire that determines the course taken by the external world. It is a wise adjustment between your desires and external realities that leads to great success. It is a fact that no one can overrule your ambitions but it is also a fact that you cannot overrule the laws of nature. So always be a realist. Acceptance of reality is the most important principle of any kind of success.

Every human being, great or small, is determined to live between two different sets of compulsions – limitations and advantages. So you should know your limitations while you avail of the advantages. Never go beyond your limits and never try to avail of that which is ultimately beyond your reach. Always try to maintain a balance between these two different aspects of life, and the result will certainly be success.

Life is not a smooth journey, being fraught with all kinds of odd and unwanted situations. Accept the reality rather than try to fight it. Don't forget this wisdom, if you want to see your name listed along with the super-achievers.

Motivation is Greater than Favour

One who is born in a state of affluence is bound to become intellectually dwarfed, while one who is born in poor circumstances emerges as an intellectual giant.

According to a survey, out of the world's hundred richest people today, 27 are heirs and 73 are self-made. Of the self-made, 18 have no college degree and 36 are children of poor parents, but some billionaires had neither a degree nor wealthy parents. (*The Times of India*, August 18, 2013).

In other words, super-achievers are not born, they are self-made people. It is not external favour that makes one a super-achiever, but one's own struggle. Super-achievement is not achieved through inheritance, but is a self-acquired success.

It is a fact that no one is a born billionaire, but it is also a fact that everyone is a potential billionaire. It is the unfolding of one's own potential that makes one a billionaire or super-achiever. Nature does not discriminate between one person and another. Nature's gifts come to everyone on an equal basis. It is the receiver himself who either utilizes them or fails to do so.

The so-called deprived persons are in fact privileged persons. Their state of deprivation serves as an inner motivation. When they see others are progressing, it creates a strong incentive in their minds. It is this incentive that makes a man a superman. It inculcates in him a strong urge to make himself successful.

Their state of deprivation brings about a kind of brainstorming which enhances their inner spirit. They enter the world of competition working to their full capacity. They develop the spirit of do or die. It is this great spirit that leads them to great success.

There is a saying that 'Mr. So and So was born with a silver spoon in his mouth'. This kind of birth creates a kind of contentment in the concerned person, and contentment is the killer of motivation. While one who was born in a poor family without a silver or golden spoon, develops a kind of discontent. And it is a psychological fact that discontent activates one's mind and triggers a fire within one to do hard work.

You can seldom find a family that started its history with a treasure of gold and diamonds. For every family, the treasure of gold is a phenomenon of the future, not of the present. Every family initially started its history from rags, and not from riches. The story of rags to riches is not the story of some exceptional persons, but is common to all. In fact, the story of rags to riches is the story of every successful family or successful person.

There are numerous examples of one rising to a high position through one's own struggle, while one's children turned out to be dull. The reason was very simple. The father started his life with the spirit of discontent, while his children started their lives with the spirit of contentment. It was this reason that was responsible for the difference between father and sons. A person who is born into a poor family and achieves success by way of struggle, achieves one more thing, which is more important than wealth – that is, intellectual development. His circumstances automatically develop an intellectual struggle in his mind. This struggle unfolds his inner capacity, and consequently he emerges as an intellectually developed person.

One who is born in a state of affluence is bound to become intellectually dwarfed, while one who is born in poor circumstances emerges as an intellectual giant. The laws of nature are greater than everything else. They are eternal: they cannot be changed. The law of nature in this regard tells that it is not ease but effort, not facility but difficulty that makes men.

Schooling versus Training

Parents must strive to develop in the child high qualities of character such as the willingness to adjust, tolerance, peace-lovingness, simple living, high thinking, and so on.

Children are the greatest concern of parents. Parents want their children to be bright, enjoy great success in life and emerge as super achievers. To this end, parents do their utmost to ensure that their child is admitted to some school of a very high standing. For this they are willing to pay any price.

But, it is important to judge the matter in terms of result. If we apply this criterion, it is difficult to find a child educated in a top school who became a great achiever, in terms of receiving the Nobel Prize or making any important scientific discovery.

Judging by the result, training for a child is actually of greater importance than schooling. What is training? Training here does not mean equipping children to enter a profession. It means rather parents becoming home trainers for their children. Parents should attach the greatest importance to imparting wisdom to their children rather than pampering them. They should plan wisely for their children's education, laying great emphasis on how essential hard work is. They should foster the spirit of positive thinking in children, so that they may lead their lives along healthy lines. Parents must strive to develop in the child high qualities of character such as the willingness to adjust, tolerance, peace-lovingness, simple living, high thinking, and so on. They must teach their children values that will prove to be beneficial for them in every situation, such as the art of introspection and the habit – in moments of adversity – of blaming oneself rather than others for unfortunate occurrences.

We learn that training is more important than schooling when we apply our reason and pay heed to the experiences of human history. For instance, men such as Dr. B. R. Ambedkar, Dr. Rajendra Prasad, Dr. APJ Abdul Kalam and many others received their education in ordinary schools but nevertheless reached great heights of success. Parents' laying too much emphasis on schooling is, in actual fact, handing over own responsibility to others. But, the law of nature tells us that, in reality, in the sphere of children's upbringing, there is no other person who can satisfactorily take over the parents' responsibility.

The Definition of a Great Mind

We have to develop that sagacity which differentiates between trivial matters and real issues. Without this, you cannot do anything worthwhile for yourself or your society.

François de La Rochefoucauld (1613 – 1680), the noted French author of maxims and memoirs, once said: 'Small minds are much distressed by little things. Great minds see them all but are not upset by them.'

Life brings us all kinds of experiences. We have to live in a jungle in which all kinds of things, great and small, are intermingled. But, we have to be selective. We have to differentiate between things that are really great and things that have no importance at all in life. If you take everything seriously and without discernment, your focus will be scattered. You will give equal attention to everything without making any assessment of individual worth. In that way, your time and energy will be wasted. And you will not be able to accomplish anything of any value.

We have to develop that sagacity which differentiates between trivial matters and real issues. Without this, you cannot do anything worthwhile for yourself or your society.

If you board an express train, you will learn that express trains always ignore small stations, stopping only at large stations. Do as the express train does, and you will be able to reach your destination rapidly and in a frame of mind which will enable you to do much which is of value both to yourself and society.

The Limitations of Man

Realistic planning has every chance of being successful, while emotional planning is almost certain to be doomed to failure.

Napoleon Bonaparte (1769 - 1821), the erstwhile Emperor of France, is famously known to have said: 'Impossible is a word to be found only in the dictionary of fools.' However, Napoleon's own history refutes the veracity of this saying. In 1812 Napoleon invaded Russia with an army of 600,000 men. But, his plan to capture Russia was unsuccessful, because he could not foresee the harshness of the Russian winter which proved overwhelming for the French army. The majority of the troops died and Napoleon's invasion failed miserably.

As a general principle Napoleon's saying was correct. However, human beings have certain limitations. When you are planning your goal or target, you should be determined and look on the bright side of things. But, at the same time, you have to take into consideration the practical realities you may have to face in the course of executing your plan. Therefore, you have to plan for your goal in a realistic manner and not simply on the basis of your aspirations.

Every goal is achievable in this world, provided your plan does not derive solely from your ambitions. This means that you should carefully study the pros and cons of the situation and allow for all those practical hurdles which you may have to surmount in the implementation of the plan.

There are two kinds of planning: realistic planning and emotional planning. Realistic planning has every chance of being successful, while emotional planning is almost certain to be doomed to failure.

But it is Very Difficult

~❦~

Living in a state of negativity, is a kind of self-killing.

I once happened to meet a young employee of a multinational company, who complained that his boss promoted other employees, while denying him promotion. I advised him that instead of complaining about his boss, he should improve his own performance, and then the boss would be compelled to acknowledge his good work and would certainly give him in the future what he didn't give him in the present. In response to this, he said, "You are right, but that would be very difficult to do."

If those engaged in fighting for their rights were told that the better way to get what is due to them was through their own efforts and struggle, and that demands and protests would not work, they too would say that that was right but that it would be very difficult to do.

If someone is living in a state of negativity, and you tell him that negative thinking is a kind of self-killing and that he should forget the past and try to live in the future, he too would say: "You are right but that would be very difficult. "

'But it would be very difficult' is a wrong conception.

What people consider as difficult is, in fact, the only option for them. Our world is one in which we must necessarily make difficult choices. The only thing that you should consider is which one, out of all the different options, it is possible for you to achieve. Going against this principle is going against reality. And no one can afford to do so.

Also, the term 'difficult' is a relative term. If you are able to manage the problem, then it is not difficult. It is difficult when you are unable to manage it. Don't say, 'It is difficult', but develop that kind of wisdom which is greater than all problems. It is all a matter of management. Learn the art of problem management and you will certainly be able to deal effectively with all your difficulties. The concept of difficulty only arises from a way of thinking. Change your way of thinking, and very soon you will find that the difficulty has disappeared.

A Power that Can Move Mountains

When there is strong will power, nothing can stand before it, neither habit nor addiction nor anything else.

Ram Kapoor (b. 1973) is an Indian television actor about whom *The Delhi Times* published an interview on March 29, 2015. In the interview he says, "After 20 years of smoking I quit it overnight. From 40 cigarettes to zero, only because my daughter said to me, 'Dada, you want to die. You want to leave me.' It has been one year, three months since I stopped smoking."

Ram Kapoor was addicted to smoking and under normal circumstances it was not possible for him to overcome his addiction. But one sentence from his beloved daughter had shaken him and a strong will power emerged in him. And when there is strong will power, nothing can stand before it, neither habit nor addiction nor anything else.

Often people say that they cannot give up a habit. For example, they say, I cannot stop being angry, or I cannot prevent myself from becoming tense, or I cannot stop hating others, or I cannot agree to humble myself before another, and so on.

All this is not because it is impossible for the person in question to do these things. The real reason is that he is not serious about developing strong will power. If he developed strong will power, he would be able to give up any habit in the same way in which Mr. Kapoor overcame his desire to smoke.

There are two kinds of strong will power—emotion-based and reason-based. There are many people who are motivated by an emotional moment and so abandon their habit. But it is better to abandon something on the basis of reason: a person should think and apply reason to his behaviour, then give up his habit as the result of a well-considered decision.

For example, people often develop complaints about others and go on living in the complaint culture. The habit of complaining is an issue of reason and not of emotion. That is, if a person just thinks about it, he will realize that to go on complaining means being a bad member of society. A good member is one who wishes others well. This kind of thinking is possible through rational analysis. If a person thinks in this manner, he will surely develop strong will power and instantly abandon the complaint culture.

I once met a person who told me that he used to constantly feel angry with others. One day he thought that although he was the one who was angry with others, but it was actually he alone who paid the price for this because he constantly lived in a state of tension and stress. When he realized this, he instantly took the decision to change his attitude and stop being angry.

It is commonly seen that people easily develop strong will power for their own personal interests, but where it concerns another's interests, they do not do so. Such a person lives by double standards. If he uses his reason and recognizes this as a weakness, then surely he will develop strong will power and will abandon his wrong habit.

Often after marriage rifts develop between husband and wife and then their married life is filled with bitterness. If both were to reflect that if, after marriage, they could not live in the same happy way as before marriage, it was because they had been living with their own family members with whom they had a blood relationship: now there was no such relation. Once they acknowledge this, they would be able to summon the will power to correct their behaviour and so manage to lead a normal happy married life.

Develop strong will power and you will certainly be able to move mountains.

Where There's a Will There's a Way

❦

Strong will makes you able to learn from experience, and it is a fact that for a sincere person, experience is a successful teacher.

Some years ago I spent a few days in Kigali, the capital city of Rwanda in central Africa. During this visit, I happened to meet a Gujarati Indian, who was living in Kigali as an immigrant. He was running a cloth shop in the city.

One day I visited his shop and found that he was able to deal with his customers in fluent and understandable English. He seemed to have a good working knowledge of the language. One of his friends told me that there was an interesting story behind his English. When this Gujarati Indian first came to Kigali, and opened his shop, he was ignorant of the English language. But a large number of his customers were English-speaking, so he felt compelled to try to speak in English. During the early days, his English was far from correct. One day someone said to him, "If you are not in a position to speak correct English, why are you trying to speak in English?" The shopkeeper simply replied, "I speak incorrect English so that I may be able to speak correct English."

And so it came about. In two years' time, he was able to deal with his customers in the English language. When I met him, he was fluent in English as a means of communication, and for a shopkeeper that was quite good enough.

This success story bears out the old saying, 'Where there's a will there's a way'. If you have a strong enough will to achieve something, you will do so, sooner or later. Strong will itself is like successful schooling. Strong will makes you able to learn from experience, and it is a fact that for a sincere person, experience is a successful teacher.

Studies of the human brain tell us that it contains numerous windows. Some are open and some are closed. It requires a compelling situation to open the closed windows of the mind. If one has a shocking experience and takes it quite seriously, that will automatically open those closed doors of the mind. This process can sometimes bring about miracles: a person can then play a role that was unimaginable prior to that experience. This principle can be applied to almost every situation, big or small. Anyone can perform a miracle, the only condition being that he should have the capacity to turn the shocking moment to good account.

In psychology there is a theory that is called the brainstorm theory and this explains such abnormal events. According to psychological studies, when there is a shocking experience, there is a storm in the human brain. This brainstorm activates the dormant cells of the mind, and the result is that one becomes capable of doing what one could not have accomplished in a normal situation.

There are numerous examples in history that confirm this theory. One Indian example is that of Bhimrao Ramji Ambedkar (1891 – 1956). He was born into a poor untouchable family. As a boy, he found himself rejected in his own society. This sad experience was very strong, but he decided to overcome this situation. After much hard work, he successfully completed his education, and finally emerged as a great mind in the drawing up of the Indian Constitution. After Independence he was appointed as the Chairman of the Drafting Committee of the Indian Constitution.

What is imperative in such a situation is that one who faces such adversity should not become demoralized, but should try to overlook other people's behaviour towards him, so that he may unfold his own potential. Soon he will find that he is at the top of the ladder of achievement.

The will, if it is strong, can unfold one's hidden potential. But there is a difference between willing and wishing. Do not follow any unrealistic wish: follow your true will and you will be able to add your name to the list of super achievers.

Something More than Money

❦

If you are born to a life of hardship, it will activate you and this will give you the incentive to work.

It was May 7 of 2012. After a foreign tour, I landed at the Delhi airport, where I used a wheelchair. At the exit, my companion offered some money to the boy who was manoeuvring my wheelchair. The boy refused, saying, "Don't give me money, but give me your *ashirwad*. I am appearing for an examination, please pray that I pass it." I placed my hand on his head and prayed for him.

What the airport boy said was not something simple. It represents a creative mindset. It is to opt for hard work instead of opting for easy money. It is to opt for a 'self-made man' formula, rather than trying to find some favour.

When you try to live on your own, you are trying to tap your own potential. Everyone is born with enormous potential, but potential can be developed only by hard work. The best policy for anyone trying to succeed in life is to try to unfold his potential rather than try to receive any advantage from elsewhere.

People generally say with envy that Mr. So and So was born with a silver spoon in his mouth. But this is wrong. Fortunate is one who is born with an incentive spoon in his mouth. If you are born to a life of hardship, it will activate you and this will give you the incentive to work. On the other hand, if you are born to a life of comfort, it will kill your motivation. It is a fact that self-motivation is far greater than external support.

Every favour is limited in nature. There is no favour that has unlimited scope. But when you try to unfold your own potential, that is like embarking upon a journey that has no limit. Favour may give you temporary relief, but hard work is the only way to achieve great success. All the super achievement in history was the result of hard work rather than favour.

It has been rightly said: 'It is not ease but effort, not facility but difficulty that makes men.' Facility may seem to be good, but difficulty is better in terms of result. Opting for effort is good for both physical health and intellectual development.

Living on favour means living as a taker in your society. But living as a hard worker means being a giver in your society. And it is a fact that the giver is better than the taker.

When you achieve something by dint of hard work, it gives you one precious thing, and that is confidence. Hard work is always accompanied by confidence. And, confidence leads to peace of mind. Nothing is better than peace of mind.

Once a man came to the Prophet of Islam. He said: "I am a pauper. Give me some money for my livelihood." The Prophet said: "That would not be good for you." Then he told him a formula for dignity: "The upper hand is better than the lower hand." Then the Prophet gave him a few silver coins, and said: "Go to the forest, cut some wood, and sell it to earn your livelihood. And meet me in two months' time."

The man accepted the Prophet's words. He led his life as advised by the Prophet. Then two months later, he came back to the Prophet and said: "I am happy with my job. Now I have decided not to ask for anything from anyone."

By hard work you can earn money, but through money you cannot achieve hard work. The best formula of life is this: Do not try to obtain favours from others, but rely on your own efforts.

Welcome Criticism

Criticism is a process rather than an end. It entails discussion and discussion leads to intellectual development. It is intellectual development that makes a man a superman.

Criticism, as a rule, is disliked by all and sundry. Some people go to the extreme of abhorring criticism. But that is an unhealthy response, for criticism and dissent are positive elements in the lives of individuals and in society at large.

I happened once to meet an American scholar to whom I put the question: "What is the most important aspect of western culture?" He replied: "Freedom of expression." Elaborating on this point, he stated that in the west dissent was taken – right, wrong, good or bad – as a sacred right of the individual.

What is criticism? It is a part of intellectual exchange. When you discuss some issue with anyone without any reservation, what you have to say is very likely to take the form of criticism. In any critical process there are two parties. One who criticizes and one who is the object of criticism. The former may expound a divergent viewpoint in a frank and open manner, and this encourages the latter to discover some new aspect of the subject under discussion. So criticism is good for both of those concerned.

The universe of thought is vast. No single person is able to cover all of the arenas of thought or knowledge. Given this situation, criticism affords the opportunity to broaden and enhance your field of knowledge. It is a kind of give and take process.

Let us take the example of a mirror. A mirror is also a critic – in a purely physical sense. If you have a spot on your face, the mirror will instantly draw your attention to it. And you accept this without the slightest reluctance. The same is true of the critic, who is like an intellectual mirror. If he points out some fault in your thinking, then you have to accept it. If you are not in a position to accept it instantly, you have at least to give thought to the point he makes. A negative reaction is not good because it is infructuous, both in the case of the intellectual mirror and in the case of the physical mirror.

Criticism is a process rather than an end. It entails discussion and discussion leads to intellectual development. It is intellectual development that makes a man a superman. Indeed, through the process of criticism we embark on an intellectual journey, trying to find answers to our questions. Criticism, opening the closed doors of a mind, enhances the human thinking capacity. As such, criticism is always good. There is nothing bad in criticism.

Criticism promotes thinking along new and different lines. It is the result of thinking in a fresh and original way and, as such, it is a healthy factor in a society. Someone has rightly said that when all think alike, no one thinks very much.

Critical thinking is constructive thinking. It is a phenomenon of creativity. And creative thinking is the only way to intellectual progress. Creative thinkers are always able to discover new things, but creative thinking cannot be developed without critical thinking. You should, therefore accept criticism with a tranquil mind and you will soon discover that your critic was an intellectual enabler.

The greatest weakness of every man or woman is that he or she lives within the boundaries of his or her own mind. This kind of thinking tends to induce self-conditioning, which is not always of a positive nature. No one, except your critic, can de-condition your mind. That is, he points out those negative aspects of your intellectual make-up that had hitherto been hidden from you. Everyone must, therefore, welcome the critic. The critic is the only one who can help you to rid your personality of undesirable traits. So, be eternally grateful to him.

There is a saying: 'One who criticizes you is better than one who praises you.' This saying is very correct and is also very meaningful. One who discovers the value of criticism will surely appreciate criticism and will accept what a critic has to say just as happily as if he were being given a make-over in a health spa.

Living in the Culture of Discovery

If you are an intellectually awakened person, then it is quite possible to extract new things from your observations every day and night.

There is a Japanese saying: 'Discover something new every day, even if it be a new method of threading a needle.' This saying is based on nature. According to nature, everyone should develop his mind. Intellectual development is a continuous process that goes on day and night.

The universe of facts is replete with points of interest. If you are an awakened person, if have a curious mind, and you are sensitive about your learning, then it is quite possible that every experience, every observation will teach you a new lesson. Each time you cogitate, you will be able to discover a new idea.

Discovery is food for the mind, just as physical items are food for the body. When we take lunch or breakfast, we take physical food and thus we energize our bodies. Similar inputs are required for intellectual health. We must be so conscious about this fact that we should derive something new from every experience. It all depends upon our intellectual awakening. If you are an intellectually awakened person, then it is quite possible to extract new things from your observations every day and night.

Without this daily discovery, your mind will become so dull that you will be just like an animal. Ostensibly, you will appear to be a human being, but in actual fact you will be something of a lesser being altogether.

All the animals need physical food, but they have no need of intellectual food, whereas it is in the nature of man to need intellectual stimuli. And for this purpose, he must discover new things every day. This habit makes one a creative person. And only a creative person can do great things in life.

Being Master of the Situation

Control your emotions and you will be able to deal effectively with all kinds of situations. This is the master formula for high achievement.

Who is the master of any given situation? One who is able to turn an unfavourable situation to good account. This is possible for anyone. One just has to control one's feelings and be able to think in an unbiased manner.

Swami Vivekananda, a great soul of India who lived in the nineteenth century, was once put to the test by a friend of his. He invited him to his house and asked him to sit in a room where there was a table laden with books. These books were the ten sacred books of different religions, one on top of the other. The sacred book of the Christians, the Bible, was placed on the top, and the sacred book of the Hindus, the Gita, was placed at the bottom. Obviously, this arrangement was intended to provoke his guest. Pointing to the pile of books, the host asked Swamiji to give his comments. Swamiji just smiled and said: "The foundation is really good."

This story gives a good example of how one can become the master of a situation. Basically, it requires

us not to become provoked, even in a provocative
situation. When you become provoked, your mind
suffers a kind of paralysis; it cannot work properly, so
you find yourself at the mercy of the situation. But,
when you do not allow provocative situations to affect
you, your mind can work at its full capacity. When the
mind is free to work, it is like a super computer and can
solve all problems.

The most powerful faculty of a man or a woman
is his or her mind. In capacity, it is of unimaginable
scope. It is the mind that successfully controls the body
and, through scientific advances, has come to grips
with the vastness of space. Through the mind, man
becomes a superman. By contrast, it is the feelings, or
emotions, that render human beings vulnerable. They
are the weakest part of the human personality. He who
can prevail over his own feelings can prevail over the
whole world. This is the simple formula for mastering a
situation: control your emotions and you will be able to
deal effectively with all kinds of situations. This is the
master formula for high achievement.

Man's personality is paradoxical. He is intellectually
the strongest creature in the world but, at the same time,
he is the weakest of all creatures. He who is controlled
by his mind, is a strong person, while he who becomes
the victim of his emotions, is a weak person. It is in
your own hands to become either strong or weak.

People generally complain about others; but no one
is stronger than you. No one can create problems for
you. It is your own unwise or emotional actions that
give others the scope to do mischief. So don't complain.

Always look to yourself, always review your own actions, and be ready at all times to re-assess your planning and then you will have no complaint against anyone.

There is a terse but meaningful saying: 'Blame thyself.' This means that in all situations you should not try to see others' mistakes but identify and acknowledge your own mistakes. This is the simplest formula for a successful life.

Never say that this situation is favourable or that situation is unfavourable for you. It is you yourself and not the situation that can create a better future for you. So learn the art of situation management. Those who can manage situations successfully are bound to emerge as masters of their own destinies.

Almost all the great men were born in unfavourable conditions, but they took control of their circumstances and became super achievers.

The Haves and the Have-Nots

The greater the incentive, the greater the development, the poorer the incentive, the poorer the development.

It is said that Mr. So and So was born with a silver spoon in his mouth and that Mr. Such and Such was not. In this way, people generally fall into two groups – the haves and the have-nots. But history shows that this kind of categorization fails to explain the real situation. There are many people who were born in the have-not group but, by the time they died, they had become honourable members of the group of haves.

One great example of this is the late Dr. APJ Abdul Kalam. Dr. Kalam was born into a family so poor that they were unable to pay his school fees. Yet, in the latter part of his life, he rose to the highest position in the country, that is, he became the President of India. In his youth, he was an unknown person whereas, towards the end of his life, he became an internationally well-known figure.

This means that the 'haves and have-nots' equation is wrong. It is better to categorize people as 'potential haves' and 'actual haves'. When Dr. Kalam was born, he was a member of the 'potential haves' category but, at a later stage, he became a member of the 'actual haves' category.

The fact is that all men and women are born with great potential but it lies dormant. In this sense everyone belongs to the 'potential haves' category. If one is able to activate one's capacity, and is able to plan one's life, one is bound to become a member of the 'actual haves' category. Almost all the super achievers were super failures in the early phase of their lives but, in the later phase, they emerged as super achievers. If you have been born into a so-called poor family, don't say that you belong to a poor family. You should say rather that you belong to the 'potential haves' group.

Nature is not unjust to anyone. It is generous to

all men and women. But nature gives you things in potential terms and not in actual terms. It is up to you to turn your potential into a reality. Don't blame destiny but discover your own capacity: you can create your destiny on your own. The only condition is that you have to discover your potential and translate it into an actuality.

The word 'have-not' is only a negative name for those who are born with a differently-abled personality. Those who are born in poor conditions, have a greater incentive to improve their lot in life. This is in accordance with the law of nature. It is this incentive that is basically responsible for all kinds of progress. Therefore, the natural formula in this regard is: the greater the incentive, the greater the development, the poorer the incentive, the poorer the development.

Those who are categorized as have-nots are, in fact, people of who have to struggle, and it is by struggling that you can achieve all kinds of success. According to a survey, people who were born in poor African or Asian countries and then migrated to the U.S.A. are now earning more than the average American. This is the miracle of hard labour. In the past they were poor people and now they are rich people living in greatly improved conditions. What is the reason for this? It is nothing but having an incentive to do better. It is a fact that rich people are deprived of such an incentive. Incentive is the monopoly of poor people.

Seen in this perspective, the have-nots are more fortunate than the haves. In fact, the have-nots are the super haves. The have-nots have an incentive to do better, they have to struggle, they experience an intellectual awakening, and must necessarily lead an active life. They are people of vision, and this precious virtue is generally lacking in the haves.

The most important factor in our lives is the law of nature. It is the law of nature that determines the occurrence and the outcome of all events and it is a fact that the law of nature is on the side of the so-called have-nots. If you see people in terms of the future, you can say that today's have-nots are tomorrow's haves and today's haves are tomorrow's have-nots.

The De-Conditioning of a Conditioned Mind

De-condition your conditioning and you will instantly emerge as a new person – better than what you were in the past.

American psychologist, Broadus John Watson (1878 – 1958), after lengthy experimentation, discovered that conditioning is an integral part of life. Every human being is born in an environment, so everyone is subject to environmental conditioning. There is no exception whatsoever. So everyone is either Mr. Conditioned or Ms. Conditioned.

Professor Watson's finding was quite correct. It

is a fact that everyone is a case of conditioning. But Professor Watson's finding related only half of the truth. He discovered the law of conditioning, but he failed to discover the law of de-conditioning. According to his research, everyone is bound to live in a conditioned state. It is everyone's fate and no one can escape from it. But it was certainly an unnatural statement. It is a fact that everyone is subject to conditioning but it is also a fact that every form of conditioning can be reversed. Conditioning is a phenomenon of thinking and it can be changed by counter-thinking. Thinking and counter-thinking are both well within the capacity of the mind.

The modern computer is a small mechanical model of man's mind. Everyone knows that a computer can delete anything that you want it to delete. If you feed some item into the computer, and then you want to delete it; this can be done, simply by touching a small key. Man's mind is an inconceivably large model of the computer. If a small mind can delete an item without failure, how can a big model not do the same job? The de-conditioning of a mind also has a small touch-button. This touch-button is a simple phrase of just three words: 'I was wrong.' Say with complete sincerity: 'I was wrong' and you can delete any type of conditioning within a second.

Watson himself is a proof that environmental conditioning can be reversed in the later period of one's life. As a matter of fact, Watson first de-conditioned himself, consciously or unconsciously, and only then was he able to discover the phenomenon of conditioning.

So, if this de-conditioning was possible for him, why should it not be possible for others?

What is the importance of de-conditioning? It is the only way to intellectual development. It is a generally accepted fact that education is an important tool for personality development. But at the same time, one must try to de-condition one's mind; otherwise one cannot receive the fruits of education in their totality.

I know a person belonging to a minority community who was obsessed with the concept of discrimination. He said that, without there being positions reserved for members of minority groups, he could not find a good job in this country. I said: "No, at present you are thinking in terms of discrimination, but please revise your thinking and try to understand the matter in terms of excellence." I reminded him of a well-known saying: 'There is always room at the top.' I said that if you were an average student, then you might face some kind of discrimination, not only in this country but elsewhere in the world, but if you enhanced your efforts, if you became a topper in your institution, then you would certainly achieve the job you desired. I said that discrimination had a limit and you could cross that limit only by dedication and hard work.

The said student accepted my advice and started re-thinking. He increased his efforts and the result was miraculous. He got first class marks and, of course, he was offered a good job in some institution. Those who look only at external factors invariably underestimate their own capacity. But those who discover themselves become free of this obsession and can meet all challenges.

De-condition your conditioning and you will instantly emerge as a new person – better than what you were in the past.

Rights without Rights Activism

It is every time better to engage in the kind of activism which lays emphasis on duty and then you will have no complaints against anyone.

The well-known tennis champion, Martina Navratilova was born in Communist Czechoslovakia in 1956. Because of her pro-American ideas, the Czech authorities stripped Martina of her nationality in 1975. In 1981, she acquired American nationality. Martina worked very hard on her sport and went on to become a famous tennis star, winning several championships.

Czech citizenship was her right but, even when her right was taken away, she neither protested nor engaged herself in any activism to regain this right. She focussed on her game and went on to become a champion. This changed the mind of the Czech government. Navratilova, who was earlier considered a liability for the Czech government, later on emerged as an asset and her citizenship was restored in 2008.

In such situations, often people resort to making protests and demands. It is a matter of record that they seldom have anything positive to say. On the contrary, Martina did not launch any campaign and she had her rights restored by virtue of her own prowess.

This world is a world of challenge. This being the reality, registering protests and complaints is quite irrelevant. The only thing that can be effective in meeting challenges is to prove your competence. This is the secret of success in life. The course of rights activism should never be adopted. It is every time better to engage in the kind of activism which lays emphasis on duty and then you will have no complaints against anyone.

The Secret of Progress

To succeed in anything, it is not favourable external conditions that are crucial; it is the inner motivation that matters the most.

According to a report published in *The Times of India*, a survey of the world's 100 richest people today reveals that the vast majority of them did not inherit their economic fortunes. 73% of them were 'self-made'. Of these, 18% had no college education, and 36% were children of poor parents. (August 18, 2013, p.12)

How is it that people who were born into poor families, many of whom did not receive any higher formal education, were able to amass such wealth, and that, too, with no help from the Government or any organization? The answer is that it was because of their own efforts.

This illustrates a basic principle of nature. And that is that deprivation is not just a lack of something. Rather, it is, at the same time, also possession of something else—a strength and an incentive to overcome the sense of lack. Impelled by the law of nature itself, a person who considers himself to be deprived of or lacking something develops a strength or urge to make efforts to acquire that which he thinks he is deprived of or lacks. This inner urge keeps him active until he reaches his goal. A feeling of being deprived creates within him a strong motivation for making efforts.

To succeed in anything, it is not favourable external conditions that are crucial; it is the inner motivation that matters the most. In fact, it is often the case that favourable external conditions make people complacent and inactive. On the other hand, someone who faces unfavourable external conditions develops a certain discontentment, which, in turn, can provide him the incentive to make active efforts to change things for himself for the better.

No Shortcuts

Offering favours only paralyzes the ability of a community, whereas when a community has to face challenges, this proves to be an energizing factor for it.

November 16, 2013 was a special date for the Indian cricket star, Sachin Tendulkar. It marked the end of a career in cricket spanning 24 years, in which he emerged as a superman of India. In a short speech, he gave the credit for his success to his late father, Mr. Ramesh Tendulkar. He said that when he was eleven years old and had just started playing cricket, his father gave him this advice: "Chase your dreams, but do not take shortcuts." Sachin Tendulkar took this advice and it brought him success.

What is meant by taking a shortcut? It means travelling by a shorter route or by-pass so as to reduce the distance to one's destination. By thus avoiding the normal longer route, one spends much less time on the road. This kind of by-pass is commonly taken on road journeys. But when it comes to the purposeful journey of human life, it is seldom the best course to follow.

For example, if you are a student and try to sit for a master's degree without graduation, or if you are a moneyless person and want to become a billionaire without doing any hard work, or if you start your career in politics and try to attain a high position in the political system without doing the required field work, shortcuts of this kind will not get you anywhere in real life. In such instances, planning to reach one's goal by taking shortcuts is ill-conceived and is destined to lead nowhere.

This formula does not pertain only to individual life. It also holds true for the life of a community or a nation. Leaders of the Muslim community in India invariably insist that, for some reason or the other, Indian Muslims have become a backward community and that the only way to give them a boost is to give them reservations in jobs and services. Failing this, they will remain backward.

A demand of this nature is a demand for a shortcut. But, according to the law of nature, this is not feasible. No amount of favour shown to any community can bring about its uplift. The only way to empower its members is to enable them to meet the challenges posed to them. Life is based on competition and challenge. Without facing competition and challenge, no community can prosper. There is no escape for anyone in this regard. Offering favours only paralyzes the ability of a community, whereas when a community has to face challenges, this proves to be an energizing factor for it. Shortcut is a word that may be found in the dictionary, but it has no relevance in real life.

Abdul Kalam - A Philosopher Scientist

Be modest and you will be able to attain every kind of high success in life.

Dr. APJ Abdul Kalam, former President of India, died on July 27, 2015 at the age of 83. Throughout his life he had been a man of integrity. Two words are crucial to understand his personality—intellectually, he was scientific in temper and morally, a very humble person.

He was born into a South Indian family which could initially not even afford to pay his school fees. But he worked very hard and continued with his education, and consequently went on to become one of the highly respected aerospace scientists in the country.

Dr. Abdul Kalam was not one of those about whom it is said that 'he was born with a silver spoon in his mouth', yet he was born with a great 'incentive spoon' which was responsible for his tremendous success. His 'spoon' helped him, and he rose to the highest office of the president of India. The life of Dr. Abdul Kalam has a very significant lesson, that is, people's categorization into haves and have-nots is unrealistic.

The real categorization is that people are either actual haves or potential haves. Those who today apparently belong to the category of have-nots can convert their potential into actuality, and thus enter the category of haves.

Dr. Kalam once said, "If a country is to be corruption free and become a nation of beautiful minds, I strongly feel there are three key societal members who can make a difference. They are the father, the mother and the teacher." This statement is a very correct analysis of the issue of nation building, because a person develops his personality in his formative period, during which he is under the supervision of his parents and teachers. If these three members of society resolve to make the child a right person, then within one generation the whole situation of India will undergo a drastic change.

Regarding the youth, Dr. Kalam said: "My message, especially to young people is to have courage to think differently, courage to invent, to travel the unexplored path, courage to discover the impossible and to conquer the problems and succeed. These are great qualities that they must work towards." If we express these qualities in one word, it can be said that young people should make 'excellence' their goal, they should not accept anything less than striving for the excellent. In doing so, not only will they reach great heights of success, but will also be able to reform the society along constructive lines.

It is said that even amidst his tight schedule, Dr. Kalam found time to put pen to paper, almost every day. This is a very creative habit because if a person restricts himself only to routine office work, he will slowly experience intellectual stagnation. However, if along with work he takes out time for reading and writing, the process of his intellectual development will go on unhindered.

On one occasion, Dr. Kalam made the following point: "India has a message for the world that religion could be transformed into a mighty spiritual force." This is without doubt a realistic statement, because India has traditionally been a country of high spiritual values. If India develops in spirituality, it will certainly become a lighthouse of spirituality for the world.

When Dr. Kalam was president, a reporter began to interview him by referring to him as 'Your Excellency'. The interviewer says that Dr. Kalam cut him short, "Call me Kalam," he said. This is the key to Dr. Kalam's personality—he was modest to the core. The message he has left behind for others is: Be modest and you will be able to attain every kind of high success in life.

Time is a Treasure

You must properly regulate your life in order to use the time that you have been allotted in the most beneficial manner.

Time is our greatest wealth. All of us have been blessed with the gift of time, but few of us spend it properly. Someone has rightly said, 'Money lost can be earned again, but lost time is lost forever. So, use your time judiciously.'

It is unwise to waste and idle away your time. It is a waste of your life to spend your time on useless things. You should use your time on things that will benefit you in the true sense. Time is an external thing. It is determined according to the calendar. But the proper use of time is something that depends on an individual's own quality.

You must properly regulate your life in order to use the time that you have been allotted in the most beneficial manner. All of us have only a limited period of time in this world. And, after that, our period is up! We won't ever be able to get back the time that has passed by. So, we need to clearly distinguish between proper and improper use of time. We need to save ourselves from the improper use of time in the same way as we might want to stay away from a forbidden thing.

To be deeply concerned about not spending your time in an improper way will help you use it in the way that you actually should.

Confidence Yes, Overconfidence No

Over-confidence is a common flaw in the character of those who are lacking in humility. The virtue of modesty makes you a realist – a person who is cut down to size.

Confidence is good, but over-confidence is bad. Confidence is very important in life for both men and women. But when a person becomes over-confident, he takes such great risks as are beyond his capacity to deal with successfully. It is like fighting against the laws of nature.

Why does a person become over-confident? The reason lies in over-assessment of his capabilities. Sometimes people rate their competence too highly and plunge into situations that are beyond their control.

One historical example is that of the wrong decision-making of Napoleon Bonaparte, the erstwhile Emperor of France. He used to say that the word 'impossible' was to be found only in the dictionary of fools. This was sheer over-confidence and led him into the ill-conceived attempt to invade Russia in the winter of 1812. The Russian army at that time was not very strong, but they had the advantage over the French army in being able to cope with the severity of their winter, whereas the severe cold of that region proved to be fatal for Napoleon's army. The extreme cold accompanied by hailstorms caused most of the French soldiers to perish even before entering Moscow.

The same happened with Adolf Hitler, the dictator of Germany. It was his belief that he was destined for success. He thought he was invincible. Deluded by this obsession, he invaded Russia in the winter of 1941. His army too was caught up in a hailstorm and was crushed at Stalingrad. Over-confidence generally leads people into misadventures, which can be fatal to both nation and individuals. In this world, no one is so strong as to court disaster with impunity.

According to the divine scheme of life, any achievement is a result of two factors – one's personal planning and support by the external world. The share of personal planning is less than fifty per cent while the share of outside factors is more than fifty per cent. It is this fact which makes over-confidence untenable in this world. People, thanks to their obsessions, take into account only their own planning, generally ignoring external factors. Unable to foresee future developments, they indulge in unrealistic thinking, which eventually proves fatal. Most of the people who are prone to this kind of thinking risk being failures.

I know an educated person who was in a good government job but then, because of his political ambitions, he resigned from service and threw himself into the arena of politics. This adventure proved to be beyond his capacity and he was defeated in the elections. He lost both government service and the assembly seat.

Then there is the question of how one can cope with over-confidence. The formula is very simple. Before taking a decision, discuss the matter objectively with other people who are well-informed and when it is proved that you are about to take a step in the wrong direction, accept the reality and admit your mistake.

Over-confidence is a common flaw in the character of those who are lacking in humility. The virtue of modesty makes you a realist – a person who is cut down to size. Such people generally proceed with caution because, before taking any action, they take into consideration all of the factors in whatever situation they have to tackle and make a thorough assessment of the risks involved. Taking this realistic approach prompts them to take into account their own shortcomings. This serves as a controlling element in their lives and prevents them from having to face untoward consequences.

Overconfident people remain wrapped up in their own thoughts. They know themselves but are unaware of the lives of others. From inside their own cocoon, they are unable to draw upon others' experiences and develop the kind of inward-looking attitude which can be highly damaging to all concerned.

There is a saying that the young man sees the rule and the old man sees the exception. With a slight change, I would like to say that the overconfident person sees the rule and the confident person sees the exception. Overconfident people are always more likely than others to take risks. They hold that risk-taking is good. They say: "No risk, no gain." But taking a risk must be a well-calculated move, otherwise it could lead to disaster.

Differences of Opinion

Differences of opinion are immensely beneficial. They help bring to the fore new dimensions of issues under discussion and to uncover hitherto hidden aspects of a subject.

Once, I met a western scholar and I asked him what he thought was the secret of the West's progress in many fields. He replied that it was the freedom of dissent, which the West has come to consider as sacrosanct. Undoubtedly, what he said is true. This is not something specific just to western thought, though. It is actually a law of nature.

Differences of opinion are generally expressed in the form of critique. Ideally, intellectual critique should engender analysis and further study of issues on which differences of opinion exist. This critique should seek to facilitate an open exchange of views on such matters. It should help bring different minds together to honestly express what they know about issues and also what they feel about each other's views. This sort of open exchange of views is indispensible for intellectual development.

Knowledge as such is limitless. This is true of

knowledge of both 'religious' as well as 'secular' matters. Undoubtedly, differences of opinion are a mercy. There is only one condition for expressing such differences, though—and that is, that those who disagree with each other should do so on the basis of accepted evidence and must abstain from hurling allegations against others.

Differences of opinion are immensely beneficial. They help bring to the fore new dimensions of issues under discussion and to uncover hitherto hidden aspects of a subject. They help promote creative thinking. They also enable people to benefit from the results of the intellectual contributions of others.

No Door is Closed

Success is not the outcome of destiny: it is the outcome of effort. Pre-destination is a fact, not in terms of fate, but in terms of inborn qualities.

After finishing high school, the late R.K. Laxman (b. 1921), one of India's best-known cartoonists, applied to the J. J. School of Art, Bombay, hoping to concentrate on his lifelong interest in drawing and painting. But the dean of the school wrote to him that his drawings lacked, "the kind of talent to qualify for enrolment in our institution as a student", and refused him admission.

This was indeed a sad experience for Laxman, but he did not lose heart. He decided to try again and finally graduated with a Bachelor of Arts from the University of Mysore. He then started his career as a cartoonist and later joined *The Times of India*, beginning a successful career spanning over fifty years.

This incident teaches a great lesson. It means that a man may be born with a great talent, but may not at an early age be recognized as being talented. So he must adopt the maxim: 'Try, try, try again.' It is quite possible that he will eventually achieve a position that according to others was unthinkable for him while he was still very young.

The fact is that all men and women are born with great potential, but this potential remains hidden. Only with sincere effort can one unfold one's potential. This is a law of nature, and one should rely on the law of nature rather than on what others have to say about one. Almost all great achievers have at some time or another been underestimated by others – even by their own selves.

There are many such examples where one was rejected by others at an early age, but never lost courage, and continued his struggle till he finally reached the top. There are many who suffer this kind of rejection at an early age. The only difference is that some successfully unfold their potential, and rise as super-achievers, while others, who do not even recognize their own potential, end up as failures.

Success and failure in this world are in one's own

hands. Everyone is a born achiever, even those who are said to be disabled. And the so-called disabled are not really disabled. They are simply differently-abled.

Success is not the outcome of destiny: it is the outcome of effort. Pre-destination is a fact, not in terms of fate, but in terms of inborn qualities. Everyone is born with different qualities and it is up to each individual to discover the distinctive qualities with which he has been endowed by providence. Once he discovers them, he will be successful. But if he fails to do so, he can expect nothing but failure.

The fact is that the amount of scope for success is greater than the incidence of failure. No amount of failure can diminish this scope. Every failure is only a stepping stone to a further broadening of scope. Discover this fact of life and you will never be disappointed; you will never feel that you have reached a blind alley where there is no way to go ahead. According to the law of nature, every evening brings with it the silent message that very soon there will be a new dawn. This fact is true not only for the material world, but also – even more so – for human life.

Success is fifty per cent the outcome of one's struggle and fifty per cent the outcome of the discovery of one's potential. When you ultimately realize the full extent of your talents, you are well on the way to success.

The term 'closed door' can be found only in the dictionary – not in real life. Both success and failure are the products of one's own intellectual awareness.

More than Legal Rights

Opt for self-empowerment, and you will certainly achieve more than you could ever have expected from others.

Satyendra Nath Bose (1894 – 1974), the renowned Indian physicist specializing in mathematical physics, was best known in the early 1920s for his work on quantum mechanics. He was known to be a very hardworking student.

One of his stories from student life has a great lesson for us. While doing an MSc at Calcutta's Presidency College, Satyendra Nath Bose once performed so well in a mathematics exam that he was quite exceptionally awarded 110 marks out of 100. He was given these extra 10 marks because he had solved some complex problems by more than one method. The great lesson that we learn from this incident is that if a person proves himself competent enough, he will be awarded more than would normally be due to him. In such a world, there can be no place for complaints or protests. All those who are engaged in what they call 'rights activism', would do well to understand that they could choose to follow a better course of action, that is, 'opportunity activism'. They ought to tell people: Don't ask for your rights, but strive to do better and you will certainly receive even more than what is your due.

All men and women are born with a divine gift, that is, unlimited potential. Discover this divine gift and avail of it by turning your potential into actuality, and you will emerge as a super achiever. You can shape your future by your own efforts. Make yourself a giver member of the society rather than a taker member.

Asking for your rights is a form of begging. When you have such great potential, why do you choose to beg? There are many so-called "empowerment" movements, like Muslim empowerment, women empowerment, economic empowerment, etc. But the greatest empowerment of all is self-empowerment.

Opt for self-empowerment, and you will certainly achieve more than you could ever have expected from others. Every man can emerge as a superman, provided he discovers this law of nature and does his best to apply it to his own life.

Born as a Potential Hero

For the individual, the natural course is to discover himself through self-study. When he discovers himself in this manner, he should not become drawn away towards anything else.

Everyone is born with special qualities. But, these qualities are given to him in the form of potential. It is the duty of everyone to discover this potential and make it an actuality through wise planning. Everyone is required to play a heroic role in society. But, an individual can do so only when he discovers his unique quality and tries to realize it through objective planning.

Just as a person has been endowed with a unique quality, he has been given a unique mind. If he studies himself and discovers his special quality by objectively utilizing his mind, he will certainly be able to perform that special role for which he is destined.

To perform this task, one has to prevent oneself from becoming the victim of prejudice, distractions, reactionary thinking, a superiority or an inferiority complex, overestimation or underestimation of one's case, or allowing extraneous factors to condition one's mind. A person who can save himself from these derailing forces, will certainly discover his unique quality and emerge as the hero of his time.

Apart from these internal exercises, one has a supporting element in the external world. This external factor is the merit-based society. In a truly merit-based society, an inherent process is initiated, which can be described as automatic channelization. When a person sets out in life, there are a number of options open to him. He may enter a profession, but very soon discover that he is not excelling in it. Then he tries another option. When he faces the same experience, he will again change his vocation, until he makes that option in which he feels he is excelling and for which society is giving him exactly what he is due. He then adheres to this role and devotes his energy to it until he emerges as a hero. In this sense, society becomes a supporting factor for all individuals and helps them channelize their energies towards that for which they were born.

For the proper functioning of this supporting factor, the condition is that no favour or reservation be given to anyone in society: rather there should be a 'compete or perish' environment. The individual should know that he would not be able to gain a position unless he merits it. It is this course that I have termed automatic channelization. It is a form of internal mechanism.

Every human being is born with the great urge to achieve a high position in society. Discontent is innate in every human personality. That is why, when a person feels that he is not excelling in the course of his choice, his discontented nature pushes him towards another option. This natural course takes him toward the role for which he was born. If this course is allowed to continue in the correct way, then every person will emerge as a hero and it will become a means of superior social development at the collective level.

To develop a heroic personality and build a better society, it is important to follow the course of nature. For the individual, the natural course is to discover himself through self-study. When he discovers himself in this manner, he should not become drawn away towards anything else. He should not let any excuse intervene in this matter. He should be ready to pay any price. He should not allow any other person to dictate to him, but should rather aim at his discovered target with an uncompromising spirit.

The other responsibility is of the system. It is the duty of the system to run society on a purely merit-based principle. Society should open up all its opportunities on the sole basis of merit.

A Break in Generation

If the present generation fails to take the advice of their seniors due to their modern mindset, senior people are also responsible for their inability to convey their advice in a language that is more understandable and therefore more acceptable to the modern mind.

In the service conduct rules, there is a provision that is called a 'break in service'. If a government servant fails to report for duty for a day or more without taking proper leave, the number of days on which he is absent will be deducted from the total period of his service.

The same applies to anyone who starts a business, abandons it and starts some other job and again abandons that job and starts a new venture. This kind of practice can be described as a 'break in history'. People who behave in this way are said by psychologists to have grasshopper minds. And those who indulge in fragmenting their history in such a way cannot achieve any great success in life. Your history is your greatest asset and a break in service or a break in history deprives you of this valuable asset.

There is another 'break' which is widespread in the present world – the 'break in generation', or as it has more recently come to be called, the 'generation gap'. Over the previous centuries, it was common practice for elders to give the younger generation the benefit of their experiences. This was a healthy and instructive process. Of that there is no doubt. Young people may have a good education but, because of their lack of experience, they can easily go astray. Formerly, parents or older family members had always been there (and are still there) to communicate their experiences to the upcoming generation, so that they should take the right path in life. But now, due to modern and unnatural ideas about freedom, the new generation is reluctant to accept the advice of their elders.

They have developed the attitude of 'we know everything, we are the masters of our future; we have to stand alone.' This kind of psychology acts as a deterrent to their proper development, for all over the world, the members of the new generation are entering upon their lives without the benefit of experience. It is experience that makes you mature. In this situation the whole new generation has become immature, and the result has been disastrous.

For example, let us take the institution of marriage. In our present age, this institution has been considerably weakened. After marriage either both the husband and wife live in a state of tension, or they end their marriage by separation.

Why has the institution of marriage become so weak in the present day, when it was so strong in previous generations? The reason is very simple. Marriage in previous ages was held as a matter of adjustment, whereas the present generation is quite dismissive of this fact. Having failed to receive the benefit of the older generation's experience, they know nothing about marriage except love. And it is a fact that, in social life, it is adjustment that matters and not emotions.

Had there been no generation gap, the marriages of the new generation would have been as successful as in former times. Nowadays, this phenomenon is not so much the exception as the rule. This has done much damage to modern society. The aforementioned example is one of its harmful repercussions.

The generation gap is a very serious problem in our world. But the younger generation are not solely to be blamed. The older generation must also share the blame. So, there is fifty-fifty culpability. Old people have had their experiences – there is no doubt about that. But they are unable to express their experiences in the modern idiom that is understandable to the new generation. Thus part of the problem lies in the fact that there is a language gap between the two generations.

Old people know only the traditional forms of language, while the new generation is acquainted with language which they consider more rational. Old people give their advice in an arbitrary manner without giving the rationale behind this advice. They know only the language of dos and don'ts and the present generation can understand only that kind of language which is supported by reason. So, if the present generation fails to take the advice of their seniors due to their modern mindset, senior people are also responsible for their inability to convey their advice in a language that is more understandable and therefore more acceptable to the modern mind. So both generations are equally to blame.

Unawareness is not an Excuse

Never try to achieve the unachievable. First of all you have to assess each situation, examine the whole matter realistically, then do your best to understand your position vis-à-vis the stance taken by others.

There is a saying that ignorance of the law is no excuse for breaking it. Apparently this saying only concerns legal matters, but in fact, it is a general rule, applicable to all kinds of situations, from booking a ticket to forming state policies.

For example, suppose you are doing a job in a company in such a way that it leads to a serious dispute with your boss. If your boss takes strong action against you, in such a situation you cannot say you were not aware that the boss would take your case so seriously. This kind of excuse is not acceptable. If you are serving in a company, you have to know the principle: the boss is always right.

If you are doing business and you behave towards your customers in such a way that it annoys them and consequently your business suffers, you cannot then say that you were not aware that your customers would become angry. You have to understand from the outset that customer-friendly behaviour is essential for success in business.

This is true also of political activities. If you are the president of a democratic country, you cannot be diametrically opposed to public opinion or to what the opposition parties feel is right. If you adopt a policy that fails due to strong opposition from other parties, you cannot have any complaints about your opponents. You are, after all, living in the age of democracy and even if you are the president, it does not mean that you enjoy absolute power. You have to accept the ground realities. You have to know in advance that politics is the art of the possible.

This principle is a very common one. It is relevant to all branches of life. It is just as true for the individual, as it is for social and political matters. Of course, if you have to take decisions about your own individual life, you are free to be true to your own ideals. But, when you want to do something that affects the tenor and functioning of social or political life, you have to be practical.

Never try to achieve the unachievable. First of all you have to assess each situation, examine the whole matter realistically, then do your best to understand your position vis-à-vis the stance taken by others. Make your plans after taking all these matters into account. There is a saying in Chinese that you should start your journey from such a point that every step is a step forward.

V

Positive Aspect of Failure

Make Your Mistake a Mistake Plus

A mistake becomes a mistake plus when it awakens your mind. It thus enables you to re-plan your life. A mistake plus makes a man a superman.

The English poet Alexander Pope (1688 - 1744) said in one of his poems, 'To err is human; to forgive, divine.' This saying has now become a well-known proverb. It is a fact that everyone makes mistakes. This is a part of human nature. But there are two kinds of mistakes. The first one is simply a mistake. There is another kind of mistake, that is, a 'mistake plus'. The first kind of mistake fails to give you anything. But, a mistake plus gives you many great things. A mistake plus seems to be a mistake in the beginning, but in the end it becomes an experience of gain.

When one makes a mistake, there are two possible kinds of responses. The first response is to become regretful. One who is full of regret will become disheartened after every mistake. He will be a victim of stress. It is also possible that he may lose courage and be unable to do anything else again.

This is the negative aspect of making a mistake. But

there is also a positive aspect of a mistake. That is, it encourages you to engage in introspection and self-reassessment. When you do this, your mistake will turn into a mistake plus. A mistake plus is bound to activate your mind. It will lead to brainstorming. In return, it will emerge as a natural gift for you. It will increase your creativity and produce a thinking process that may lead to the capacity for better re-appraisal of yourself and an increased ability to analyze things. A mistake becomes a mistake plus when it awakens your mind. It thus enables you to re-plan your life. A mistake plus makes a man a superman.

Nature's greatest gift to man is his mind. The mind is the greatest miracle of nature. The German psychologist Alfred Adler observed: "One of the wonder-filled characteristics of human beings is their power to turn a minus into plus." Now there is the question of how this miracle may come about? The answer is that if a person makes a mistake and saves himself from being a victim of negative thinking, then by nature a miraculous event occurs. That is, by the law of nature a rethinking process is developed in him. He analyzes what happened with him and tries to understand where he went wrong. He thinks how he may achieve at the second attempt what he could not at the first attempt. In this way a new process of positive thinking is initiated in the mind of this person, which becomes a means for his intellectual development. Thus, this process turns his mistake into a mistake plus.

A mistake is an error or fault resulting from poor judgment. If you have a positive mind, your mistake will motivate you to try to find out where you went wrong. This kind of rethinking will open up new possibilities to you. Thus, in an indirect way, the mistake will become a means to climb to new heights of success in life.

The condition for turning a mistake into a mistake plus is that one should not take a mistake to be a full stop. Rather one should consider a mistake as a comma. If one makes a mistake ten times, one should put a comma at each instance. One should not put a full stop unless one's mistake has turned into a mistake plus.

Remember that in this world the quantum of mistakes is limited, but the quantum of achievements is unlimited. No mistake can close the door to your achievement, provided that you are able to keep your thinking positive.

Second Choice is Always There

If you try to opt for the first choice and fail, then do not consider it as the end. It is a signal that there may be another better option waiting for you.

Narendra Damodar Das Modi became the Prime Minister of India after winning the 16th General Elections in the country. During election campaigns, an instance was reported in the media that at an election rally held on 5 May 2014 at Amethi, Modi said: *Log kehte hain ki Modi haar jayega toh kahan jayega. Tum chinta mat karo. Meri chai banane ki ketli ka samaan tayyar hai.* (People ask where Modi would go if he loses the elections. They need not worry. My tea kettle is ready.)

One aspect of this utterance of the Prime Minister is that it shows the strength of India, where a person can reach the highest post having started from humble beginnings.

There is another aspect. Initially the above remark may have been considered a joke but in the extended sense we can derive from it a wise formula of life. And that formula is – if you lose the first option do not waste time in worrying; instead seek for the second option. Life is full of options. If you try to opt for the first choice and fail, then do not consider it as the end. It is a signal that there may be another better option waiting for you.

Former Prime Minister of India, Jawaharlal Nehru completed his law degree from Trinity College, Cambridge. In 1912, he started his law career in Allahabad with his father Motilal Nehru, a successful lawyer. But after some time, he decided to shift to politics. It is said that an Indian student studying law was once asked what he would do after completing his course. He replied: *Chal gayi to Motilal, nahin chali to Jawaharlal.* (If I succeed it would be like Motilal, and if I fail, then also there is an example for me in Jawaharlal!)

This is the only wise formula. It applies to both non-political and political spheres of life. This formula means that after losing the first chance, there still exists a possibility of achieving success. The law of nature is always with you. For example, in non-political life if you lose a job there might exist an option of a second job. In political life, if you do not receive majority in the assembly, there exists an option of choosing the healthy role of opposition.

Life is full of uncertainties, then what to do? It is not possible that the result of a person's striving is always in accordance with his wishes. In such a situation, the best policy is that of adjustment. This formula has many advantages. It saves you from unnecessary stresses, makes you wise enough to utilize your time and gives you a chance to re-plan your life. This formula gives you unshakeable hope. It saves you from the killer psychology of complaints and protests. Once I was in a valley where I saw rivulets cascading down from top of the mountain peaks. I noticed the way each stream flowed till it arrived at a boulder. It did not try to break the rock in order to move ahead. Rather, when it encountered the rock, it simply swerved to the left or to the right, around the sides of the rock, and kept on with its journey uninterrupted. This phenomenon has a great lesson. It teaches that nature adopts the second choice if the first choice is not workable. When you fail to attain the first option, you need to instantly divert your energy to discover the second option. Nature and history both give us a message: if you fail to achieve the first choice, try to avail of the second choice that has existed all along.

Failure is Greater than Success

The message of failure, on the contrary, is quite the reverse. It tells you that you have not yet reached your destination and you have to try again, and make far greater efforts than before.

Bill Gates (b. 1955) the American business magnate who co-founded Microsoft, once said: "I failed in some subjects in exams, but my friend passed in all of them. Now he is an engineer in Microsoft and I am the owner of Microsoft." Gates is now consistently ranked in the Forbes list of the world's wealthiest people.

Why was there this difference between two men who were following the same career path? The reason is that initial success caused Gates' friend to imagine that he had reached his ultimate destination. Therefore, his struggle ended at the point where he got a job and began to lead a 'normal' life.

Bill Gates' failure, however, gave him the incentive to accomplish more and more in order to obtain what he had failed to achieve on the university campus. It was this attitude that made Bill Gates a winner and finally he emerged as a great name in business.

There are many such examples in history that tell

us of those who faced failure in their initial years, but emerged as super-achievers in their later years.

In life, success and failure are relative. The message of success is: you have achieved what you wanted to achieve. This kind of thought paralyses the mind. It leads to intellectual stagnation. It tells you that the time for hard work is over and now you can take things easy. The message of failure, on the contrary, is quite the reverse. It tells you that you have not yet reached your destination and you have to try again, and make far greater efforts than before.

Failure is Not the Last Word in Life

Bidhan Chandra Roy (1882 – 1962) was a highly respected physician and a renowned freedom fighter. After Independence he was elected the second Chief Minister of West Bengal and is often considered the great architect of West Bengal, because he founded five eminent cities in the state.

However, the early part of his life was not at all encouraging for him. After graduating from Calcutta, Bidhan sailed for England with only Rs. 1,200, intending to enrol himself at St Bartholomew's Hospital to further his education. The Dean, reluctant to accept a student from Asia, rejected his application. But he did not lose heart. Again and again he submitted his application until, finally, the Dean admitted Bidhan to the college – after thirty admission requests.

There are many instances in history of such persons who experienced failure in their early years. But, they continued their struggle and finally became very successful. The number of opportunities is far greater than the number of failures. Given this state of affairs, no one needs to despair. One should rather carry on one's struggle in an unflagging manner. Even after failing 'thirty times', one can emerge victorious.

There is Always a Second Chance

Taking the second chance has probably brought him better results than the first one could ever have done

Former Assam Director General of Police, Shankar Barua, committed suicide by shooting himself with his licensed revolver at his home in Guwahati on September 17, 2014. He was 63 years of age. Shankar Barua was being investigated by the CBI for his alleged involvement in the multi-crore Saradha chit fund scam.

Family sources said he had slipped into a depression after his name had been linked to this scandal.

The Chief Minister of Assam, Tarun Gogoi, paid tribute to Mr. Barua, saying, "He was an upright and efficient police officer who discharged his duties conscientiously and assiduously." Perhaps Mr. Barua was himself not a corrupt person, but it seems he became involved in the scam under some pressure.

This kind of involvement on the part of Mr. Barua was certainly a mistake, but another mistake he made was totally avoidable. That is, he failed to re-think his case and re-plan his future action. It is a law of nature that if in any given situation a person loses the first chance, then there is always a second chance for him. But, Mr. Barua's real mistake was that he became so obsessed with the first mistake that he could not think beyond it.

His case could have gone to the courts and he may well have won the legal fight. There are many instances in which an individual has had to appear in court but was ultimately acquitted after the judicial proceedings, after which he was again able to lead a normal life.

Had Mr. Barua lost the legal fight and the court sentenced him to imprisonment, even then he still had a future. He could have written a book with the title, *How to Eradicate Corruption*, as he undoubtedly had many experiences relating to this phenomenon. He was very capable of dealing with this subject and his book could have become a bestseller.

Corruption is the most serious problem plaguing

Indian society. Everyone thinks about this nation-wide scourge, but no one knows how to eradicate it. Had Mr. Barua pulled himself out of his depression, he could surely have written a very valuable book on corruption which outlined a new line of action by which corruption in India could have been brought to an end. If Mr. Barua had set himself to this task with an open mind and given a revolutionary book to India on the issue of corruption, he would certainly have deserved to have the title of the 'Saviour of Modern India' conferred upon him.

Our world is full of opportunities. When anyone fails to grasp the first one that comes his way, there is always a second one in the offing. Availing of it will prevent him from succumbing to frustration and will enable him to re-plan his life. Very soon he will discover that taking the second chance has probably brought him better results than the first one could ever have done.

From Failure to Success

Almost all super-achievers were super-losers at the outset. Success always comes to those who are true seekers of success.

Mohandas Karamchand Gandhi (1869 – 1948) was born in Gujarat and after completing his early education there, he went to London to study law. After returning to India in 1891, he started attending the Bombay High Court. His first case was a simple one, for which he was offered a fee of Rs. 30. When this young inexperienced barrister of 22 stood up in court to argue his client's case, he lost his nerve. His head reeled and his mouth went dry. Thoroughly abashed, he made a hasty exit. Subsequently he undertook no further litigation in that court.

In 1893, Gandhi accepted a year-long contract from an Indian firm in South Africa to work there as their legal representative in the city of Pretoria. In 1915 Gandhi returned to India from South Africa. In 1919, the Chauri Chaura incident gave him the opportunity to assume the leading role in Indian politics, and he later emerged as the greatest leader of India. It was during this period that Tagore conferred upon him the title of 'Mahatma'.

The above event shows that failure does mean defeat. Failure can become a stepping stone to better things, provided the individual concerned does not lose courage and subsequently re-plans his course of action. It is a law of nature that the scope for achievement will always be greater than the quantum of failure. No failure can stop you in your quest for success, provided you maintain your positivity. If your first plan fails, that, in a way, is good news for you. For, according to the law of nature, your experience of failure will activate your mind. It will open up new windows that were hitherto closed. Your failure will spur you on to work in a more effective way and attain a resounding success. Thus, it is a blessing in disguise.

The journey of great achievement very often begins from great failure. Throughout the annals of history, the many people who emerged as heroes after initial failure are legion. Failure simply enabled them to re-plan their lives, and then to touch new heights of achievement. Almost all super-achievers were super-losers at the outset. Success always comes to those who are true seekers of success. Make yourself a true seeker of success and you will certainly reach your destination.

A Great Future is Awaiting You

Failure has a greater impact than success.

Hargobind Khorana (1922 – 2011), born in Raipur in West Punjab, was an Indian-American biochemist. He earned his B.Sc. and M.Sc. from Punjab University, Lahore. Then, in 1945, he went to Manchester University and obtained a PhD. Three years later, when he returned to India in 1948, he applied for the post of lecturer in Delhi University, but was rejected. This thoroughly depressed him, as he now thought his future looked bleak. However, he returned to England to carry out further research in his field. His hard work yielded fruitful results and later, in 1968, he received the Nobel Prize for an important discovery relating to DNA.

There are many such instances in history of some well-read, talented person being denied a position for which he was well qualified, but after a long struggle, emerging eventually as a super-achiever. These events tell us about a great secret of nature. That is, failure has a greater impact than success. Once you are successful, you become contented and begin to take things easy. However, if you experience failure, that gives you the incentive to put in much more effort than you normally do and such qualities come to the surface as would have remained dormant under normal circumstances. This is why failure can work as a stepping stone to great success.

No Discrimination in Divine Blessing

Abundance erodes the good qualities in one's personality while scarcity proves to be a booster for personality development.

One often hears of a certain Mr. So and So having been born with a silver spoon in his mouth. This notion conveys a wrong perception of reality. According to it, there is no equality in the divine scheme of birth, meaning that some are born with special blessings while others are not. This concept is totally wrong.

Blessings are based not on birthright but on opportunity. Opportunity is the most important thing in life. One who avails of opportunities becomes successful, while one who fails to do so becomes a failure. Success is the outcome of one's own efforts. It has nothing to do with birth.

Everyone is born on an equal basis. The most appropriate saying would be: 'Everyone is born with the silver spoon of opportunity.' There are many people who are born into affluent circumstances and have every advantage in life, but due to a combination of apathy and incompetence, have become failures. On the contrary, there are others born in straitened circumstances who, thanks to their own efforts, have emerged as super-achievers.

In fact, those who are born into abundance can actually become deprived persons, because, where there is abundance, there is no incentive to work and study hard. Because of this lack of motivation, they make no effort to go on and do better things. Sooner or later, things begin to deteriorate and, in extreme cases, one who has made no effort to enhance his existence may ultimately find himself descending into poverty. Those, on the other hand, who were born in deprived circumstances, become strongly motivated by their poverty to successfully change their lot in life.

Abundance erodes the good qualities in one's

personality while scarcity proves to be a booster for personality development. This means that in terms of results, poverty is a far greater a blessing than abundance. Deprived persons are highly blessed persons. This is the lesson taught us by long experience.

Suicide is Not an Option

Our Creator has endowed us with great qualities. It is required of every human being to unfold these qualities and play the role that is destined for him or her by providence.

Hermann Hesse (1877 – 1962) was a famous German poet and novelist. In his early years, Hesse experienced personal turmoil and conflict with his parents. This situation led to such extreme frustration that, in 1892, at the age of fifteen, he attempted suicide. But, for some reason, his attempt came to naught.

According to a study, it has been established that those who attempt suicide but do not die, become highly incentivised to do great things and later emerge as heroes. That is exactly what happened with Hermann Hesse. He completed his education and subsequently took up writing as a career. After a long struggle, he became a great writer and in 1946 was awarded the Nobel Prize in Literature.

Man is born in this world not just as a matter of accident, but in accordance with a divine plan. Our Creator has endowed us with great qualities. It is required of every human being to unfold these qualities and play the role that is destined for him or her by providence. According to this creation plan of the

Creator, every individual must live in hope. There is no excuse for becoming pessimistic.

Our world is full of opportunities. If someone fails in doing something, he should take it as a delay and not as a final failure. In adverse situations, committing suicide is not an option for anyone, whether man or woman. One should simply adopt the wait and see formula, rather than take the extreme step of killing oneself.

Positive Aspect of Negative Experience

If you save yourself from becoming the victim of negative experience and do just one thing, that is, do nothing and let nature take its own course, it would serve as a positive factor for your mind.

Thomas Alva Edison (1847 – 1931) is renowned as the most famous and prolific American inventor of all time. With his inventions, Edison exerted a tremendous influence on modern life. More than one thousand patents are registered under his name.

But the early history of Edison presents a very different picture. After a few months of his schooling, his teacher declared him 'addled' and confused, and claimed that he wouldn't be able to continue with his education. Edison's mother had no option but to take him out of school. She then decided to teach her son at home. This proved to be a great moment in Edison's life: while the door of one school was closed to him, at the same time the doors of two other schools opened up to him: home-school and mind-school. Due to this incident, Edison's mind was triggered further and he became motivated to learn on his own. This presents an example of that miraculous factor in human beings, which is known as nature. The principle we derive from here is that when man denies giving you something, nature comes into play to compensate for your loss on a far greater scale.

According to the law of nature, there is always a positive aspect of every negative experience. The only condition is that one should not become negative or succumb to despair. Life is full of unpleasant experiences. There is no escaping them. But negative experiences are not evil phenomena. They are in fact a blessing, a kind of intellectual challenge. In such situations, it is better to wait rather than opt for a reactive approach. If you save yourself from becoming the victim of negative experience and do just one thing, that is, do nothing and let nature take its own course, it would serve as a positive factor for your mind. It will certainly increase your thinking capacity and unfold your intellectual treasure.

If you have developed a strong personality and an intellectually awakened mind, then every shock will prove to be a positive shock for you. You would automatically become capable of availing the shock as a new opportunity. This is because the law of nature stands above all else and when you choose to remain un-offended by an unpleasant experience, you invite the law of nature to come to your rescue and initiate a process to compensate for your loss.

Life is full of opportunities. Even if someone takes away something that had been given to you, what nature gives you can still not be taken away. For example, if a person gave you a man-made torch and he takes it away, he can still not take away from you the divine torch, that is, the sun. Knowing this principle brings about immense hope.

The only fit response when you find yourself in a negative situation with others is to forget the unpleasant external experience and on your own take a fresh decision to improve your ability. Very soon you will find that you have gained more than what you had lost.

There is no full stop in life, only commas. No event is the final chapter of your book. Every day you are in a position to add a new chapter to it. This is due to the enormous capacity of the human mind. You must not underestimate your mind. It is underestimation of the mind that breeds frustration. If you discover the capacity of your own mind, it would give you great courage and unending strength. You will be able to take a new leap into your future from the point where apparently your life's journey had come to an end.

The First Law of Success

Those who, in spite of these drawbacks, never lose their courage and continue to make unflagging efforts, in the end emerge as super-achievers.

The British physicist and mathematician, Sir Isaac Newton (1642 – 1727) is famous for his formulation of the laws of motion. The third of law of motion states that for every action, there is an equal and opposite reaction. But, there is also another law which was demonstrated in Newton's own lifetime. This may be called the first law of human success.

Newton's father died three months before he was born. His mother soon re-married. As a result, Newton was deprived of his parents' love. A biographer of Newton's wrote: "Basically treated as an orphan, Isaac did not have a happy childhood." Apparently, this was a minus point of Newton's life, but in reality it became his life's greatest plus point.

During his childhood days, the outside world held no attraction for Newton, and he started living in his own world. He came to be called a wool-gatherer, or absent-minded person. But, it was later learnt that Newton, rather than being absent-minded was really

275

very focused. As a result of this intellectual bent, he was able to discover great scientific laws.

The lack of love and affection on the part of his parents was apparently a great drawback, but according to the law of nature, this turned out to be to his advantage. This was because it caused him to intensify his thinking capacity and he was thus able to unfold his hidden potential. In this way, his intellectual proclivities were turned to good account. Thus, in this sense, his minus point proved to be a plus point.

This is not just the story of an individual. It is more than that. It is the story of nature. Newton's life is a demonstration of a very important law of nature. That is, a human being is born with unlimited potential. Nothing can stop his journey toward success, except apathy or a sense of frustration. If he does not become frustrated or apathetic, his own true nature will automatically guide him and take him to a destination of incredible eminence.

There are many examples in history of people who, in their early years, became the victims of all kinds of adversity. Yet, they did not allow themselves to become disheartened by the difficulties they faced, and their nature ultimately guided them – continuously channelizing their energy and talents – towards a goal they could not even have thought of in their early days.

In life, people often have to face untoward situations, for example, having to live in an orphanage, suffering accidents, sustaining material losses, receiving an incomplete education, having no inheritance to look forward to, failure to get a good job, and so on. But those who, in spite of these drawbacks, never lose their courage and continue to make unflagging efforts, in the end emerge as super-achievers.

The Fall of an Apple

Nature always tries to give you a lesson, shows you the right direction and tries to unfold your potential. It tries to make you aware of the opportunities which present themselves all around you.

Isaac Newton was a great English physicist and mathematician. It is said that once when he was sitting beneath a tree, an apple hit him on the head, and through pondering over this phenomenon he discovered the Universal Law of Gravitation.

This was like a shock treatment administered by nature. This event triggered a train of thought in Newton's mind. He started thinking about why, when an apple fell, it came down and did not go up. This thinking led to the discovery of the law of gravitation. This law had always been there, but man had failed to discover it. Then, after a long time, nature hit man on the head and told him in the language of hammering: 'O Man, discover the law that has remained undiscovered till this date.'

This was like shock treatment. Shock treatment is a law of nature. This shock treatment can be called a challenge. Every human being faces this kind of challenge in some way or the other. This shock treatment is a blessing in disguise, for it always acts for the betterment of the person in question.

If you are facing some problem in your life, in your job, business or family, don't be negative. Take it as a positive phenomenon. If you turn negative, you cannot avail of the opportunity it presents. But if you are positive, you will try to understand the real message behind the challenge and very soon you will find that the challenge was nothing but a stepping stone in your life.

Shock treatment is the language of nature. Nature always tries to give you a lesson, shows you the right direction and tries to unfold your potential. It tries to make you aware of the opportunities which present themselves all around you. Don't ignore such warnings, take them seriously. They will give you right guidance and turn your failure into success.

Nature is the best guide for every human being. But nature always speaks in the language of hammering, that is, challenge. A challenge is not an accidental event. Challenge always comes from nature. In this way nature tries to awaken your mind, it tries to initiate a process of rethinking.

At first nature tries to give advice in simple language, but when you fail to adhere to that advice, it uses the method of shock treatment. This is like awakening a person who is not ready to wake up with a simple call. All the challenges in life are positive challenges. When you face any challenge, take it in a positive manner, try to understand the lesson hidden in it.

'The falling of an apple' on one's head is a very common phenomenon. Every person faces this experience, although not in the form of an 'apple', but in the form of shock. These experiences are not accidental, they are part of divine planning. They act as a booster. If you have this kind of experience, don't let your mind get disturbed. Take it as a positive sign. Try to find out the message behind this event, and very soon you will find that it was just like the fall of an apple, the sole purpose of which was to enable you to discover a great law of human life.

There are numerous people in history who failed in the first chance. But then they thought about their problem afresh and consequently achieved great success.

Sometimes people make a wrong choice, then nature hits them with an apple and gives them a silent lesson: 'Try to make a better choice!' Those who listen to this silent voice of nature are destined to emerge as super-achievers.

A Lesson from a Shock Absorber

❧

Make negative experiences grist to the mill of your own personality development. Nurture yourself on what they teach you.

If you are standing by the roadside when a car passes by, you will observe that its wheels continually move up and down over bumps in the road surface. But, if you were sitting inside the car, you would feel as if the car were running smoothly. How is this possible? It is because the car is fitted with shock absorbers thanks to which the shocks remain confined to the wheels and do not reach the passenger.

A spiritual person is one who has an inbuilt 'shock absorber'. Such a person can experience any undesirable event he faces without any disturbance either to his emotions or to his thinking processes. For such a person there will frequently be problems and unpleasant situations that he shall have to face, but because of his 'shock absorber', his mind will remain unaffected. In a world which is constantly administering shocks of one kind or another, he can live in a state of perfect equanimity.

In our society, there is no one who does not have to suffer negative experiences of one kind or another. These negative experiences generally give rise to complaints. And when the mind becomes exclusively taken up with complaining, there can be no spirituality. Spirituality and complaints cannot go together. Considering that there is no escape from such negative experiences, what should one do? The answer is that if you want to live as a spiritual person, you have to install a 'shock absorber' in your mental makeup. With this 'shock absorber' taking every shock upon itself, your spirituality will remain intact.

You are bound to live in society and much as you may want to change society, you have no power to do so. That is because social laws work independently of us. Then, what to do? You shall simply have to condition yourself to think positively, even in negative situations

Constant complaining is the greatest enemy of spirituality. But the complaint culture is a part of social living. Indeed, society is awash with complaints. It is a veritable ocean of complaints. And just as a fish cannot live out of water, its natural environment, man cannot live outside of the society to which he belongs. Therefore, rather than trying to change society, change yourself . Make negative experiences grist to the mill of your own personality development. Nurture yourself on what they teach you.

The best way to cope with the problem of complaints is to take it as a challenge. When you take a problem as a challenge, you do your best to meet it. You try to deal effectively with it, rather than try to eliminate it altogether from society.

This course of action is quite possible. For example, if a bird is sitting on the wall of your house and you throw stones at it, it will fly away from your house, sit on a nearby tree and continue its chirping. The bird always lives in a non-complaint culture. If this culture is possible for a bird, then why not for man?

Unpleasant experiences are not an evil. They cause you to think realistically. They enhance your ability to make correct judgements, increase your creativity and make you sympathetic towards those who have adopted a way of proceeding that is unfavourable from your point of view. This is the positive outcome of an unpleasant situation.

It all depends on how you look at things. Problems arise when you look at things from the wrong angle. Adjust your viewpoint and very soon you will find that everything will turn out to be in your favour.

Shock: A Blessing in Disguise

Shock is a great educator. It sets off such a process of brainstorming that a whole new mindset takes shape and as a consequence a new human personality emerges.

Alfred Nobel (1833 - 1896) was the first person to invent dynamite. He went on to establish 90 armament factories and amassed huge amounts of wealth through the arms trade. Then an incident took place which totally changed the course of his life.

In 1888, the death of his brother caused several newspapers to mistakenly publish obituaries of Alfred. One French obituary stated: *Le marchand de la mort est mort* ('The merchant of death is dead'). The obituary went on to say, "Dr. Alfred Nobel, who became rich by finding ways to kill more people faster than ever before, died yesterday." Alfred, shocked at what he read, then took a positive decision about his life. In 1895, at the Swedish-Norwegian Club in Paris, Nobel signed his last will and testament and set aside the bulk of his estate to establish the five Nobel Prizes, including the prestigious Nobel Peace Prize.

Shock is a great educator. It sets off such a process of brainstorming that a whole new mindset takes shape and as a consequence a new human personality emerges:

if in the pre-shock period he was just a man, in the post-shock period he emerges as a superman.

Shocks, great or small, are very common. Almost everyone has had experience of them. But the majority of people take these as negative experiences and are unable to learn a lesson from them.

However, shock is not an accident: shock is the language of nature. Nature speaks in the language of shocks. If one saves oneself from becoming negative after suffering a shock, this can be a highly creative experience. Shock will stimulate your mind, and will unfold your potential. It initiates creative thinking processes. It helps you to take better decisions in your life by bringing you from a state of total derailment to being right back on track. In other words, it makes you realistic in your approach.

Shock is the greatest positive factor in one's life, provided one responds positively to it. Everyone can play a high role like Alfred Nobel; the only condition being that one should take shocks as a source of learning rather than a source of anger. History is replete with instances of people who received shocks, but were able to face them with a positive mind. Shock had proved a booster to their uplift.

One such example is that of Mahatma Gandhi, who spent twenty years in South Africa. In June 1893, he had to undertake a trip to Pretoria in the Transvaal, a journey which took Gandhi to Pietermaritzburg. There, Gandhi took his seat in a first-class compartment, since he had purchased a first-class ticket. The railway officials ordered Gandhi to remove himself to the van compartment, since non-whites were not permitted in first-class compartments. As Gandhi refused to comply with the order, he was pushed out of the train, and his luggage was tossed out on to the platform in the extremely bitter cold of the winter.

What happened with Gandhi was an example of violence. Yet he decided to work for peace. He returned to India and started his movement which was based on ahimsa, that is, non-violence. Soon, he became a champion of non-violent activism.

According to the law of nature, life is not a smooth journey: it is a journey through shocks. One has no option but to accept this as a reality. Indeed, the course nature takes is determined by shocks and challenges. Anyone who seeks to make himself successful should understand this reality and take shocks as stepping stones in life.

What Makes a Man a Superman?

One who proves to be courageous enough to face the shock of unpleasant situations and takes them as challenges will find that his mind is activated by the experience and this will certainly unfold his potential.

M K Gandhi, a great leader of India, said at a meeting in New Delhi on June 28, 1946, that he was born in India but was made in South Africa. (*Gandhi and South Africa 1914-1948*, edited by E S Reddy and Gopalkrishna Gandhi)

This statement is correct, but it only tells us the location of a great event, and not its real reason. It was not the soil of South Africa that gave rise to this miracle, but rather the workings of nature. And, almost all the super-achievers were created by the same natural process.

When the American missionary Dr. John Mott visited Mahatma Gandhi at his Sevagram Ashram in central India, he asked him, "What have been the most creative experiences in your life?" Gandhiji replied, "Such experiences are in multitudes. But as you put the question to me, I recall one experience that changed the

286

course of my life." Then he related the Pietermaritzburg incident. (*Gandhi Katha*, Umashankar Joshi)

In 1893 Gandhi went to South Africa to take up a job in the legal profession. In June 1893, he had to go by train to Pretoria in the Transvaal, a journey which would take him to Pietermaritzburg. Having purchased a first-class ticket, Gandhi took his seat in a first-class compartment. He was thereupon ordered by the railway officials to remove himself to the van compartment, since non-whites were not permitted in first-class compartments. Gandhi protested and produced his ticket, but was warned that he would be forcibly removed if he did not make a gracious exit. As Gandhi refused to comply with the order, he was pushed out of the train, in the extreme cold of winter, and his luggage was tossed out on to the platform

It was this shocking incident that made him decide to remove racism from the world. He became a man with a mission and, in 1920, began to take action in India, where at that time India was ruled by the same racist colonial power. When he went to South Africa, he was Mr. Gandhi, but when he started his mission in India, he very soon emerged as Mahatma Gandhi.

History tells us that many individuals attained to greatness because of having received some kind of shock. This is a law of nature, and it is this law of nature that has produced so many great personalities of history.

It is a fact that shock treatment is the greatest factor in the process of 'man-making'. But, there is a condition. This law of nature works only in the case of those who take shocks in a positive manner. If an individual takes the 'shock treatment' negatively and becomes dejected, he will develop a negative mindset and will go on living in a state of total frustration or will ultimately die by his own hand.

On the contrary, one who proves to be courageous enough to face the shock of unpleasant situations and takes them as challenges will find that his mind is activated by the experience and this will certainly unfold his potential. His sense of shock will give rise to a new kind of motivation to deal effectively with the situation, and, in the process, this will lead to the development of a creative personality.

One who gives this kind of positive response to shocks, will be enabled to initiate a new, great struggle in his life. If, in the pre-shock period he was just a man, then in the post-shock period he will become a superman. Shock treatment is obviously an unwanted occurrence, but it is this very shock treatment that leads to the kind of superlative creativity which can be of immense benefit to humanity at large.

We Have the Ability to Bounce Back

Remain silent, make your mind empty and the mind will pacify everything within a minute. Very soon your mind will make you normal.

Resilience is a law of nature. It means the ability to recover quickly from illness, change, or misfortune. It can be found everywhere – in the physical world, the plant world, the animal world and the human world.

Resilience in physics means the ability to return to the original form after being bent, compressed or stretched. The same is true of the plant world and the animal world. Every creature inherently possesses the power of resilience.

Man has the lion's share in this gift of nature. Dr. Bruce McEwen, Head of Laboratory of Neuroendocrinology at the Rockefeller University has researched this subject and has concluded: "The human brain is very resilient. Give it a chance and it will make every effort to repair itself."

We are living in a world of challenge and competition. Due to this, every day we experience something unpleasant. Every day we suffer some kind of damage both intellectually and materially. This is a problem for every man and woman. Such problems are a part of nature. But nature has also provided the remedy for this problem, and that is, the power of resilience.

The only thing that is required is an eight-lettered mantra, that is, patience. When you suffer some kind of damage, either internally or externally, keep your patience. Be empty-minded for a while. This is what Dr. McEwen has called giving the mind a chance. If you give this chance to your mind, it will soon release a strong energy and this energy will provide you the help required in any untoward situation. For example, in the case of anger, the mind will readily manage it, in the case of material loss, it will enlighten you as to how to do new planning, in the case of tension, it will provide you the formula to forget, and within minutes you will become tension-free.

The formula of resilience is also applicable to the problems of nations. One such example is the recent history of Japan. Japan was the first to suffer the dire effects of the nuclear bomb. During the Second World War, the Allied powers dropped two atomic bombs on Japan, and apparently Japan became a ruined country. But the Japanese leaders, consciously or unconsciously, followed the formula of resilience. They were able to re-plan their national targets and the result was miraculous: after just thirty years, Japan emerged as an economic superpower.

A recent example of the power of resilience is what happened in the aftermath of Hurricane Sandy in the US. During this catastrophe the US lost about 110 lives and suffered losses of $50 billion. But, within a month, the US was able to bring things back almost to normal. How did this miracle happen? The answer is again that it was due to the secret power of resilience.

Studies show that our mind has enormous potential, perhaps unlimited potential. And that potential is tapped by the power of resilience. In a normal situation, this potential remains dormant. When one has any kind of unusual experience, the brain becomes active and starts unfolding its hidden energy. And if it is given a chance, it will certainly recover all the losses. The only condition is that you should not disturb its natural process or stop it by some unnatural activity.

A simple demonstration of resilience is your remaining silent when you become angry. Remain silent, make your mind empty and the mind will pacify everything within a minute. Very soon your mind will make you normal. On the contrary, if you become provoked and react negatively, your anger will persist, and will very soon turn into malice and even violence.

Remember, Everything is Temporary

───❦───

Optimism means knowing that one will eventually be rescued: that the waiting period will only be temporary in nature.

Ernest Shackleton (1874 - 1922) is best known for his expeditions to Antarctica. On his third expedition, he faced a very serious situation when his ship sank. He and his group of twenty-seven men were literally stranded on ice, drifting aimlessly in the wild southern seas. Apparently, they had no hope of survival. They remained on the floating ice for six months and spent the next four months on Elephant Island before they were rescued. Yet, in the end they returned safely to their homes.

Now the question is: how did this miraculous escape come about? Alfred Lansing in his book Endurance: Shackleton's Incredible Voyage explained it in these words: 'Underlying the optimism of the party was the confidence that their situation was only temporary.'

This miraculous formula is applicable not only to Shackleton's crew, but to every single man and woman. Everyone has the experience of facing serious situations in life. But if you believe that every situation is only temporary, and that it will last for only a limited number of days, then you are able to repeat the story of Shackleton's party.

Every dark night is a temporary phase in this world, and the same is true of human difficulties. Every human difficulty is temporary in nature. Every difficulty is bound to disappear after some time. It is a law of nature that no difficulty goes on and on forever. So, you have to feed this simple formula into your thinking: 'It is all but temporary'.

Ghalib, the Urdu poet, says in one of his verses: *Raat din gardish mein hain saat asmaan, ho rahega kuch na kuch ghabrayein kya.* (The seven heavens are active every day and night, something new will emerge, then why this anxiety?) History only verifies this formula. Difficulties come and go, just like day and night. This is the universal law that applies equally to every human being.

Optimism means knowing that one will eventually be rescued: that the waiting period will only be temporary in nature. The only thing that can create a serious problem for you is to lose your patience or to lose your hope or to forget that the situation is temporary and not permanent.

When you save yourself from being upset, you are in a better position to keep your energy intact, to keep yourself from being a victim to frustration, for frustration is certainly a killer frame of mind to be in.

At every point in life there are serious difficulties, on the home front, the social front, the national front and the international front. The simple formula for facing these difficulties successfully is: think that, like the human being himself, one's problem is also temporary, that is, lasting for only a limited period of time, not permanent. Death is the ultimate fate of man, and the same goes for his difficulties. Difficulties are also doomed to pass away, sooner or later.

In fact, difficulty is state of mind. It is the mind where difficulties are created, and where they can be killed too. When one faces a difficulty, one generally forgets a very important fact: that man himself possesses a difficulty-solving machine, that is, his mind. The mind is greater than everything, including difficulty, however severe it may be. So, in such situations, try to focus on your mind rather than on the difficulty. And very soon you will find that the difficulty has disappeared, first psychologically and then physically.

Moreover, difficulty has a plus point. Difficulty unfolds your hidden qualities: it is a boon rather than an evil. Difficulty makes an ordinary Shackleton into a hero Shackleton.

Here is a Silver Lining

Positive leadership gives the right direction to its people, so that they set about struggling for what is right, rather than just register complaint after complaint.

The British historian Arnold J. Toynbee (1889 – 1975) is best known for his 12-volume work, A Study of History, which was published from 1934-61. In this work he has examined the rise and fall of 26 civilizations throughout the course of history and has developed a theory regarding the growth and disintegration of these civilizations. According to his analysis, history is governed by a law of nature. This law is based on what he terms, the 'challenge-and-response' mechanism. According to this theory, all the great civilizations were created by minority groups.

A minority always comes under the influence of historical factors, which have a profoundly motivating effect upon it. This motivation enhances the minority community's general capacities until it is finally recognized as the most creative segment of the country or region to which it belongs. All civilizations have been the culmination of the efforts and struggle of some such minority.

This law of nature itself is not enough to make the

minority a creative one It requires wise leadership. It is a fact that the minority is always under pressure from the majority. This is but natural and there is no exception to this rule. It is a very critical situation. At this juncture, the leadership of the minority community is put to the test. If the leadership of the minority takes the pressure from the majority as a negative experience, and resorts exclusively to complaining and protesting, the minority will ultimately face disaster. Such leadership plays a negative role in the life of its people. It is this kind of leadership that is thus referred to in a verse of an Arabic poem: 'When a crow becomes the leader of a nation, it will certainly lead its people to a disastrous end.'

The reverse of this situation is one in which, when a minority comes under pressure from the majority and is beset by problems, its leadership plays a positive role. It is then that the leaders of the minority community tell their people that the situation they are facing is not a problem, but is rather a challenge which the people should try to meet with all their might. This kind of positive leadership gives the right direction to its people, so that they set about struggling for what is right, rather than just register complaint after complaint. It is this kind of positive leadership that leads its people toward playing a healthy role, and thus giving rise to a new civilization.

This law of nature means that the minority is always in an advantageous position from which it can overcome the majority. Every minority is potentially in a position to give a gift to the world, that is, a new civilization.

The Survival of the Fittest, the Survival of Both

⁓⁂⁓

Competition creates challenges, challenges act as incentives to increased effort, and this leads to reaching new heights of success.

Modern industry was a boon for mankind, but at the same time its existence created a bad and unfair situation. Those who were able to invest more money in industry emerged as masters of the market, while moneyless people were seen as a deprived group. This situation in the economy created a new saying, that is, compete or perish.

An English thinker, Herbert Spencer (1820 – 1903), justified this development by a theory which he termed Social Darwinism. This theory, according to him, means, "Society is like a living organism. Just as biological organisms evolve through natural selection, society evolves and increases in complexity through the survival of the fittest, that is, the preservation of favoured races in the struggle for life." Where Darwin had applied this concept to biological phenomena, Spencer applied it to socio-economic phenomena.

In science, Darwinism is still a controversial theory. At present I have nothing to say on this score. But I would like to say a few words about Social Darwinism.

It is a fact that there is competition in socio-economic life. But this competition is not evil. It is good for every society. During the process of competition, one group may temporarily emerge as a privileged group, while other groups may in comparison seem to be underprivileged.

However, this state of affairs proves to be positive in terms of its result. According to natural law, sooner or later, the underprivileged group is bound to become infused with a new spirit, which will play a revolutionary role in enabling it to prevail over the negative aspects of its present situation. If the underprivileged group was earlier an uncreative group, it will now emerge under the pressure of circumstances as a creative group.

Keeping this in mind, one can safely say that 'compete or perish' is a wrong saying. In economy, victory and defeat come and go on an alternate basis.

Competition is not just the byword of capitalism. It is a phenomenon of nature, which inevitably fosters competition. Competition creates challenges, challenges act as incentives to increased effort, and this leads to reaching new heights of success. In this sense, a better maxim than 'compete or perish' is, 'compete and grow'.

So, by following the law of nature we can say that the survival of both and not the survival of the fittest is the best formula.

In the End There is Always Light

Failure makes you all the more keen to attain your goal. Moreover, it brings about brainstorming - the best source of intellectual development.

There is a saying that there is always light at the end of the tunnel. If you enter a tunnel, you will feel first of all that there is darkness everywhere. However, if you go on walking, after some time you will begin to notice a small circle of light ahead of you. And when you come to the end of the tunnel, you will find yourself in broad daylight and open air.

The tunnel is an example from the physical world. The same example is also applicable to the human world in which life is a journey for which there is seldom a smooth path. Everywhere on this path there are problems, unwanted situations and sometimes darkness. But, if you do not lose courage and hope, the moment will certainly come when you have reached the light at the end of the tunnel.

Why are there difficulties along the road to any given destination? Consider that difficulties give you experience, make you earnest with regard to your goal and enhance your creativity. Difficulties, thus, reinforce your powers of perseverance, and inculcate the highest values of life. Great qualities cannot be cultivated without the experience of a difficult journey. All is for your own betterment. The Scottish author Samuel Smiles once rightly said: 'We learn wisdom from failure much more than from success.'

What is the reason behind this? The reason is that failure makes you all the more keen to attain your goal. Moreover, it brings about brainstorming – the best source of intellectual development – and stimulates you to revise your planning so that it may the more effectively enable you to achieve your goal.

Success brings you contentment, and this eventually brings to a halt your thinking processes. On the other hand, failure makes you discontented, and discontent is the greatest source of continuous effort in life.

VI

The Formula for Happiness

Happiness in Your Hands

When you call a problem a problem, it seems to be an evil, but when you call it a challenge, it becomes a useful part of life, something that spurs your intellectual development.

A report published in a US journal, the *Journal of Positive Psychology*, gives details of experiments conducted on 'trying to become happier'. The participants were made to listen to 'happy music', and those who actively tried to feel happier subsequently reported the highest levels of positive mood. (December 19, 2012)

Such happiness is certainly of an artificial kind. Life is full of problems. When one is living with the so-called 'feel-good' factor brought on by 'happy music', problems still exist all around you. It is but natural for your mind to keep on reacting to these problems, as you cannot stop the thinking process of your mind. Therefore, this happiness through music will be artificial and unrelated to reality.

It is not possible to achieve absolute happiness by using this procedure. It is like wearing an artificial smile on your face while you are sad within. And anything less than real happiness cannot satisfy you. What is achieved by this method is only a temporary state of happiness. It is better to recognise it as self-deception rather than happiness.

If these researchers were to extend their investigation to the entire life of the participants, they would certainly find that these people in the long run had become dull. In actual life, there are always problems. If you want to live in a state of happiness, that will be possible only if you stop the thinking process. And, when your thinking process is stopped for long periods, it is but natural, that you will become intellectually dwarfed.

The only formula for happiness is to manage the problems rather than forget about them. Problems are created not by man but by nature. Because according to nature, problems are nothing but challenges. When you call a problem a problem, it seems to be an evil, but when you call it a challenge, it becomes a useful part of life, something that spurs your intellectual development.

Take a common experience which needs no lengthy research. Select two persons from your neighbourhood: one, who was born in affluence and never experienced any kind of difficulty, and the other born into difficult circumstances, who had no choice except to face the difficulties as a challenge and tried to achieve success. You will certainly find that the first person is intellectually dwarfed, while the second will be intellectually enhanced.

The British historian Arnold Toynbee has insightfully formed his well-known formula which he calls the mechanism of challenge-response. According to this, the formula is: a problem creates a challenge, the challenge leads to a response and the response results in success. This is the scheme of things in nature. And, in this world, a positive result can be achieved by following the path of nature. No one can develop a formula better than that which nature has developed.

According to the law of nature, happiness is not the greatest good, struggle is the greatest good. One who escapes from struggle and tries to live in happiness, is trying to live in a fool's paradise. This kind of artificial living is bound at some point to fall apart. Such people can live in a state of happiness for a temporary period, but then they are doomed eventually to become sad.

It is not happiness but seriousness, it is not an easy-going life but struggle, it is not living in comfort but being involved in hard work that matter in life. This is the natural path and it is by following the natural path alone that can one attain any real success.

Old Age – A Blessing

It is a fact that old age does create some problems but it is quite possible to take this as normal and save yourself from negative thinking. By awakening your mind, you can live with a positive outlook.

In the USA a series of research projects under the heading of *Progress in Brain Research* (2008), were conducted under the patronage of Yale University. Its findings were reported in the *New York Times*, with the meaningful title *Older Brain Really May Be a Wiser Brain* (May 20, 2008). According to their investigations, researchers have found that old age is not any kind of curse for man but is rather a blessing.

In essence, old age is the advanced stage of one's intellectual development and of one's intellectual journey. Old age, in fact, is a symptom of maturity, increased experience and wisdom. The well-known saying, 'Old is Gold' expresses this perfectly.

While the health of the physical body depends on how many calories we are taking in, the brain is an independent part of our being. Therefore, our mental health depends entirely on positive thinking. If you maintain your positivity in pre-old age, then you will enjoy mental health in the period of old age, even if your body is deteriorating. All those who reach an advanced age are potentially cases of the kind mentioned above. The only condition is that you must maintain your positivity.

It is a fact that old age does create some problems but it is quite possible to take this as normal and save yourself from negative thinking. By awakening your mind, you can live with a positive outlook. This is the only course to take, and if an aged person is able to do so, he can certainly emerge as a wise person.

Indeed, old age is the best phase of one's life. Old age means having more experience, more learning and greater sincerity, wisdom and maturity. All these qualities are enough to make one a great person. According to his situation, the mature individual can do worthwhile things, like founding an NGO, writing his memoirs, opening a counselling centre, etc. An aged person is better placed to give his society or humanity the kind of precious gift that it was not possible for him to give in his youth. One must recognize this opportunity given by nature, and try to utilize it in whatever form suitable to one.

For people, old age all too frequently becomes a liability for themselves and others. The old person tends to think that he is no longer of any use. This phenomenon is not due to ageing. It is due rather to people becoming negative in their old age and failing to turn negative into positive thinking. It is an intellectual problem rather than a physical one. I know many aged people who are capable of performing useful tasks but, because of their negative thinking, they have failed to avail of this opportunity.

I am a writer, now in my nineties. Those who read my articles say that the articles that I write now are clearer and more profound than my earlier writings. According to my assessment, the only reason is that I always try to live as a tension-free person. I face all those same problems in life that make people negative, but I have learnt the art of negativity management. This is the only reason I am living with a totally positive mind, even in this old age.

In my experience, most problems are imaginary rather than real. If you are able to differentiate between what is real and what is imaginary, you will soon discover that what you had been considering to be a real problem was, in fact, a non-real problem.

Learn to sort things out and you will be able to live in a state of normalcy and positivity till you breathe your last breath.

The Formula for a Happy Life

Every problem begins in the mind, and it is also in the mind where problems can be solved. So it is like changing your intellectual gear. If you are able to change your intellectual gear, then you have found the super-formula for de-stressing.

On a visit to the USA I happened to meet an Asian immigrant, a Mr. S.A. I found that he was a man with a difference. At all times he was in a happy mood. His colleagues also affirm that he is quite different from other people.

In the course of conversation, I asked him how he was such a stress-free person, while others were living in stress. He smiled and said: "God Almighty made me and threw the mould away."

It was then my good fortune to be invited by Mr. S.A. to stay with him for a few days. Accepting this offer allowed me to discover the secret of his different personality. My stay with him proved to be one of discovery. I discovered the formula for his happy, stress-free life.

When I was with him at his home, one of his relatives came to him in an angry mood. He said, "Mr. So and So is trying to distort your image. He is engaged in negative propaganda against you." The visitor continued in this way, but Mr. S.A. listened to him dispassionately. Finally the man said in annoyance, "I am telling you something as serious as this, and you are not responding." Mr. S.A. said in an unruffled way: *Yeh unka problem hai, mera problem to nahin.* (It is his problem, and not mine.)

The next day we had planned a sight-seeing trip to a number of places, but for some reason at the eleventh hour, I said, "I'm not in a mood to go out. Let's stay at home." Mr. S.A. replied very calmly: *Chalo yeh bhi theek hai.* (No problem, this is also okay.)

During my stay with Mr. S.A., I discovered these two formulas for his happiness. I think these are applicable to every man and woman. Everyone can adopt these formulas, achieve a stress-free life and live in happiness.

The first principle ('It is his problem, and not mine') can be formulated in these words: the art of problem management. In life there are always problems, and the best formula is to try to manage them rather than try to eliminate them. You have to learn the art of problem management, and then you can have a life where there is no stress or tension.

The second principle ('No problem, this is also okay') can be formulated in these words: if you don't get the first good, be content with the second good. It is a fact that in every situation there is always something that can be called the 'second good'. All that is required is to opt for the second good and forget the first good.

According to psychological studies, every problem begins in the mind, and it is also in the mind where problems can be solved. So it is like changing your intellectual gear. If you are able to change your intellectual gear, then you have found the super-formula for de-stressing.

Man is greater than everything. You are more precious than everything else. So always try to save yourself. If in any situation, you have lost something, even then you have something, and that is yourself. So forget what is lost and take that which still exists for you. This is the best formula for attaining a happy life.

A happy life can often only be achieved in unhappy conditions. Life is an art of management. You cannot change the world, but you can manage yourself in order to find a happy place for yourself in the world. This is the only workable formula for happiness in this world.

Live on Your Own

You have no option other than to discover your true self and to stand up for yourself with determination.

Consider a situation in which someone provokes you and you become incensed; someone makes you angry and you are ready to explode; or someone speaks offensively to you and you take umbrage at this; someone does something damaging to you and you are filled with a desire for revenge. In all such cases your feelings are living proof that you are in a state of subjection to others. Under their Influence, you have become what they   want you to become. You have accepted them as your masters.

In all such situations, you are being dictated to by others. In this case, the right thing for you to do is to refuse to be influenced by others and to live your own independent life. You have to develop yourself as a self-made person. You have to adopt such a course as will not permit anyone to dictate to you or reduce you to living in a state of mental disarray.

This world is full of people who, having no interest in you, ride roughshod over your feelings. Everyone is intent upon his own interests and no one is concerned about your personal welfare. You have no option other than to discover your true self and to stand up for yourself with determination. It is you alone who matter; you are not anyone else's concern. In such a situation, you have to realize what is good and what is bad for you. And, having resolved this matter in our own mind, you have to be wise enough neither to be riled by others' jibes at you, nor to become perturbed at attempts to tarnish your good name.

There is a saying of Benjamin Franklin, 'God helps those who help themselves.' This saying is entirely in accordance with the law of nature, according to which everyone is responsible for his or her own well-being.

How to Develop Positive Thinking

Negative thinking can all too easily overwhelm one's better self, therefore, concerted effort is required to keep it at bay. For positive thinking you need only to 'open your eyes'.

Positive thinking, the source of all kinds of good things, is the most important habit in a man or a woman. It ensures good health and a sound mind, it enables you to plan competently and helps you in crisis management. Indeed, positive thinking results in super achievement.

Positive thinking is the other name for natural thinking. Positive thinking cannot be acquired from the external world. It is your inner nature that provides a reservoir of positive thought. Preserve your inborn nature and you will surely emerge as a positive thinker. Every human being is born with great potential. Allow your potential to unfold and you will become a positive thinker in the perfect sense of the word.

Why are men and women so often incapable of positive thinking? The sole reason for this is that they fail to draw upon the reservoir nature has given them. Everyone is born with eyes, but if he closes his eyes, he will not be able to see anything. The same is true of positive thinking; it comes naturally to every individual, provided he does not 'close his eyes' to it.

The opposite of positive thinking, negative thinking, is like shutting one's eyes. If you want to live as a positive thinker, try to distance yourself from negative thought. Positive thinking enhances the inner qualities of every human being, while negative thinking does the very opposite. Negative thinking can all too easily overwhelm one's better self, therefore, concerted effort is required to keep it at bay. For positive thinking you need only to 'open your eyes'.

The problem here is that we are living in society. Man is a social animal. He is bound to live in society. What is society? Society is a construct whereby human beings live in congregation for mutual benefit. But all of its members have their differences. Difference is a part of nature. Every man is born as Mr. Different and every woman is born as Ms. Different. Indeed, society is an amalgam of highly disparate elements.

It is this difference that creates problems. When you face a situation which is not in accordance with your desires, you become irritated. Then a chain reaction sets in—leading to anger, vengefulness, negative thinking, and violence. It is this phenomenon that prevents you from thinking positively.

Then, the other problem is that everyone is prone to conditioning. The process of conditioning starts with every negative experience. And, conditioning gradually becomes a part of the unconscious mind. The occasional negative experience, because of the conditioning process, comes to affect one whole side of our personality, until a time comes when it becomes integral to one's personality. One loses sight of the fact that it is an evil of which one should rid oneself as soon as possible.

To overcome this problem, one has to learn the art of remaining silent. When any negative thought comes to your mind, do not react. Say nothing. Make your mind empty for a moment. Then the whole matter will settle down. If someone makes a harsh remark about you, you should not take it seriously. Things not taken seriously do not become registered in the mind and thus do not continue to rankle.

Fortunately, nature is very helpful towards us in this regard. Apart from other qualities, there is a unique quality in human nature, that is, the ability to cool down. The only condition is that we should give nature a chance. When we are faced with some unwanted situation, our powers of reasoning are generally swamped by a flood of negative thoughts. But if we can only keep quiet, the cooling down faculty of its own dispels the negativity. It changes the direction of the flood and within seconds, it is gone. Keep silent for thirty seconds. Everything will return to normal, as if nothing at all had happened.

Unnecessary Complaints

Challenges are for our own good. They come into our lives in order to train us, to increase us in wisdom and to strengthen us.

The British MP Enoch Powell (1912 – 1998) once made an interesting comment about political leaders who complain about the media. He felt that such complaints were unnecessary or unjustified. 'A politician who complains about the media,' he said, 'is like a ship's captain complaining about the sea.'

This comment is absolutely true. It applies, however, not just to political leaders, but, actually, to every person. Whenever someone complains about someone else, his or her complaint is actually a needless complaint. He or she turns an issue into a cause for complaint, although the issue is actually not something to complain about at all.

This world is established on the principles of nature. Life in this world is like a vast ocean, always full of waves. Living in society, we will always have to face one wave after another. The only sensible way to deal with the waves that appear in our lives is to consider them as challenges. Instead of complaining about the waves that come our way, we should learn the art of successfully going over or bypassing them.

The fact that we have to face many waves or challenges in life is not something bad or wrong. In fact, challenges are for our own good. They come into our lives in order to train us, to increase us in wisdom and to strengthen us. The difficulties that we face in life are experiences, and without going through such experiences one cannot become a more complete person. We should learn lessons from our experiences. At the same time, we should abstain completely from complaining about them.

Happiness: Another Name for Contentment

⁓§§§⁓

The meeting of needs is achievable for most people, but the satisfaction of greed is hardly achievable for all and sundry, even for the wealthy and the politically powerful.

Happiness is the cherished goal of every human being, whether man or woman. But, it is a fact that the majority of them fail to achieve happiness. They begin their day with unhappiness and end it with unhappiness. It is a sad aspect of the life of almost every human being. So, what is the solution to this widespread problem?

By applying the well-known formula: 'It is by making comparisons that we understand', we can explain this phenomenon. Animals are in many ways like human beings, but with the difference that all animals live in a state of happiness. The word 'unhappiness' is not found in their dictionary. What is the reason for this difference? It is because animals are always contented. They are satisfied with whatever they get, be it more or less.

This tells us that the secret of happiness is in contentment. If you are contented, you will be happy. But if you are discontented with what you possess or have achieved, then you are bound to live in a state of unhappiness.

Studies show that there are two levels of achievement: one based on need and the second on greed. As far as need is concerned, very few are in a truly deprived state in this world. But, the pursuit of greed has no limit. No amount of achievement can satisfy one's greed. It is this streak in man's nature that makes him unhappy.

In this matter, everyone should be very practical. All must differentiate between the achievable and the unachievable. The meeting of needs is achievable for most people, but the satisfaction of greed is hardly achievable for all and sundry, even for the wealthy and the politically powerful.

Although the number of things about which one feels greedy is finite, there is no end to greed itself and the attempt to satiate one's greed is an unending quest. Man demands are unlimited. This is part of his nature. But the world in which he lives is a limited one, and is very seldom geared up to meet his demands. It is this difference that leads to that unenviable state called unhappiness.

Both happiness and unhappiness are states of mind. If you acknowledge this fact, you will easily be able to keep your ambitions in check and will instantly achieve happiness. Happiness is an internal phenomenon, it is not an external achievement.

Acharya Rajneesh was an Indian mystic guru. He wrote a book called, *Kundalini Andar Base*. This title is based on a story of the musk deer. When it smells the odour of its own musk, it runs here and there in search of the source of the fragrance, although it is actually coming from within it. The same is true of happiness. Man searches for happiness outside himself, unaware of the fact that happiness dwells within him.

Happiness is everyone's greatest desire, yet there are few who ever achieve it. Why is this so? It is because man is searching for it outside of himself in the external world, although happiness lies in his inner world, that is, in his state of mind. Make your state of mind healthy and you will certainly achieve happiness.

Happy Married Life

The best way to enjoy life is to play the role of intellectual partner. Men and women must live as intellectual partners.

Men and women were both made as a special creation and created of the same substance. Life is like a cart with two wheels. The cart cannot move without the joint action of both the wheels. No wheel is superior or inferior, both are equal and both have equal roles to play.

It is said that man is a social animal. It means that a man or a woman cannot play his or her role alone. To fulfil their purpose in life, they must join each other. Every successful venture, be it launched by a man or a woman, has to be a joint venture. Without joint effort, no one can achieve any great goal.

A joint venture does not mean that both the genders must do one and the same job. This kind of absolute equality is against nature, and is thus impracticable. In life, there is no such thing as can be described as job equality. True equality is equality in status or respect. Here, joint effort means that both the genders, like the two wheels of the cart, must unite in their life's mission.

The role of a man or a woman in life is not simply to earn money, to accumulate material things, enjoy life, and have what is called entertainment. The purpose of life is greater than these things. Man is not simply a physical entity, but an intellectual being. A man or a woman must enjoy life, not only on a material level, but on an intellectual level. The best way to enjoy life is to play the role of intellectual partner. Men and women must live as intellectual partners.

The universe of facts has far more items than are found in a shopping mall. The universe of facts has billions and trillions of things which are spiritual and intellectual in nature. And, man and woman must embark their journey on this path, in order to discover higher facts and to enjoy life on a higher plane, thus unfolding the hidden treasures of life.

Jesus Christ rightly said that man does not live by bread alone. Here 'bread' is a symbolic term, meaning material goods. Experience shows that those who focus entirely on obtaining material things die in a state of dissatisfaction. No amount of material goods can give you real satisfaction or real peace of mind. Man cannot live on material things alone.

The real goal for a man or a woman is to achieve peace of mind—the most valuable thing in our lives. Peace of mind is spiritual in nature, and it is only spiritual attainment that can give you peace of mind. The mind can become peaceful only by feeding more and more spiritual things into it. And, man and woman are two natural partners in this regard. They are born to make a joint effort to achieve this goal.

Spiritual attainment is not a mysterious word. It is one and the same thing as intellectual attainment. Spiritual attainment, or intellectual attainment, can be had through intellectual exercise, and such an exercise is a joint effort. Everyone needs a partner to proceed with such a journey. And, nature has provided us with this blessing in its pairing of man and woman.

Intellectual partnership is very important and the highest goal for a man or a woman. But there is a condition for this to be successful, and that condition is a ten-lettered miraculous word, that is, adjustment.

Adjustment is not submission or surrender. It is rather the greatest joy. And it is more than that. It is the acceptance of reality. When you adjust with the other partner, you prove that you are living at a higher level of intellect. Adjustment results from high thinking and is a highly enjoyable experience.

The British hunter Jim Corbett (1875 – 1955) was a great expert on tigers. He states in his book, *Man-Eaters of Kumaon*, "The tiger is a large-hearted gentleman with boundless courage." Contrary to the popular notion, the tiger always adjusts, it never invites fighting. So adjustment is characteristic of the tiger. Live like a tiger and adopt the high culture of adjustment. The tiger is the king of the jungle, and by adopting this culture, you can also live like a king.

Touch Me Not

Having a tension-free mind is the greatest need for us all. The only way to achieve this is to learn the art of management of human situations.

There is a small plant with the botanical name of *Mimosa pudica* which is found in shady areas. On account of its sensitive nature, it is popularly called 'touch-me-not'. Its leaves fold inward and droop when touched, and then minutes later they re-open on their own.

This is a phenomenon of nature. It is an illustration of how to successfully tackle men and women. By nature, women are emotional and men are egoistic. This is the basic nature of both. Allowances must be made for both the sexes in this matter. Don't touch women's emotions or men's egos, and then you can successfully deal with them. This is the surest formula for having good relations with both the men and women whom you are bound to come across, whether at home with your family, out in society or on your travels. If you follow this formula, you will never have a bitter experience. You can have a balanced life in every situation, both at home and outside.

All too frequently, people live in a state of tension. In the majority of the cases, the reason is the bad handling of others, whether men or women. Intentionally or unintentionally, people touch a woman's emotions of or hurt a man's ego, and it is this wrong approach which leads to breakdown. The result is that both the parties unnecessarily start suffering from tension.

But there are simple remedies for this. For example, if a man comes home late from his office, and his wife becomes angry, he should not become provoked, but should rather reply with a smile: "Right now I'm hungry, so let's eat something and we'll talk about this later." On the other hand, if a woman insists on going shopping, but her husband doesn't feel like going out, the husband should not refuse downright. He should say: "Good idea! But please not today. I'll go along with you tomorrow." This is the easiest way to settle the matter between a husband and wife.

Having a tension-free mind is the greatest need for us all. The only way to achieve this is to learn the art of management of human situations. This art often requires only a few well chosen words to be uttered to smooth the ruffled feathers of others and to stop tension destroying your own peace of mind, as well as adversely affecting your physical health.

Peace of Mind - For What?

The first task for every man and woman is to stop their thinking from taking a negative turn and instead direct it into positive channels. This should be an imperative for every human being.

P eace of mind is a condition that can be defined as the absence of anxiety. It is good to have a tranquil mind. But, what is the purpose of this? It is generally believed that peace of mind is essential to making us tension-free, helping us to lead a joyful life, enabling us to do our job well or carry on our business in a better way, ensuring our good health, and so on.

It is true that a peaceful mind makes all these things possible. But, this is an under-valuing of the blessing called a peaceful mind, for a peaceful mind is a positive mind. In reality, it is this peaceful mind that makes us capable of living life at its highest level.

The fact is that our mind is a non-stop thinking machine, just as the heart never stops beating. But it is very important to give our thinking a positive direction. If we fail to do so, our thinking process will start moving in a negative direction. Once this happens, the whole functioning of our nature will be thrown into disarray.

The problem is that we are living in a world in which

everyone is free to act as he or she pleases, and which is consequently fraught with challenge and competition. This state of affairs creates all the social problems which are generally described as 'social evils'. It means that the happiness of one person may mean unhappiness for another. Indeed, this happens all too often. In this situation, it is quite natural that when the mind is perturbed, it should slip into negativity. This comes about far too easily and is a very common experience. For all human beings, not being able to develop oneself as a positive personality is a great loss. It is only when you are a positive personality that you can be the beneficiary of all those bounties which are destined for you by the law of nature. If you have allowed yourself to turn into a negative personality, you will never have the blessings which are your due. You will live in frustration and die in frustration, without achieving the high goal for which you were born.

In this situation, the first task for every man and woman is to stop their thinking from taking a negative turn and instead direct it into positive channels. This should be an imperative for every human being.

There are three major sources of intellectual development – study, observation and discussion. All three are nourishment for the mind. If the mind is peaceful, it will be able to take the right lessons from these sources. But if the mind is not peaceful, it will not be able to avail of whatever intellectual food is on offer.

The mind is the greatest shaper of all kinds of personality development. Everyone knows that for good health, we need to take great care that nothing of a damaging nature will affect our physical organs. Similarly, for better personality development, we need to take care that our minds are protected from anything which will disturb its thinking processes. The mind is your engine. Do not let the engine get derailed, for then you will not be able to reach your destination.

Wisdom is the greatest asset of all men and women. Wisdom, the ability to judge or discern what it true or right, has its source in the mind. A healthy body gives you physical energy, while a healthy mind gives you wisdom. If you fail to preserve your mind, you will be deprived of wisdom. And, to be deprived of wisdom is to be deprived of all good things. Wisdom can be the product only of a mind which is healthy. And a healthy mind is one which has developed through the positive thinking process.

How to Attain a Peaceful Mind?

Depression is the result of non-acceptance of reality. The real solution to this problem is then acceptance of reality. While non-acceptance creates the problem, acceptance of reality will solve it.

Depression is a common problem of modern times. Both the rich and the poor suffer from it.

According to the World Health Organization, by the year 2020 depression will become the second leading cause of disease in the world. Many solutions have been prescribed for the problem of depression but have proved to be ineffective. They may offer temporary relief but fail to resolve the problem permanently.

Meditation is often advised to treat this problem of depression. But meditation focuses on the heart, and the modern scientific age has discarded this solution. Science has established that the heart is merely an organ that pumps blood, whereas depression is a mental problem. It is the mind that controls the heart and not vice versa. Depression is non-physical and the heart is physical. How can a physical organ resolve a non-physical problem?

We also often hear about physical techniques to counter depression. But the reach of physical techniques is confined to the body and does not extend to the mind. How can these physical techniques then address the issues of the mind?

Depression is the result of non-acceptance of reality. The real solution to this problem is then acceptance of reality. While non-acceptance creates the problem, acceptance of reality will solve it.

Our world is a world of freedom, competition, challenge and clash of interests. This nature of human life is bound to create problems. No one is exempted from this process. This being so, there is only one formula for de-stressing – learn the art of stress management rather than trying to eliminate the stress.

A person may become sad upon facing a loss in business or feeling discriminated against at work. He may give in to anxiety and frustration if he suffers a loss in an election, or his love marriage turns into a problem marriage or if he is offended by criticism. In all such cases, a person becomes negative because of being unaware of the real cause. He attributes the cause to another person and holds this person responsible for his difficulties. He fails to realize that all these instances are due to the law of nature. If you attribute the cause of the problem to the law of nature laid down by the Creator, it will arouse no negativity, but when you attribute it to a person, it brings on negative thinking. This is because the law of nature is not your rival, whereas another person is your competitor.

When you attribute the cause of your problem to a person, who is your rival, it will invariably arouse negative thoughts and lead you to anger. But when you attribute the cause to the law of nature, because the law of nature is not your rival and equal in its treatment of all, it will lead to introspection.

When you follow nature-based thinking instead of person-based thinking, you will try to discover its wisdom and will realize that whatever has happened is actually for your betterment. The purpose of this occurrence was to activate your mind and enhance its creativity. It was a means of developing a realistic approach, fostering incentive, making you realize your mistake and helping you to re-plan along the correct lines.

When this thought comes to you, your mind will automatically change from the negative to the positive.

You will be grateful towards the law of nature for bestowing this blessing in disguise. What transpired was for your benefit and not to your detriment. This thought will eliminate your stress and you will be able to live with a normal mind. This is the only method of de-stressing. There is no other technique or method that can help de-stress the mind.

No Complaints

There are untold blessings that are enjoyed by almost every man and woman. If this fact were not so often lost sight of, people would never become victims of negative thinking or take to constantly complaining. In their thinking, they would always be positive and positive thinking is undoubtedly the source of all kinds of good things.

Medical records show that there are no less than seventy-eight organs in every human body. All these organs work in perfect coordination. This is why man is able to perform his innumerable activities so smoothly. If one or more organs were to fail, untrammelled living for human beings would become almost impossible. Moreover, these organs of the human body function automatically and unflaggingly. If these organs had to be operated in the way that a machine has to be, then man would never have been able to do any other work. He would be too busy making all these organs function.

This realization makes us conscious of two very great things. Firstly, that here there is a beneficent Creator. Hence, a strong affection is produced within each individual for his Creator and he will feel eternal gratitude towards Him. Secondly, the realization of being endowed with such great blessings will make a person a positive thinker in the complete sense of the word. Thus, he will become a healthy member of society.

God – A Source of Conviction

In this vast universe, God is our support. He is the one who supports us in the journey across the river of life and brings us to the other shore. Faith in God is everything for man. Without this conviction, man is nothing.

If you are somewhere in space and you look into a powerful telescope, you will notice our exceptional and relatively tiny planet—earth—standing out amidst an otherwise vast lifeless universe and filled with all things that are needed to sustain life. This amazing sight will leave you stunned!

If you look closer, you will notice even more startling things. For instance, you will notice that Earth and its moon and other planets are constantly moving. You will see them rotating on their own axes, as well as revolving around the sun. Moreover, you will see the entire solar system orbiting around the centre of the galaxy of which it is a part. And, further still, you will find that this galaxy itself is also moving, along with many more such galaxies across the vast universe.

You are bound to be awe-struck seeing all of this! And when you find innumerable and massive balls of fire that we call stars racing about, here and there, and in front of which our Earth appears as just a tiny speck, you will find the scene so frighteningly amazing that you will be forced to admit that in front of all of this you are absolutely valueless and insignificant!

This experience will lead you to realize that there is a mighty God of this entire cosmos, who is its Creator as well as its Sustainer. If you try to visualize the vast expanse of the cosmos in your mind, your heart will cry out, declaring that the cosmos itself is a clear proof of its Creator. After this, there is no need for any more such proof. And along with this, you will realize that in this vast cosmos, human beings are actually utterly helpless and insignificant creatures and that God is an indispensable necessity for us, for without God, it is simply impossible for us to exist.

This, undoubtedly, is the most important fact of life. When someone realizes this fact, he throws all inhibitions to the wind and rushes towards God. He cries out with his whole being, "O God! Help me! Without Your help, I can do nothing."

In this vast universe, God is our support. He is the

one who supports us in the journey across the river of life and brings us to the other shore. Faith in God is everything for man. Without this conviction, man is nothing.

All of us experience in our daily lives something of the utter helplessness that one experiences on seeing the enormous cosmos through a powerful telescope. Every person repeatedly faces experiences that force him or her to become a victim of limitations. For instance, we do not always get what we want. We often find ourselves in situations where we feel totally helpless. We all experience fear of loss, sickness, injury, old age and death. All of these give us a feeling that we are dependent on some superior force, and that without the help of this superior power we cannot succeed in any way. This feeling can be said to be a psychological proof of God's existence.

Every person definitely experiences this feeling. Every one of us finds within our own selves indisputable evidence for God's existence.

The inner being or nature of every person tells him or her, "You need God. Without God, your life cannot be complete. Without God, you cannot succeed."

The Key to Happiness

If you want to live in a state of happiness, you must learn the difference between need and desire.

If you can be satisfied with what you already have, you can certainly achieve happiness. But if you can only be satisfied with more and more material things, you can never achieve happiness. Happiness is a state of mind. Nothing of a material nature can bring you happiness.

If you have in your mind a list of all the material things that you want and you believe that by acquiring every single thing on that list, you will be happy, then it will be impossible for you to attain happiness. The fact is that this material list has an end on paper, but not in your mind. If you do not learn to stop your mind running on in this way, it will keep on adding on more and more items. And, you will always remain insatiable.

If you want to live in a state of happiness, you must learn the difference between need and desire. The real needs of a human being are quite limited. There is always a full stop in the list of real needs, but the list based on desire has no full stop. Every day you will include a comma, and this will continue endlessly till the day you die. A human being, by nature, is insatiable.

So, it is not abundance that will give you happiness – only contentment.

For my part, I can say that I am living in a state of happiness in the sense that I am contented. I believe that what I have is quite enough for me. This formula has given me an everlasting sense of fulfilment. I say of myself that I am the greatest 'status quoist'. And it is having such a nature that has given me lasting contentment.

Being a 'status quoist' is not a minus point in one's personality. It is rather the greatest plus point. One who is a 'status quoist' is saved from all kind of distractions, and when you are saved from distractions, you have enough time to do all kinds of good things, for example, study, think positively, perform social service, and so on.

Happiness is not simply a personal condition. Happiness is of great and far-reaching value. If you are unhappy, you are bound to live in a state of tension and stress, which is of no good either to yourself or anyone else. But if you are happy and are tension-free, you will have no stress, you will be free of pessimism and you will be able to reach out to other people. Then you will have a positive personality, and a positive personality is the greatest asset to human development.

The Goal of Married Life

❧

Life is like a cogwheel. If man has one cog, the woman has the other cog, and both are in need of communion so that a joint effort may be possible.

It is true that adjustment is the only formula for a successful married life. But adjustment for what? It is not adjustment for the sake of adjustment. It is adjustment for a higher purpose, that is, to create a normal environment in which it will be possible to achieve the real purpose of married life.

Married life is not simply co-travelling. It is rather co-sharing. Both partners after married life possess something unique and each needs to share that with the other. Every one of us is born with different qualities, and each one is in need of having a share of them from one's partner, so that both the partners may develop their personalities in a better way.

In married life both the partners are givers and at the same time takers. So, both the partners need favourable conditions in which it may be possible to benefit from each other.

Life is like a cogwheel. If man has one cog, the woman has the other cog, and both are in need of communion so that a joint effort may be possible.

I know a number of marriages in which both the parties, being aware of this fact, tried to make adjustments. But they were quite conscious that their doing so was not merely for the sake of adjustment, but for the sake of mutual sharing. Thus, their marriage proved to be successful.

One very important aspect of marriage is what I call intellectual partnership. Every day we face problems, every day there are some new issues, every day we have to take some decisions, every day we want to explore some new area in the world of ideas. This is important for everyone, man and woman both. And every one of us needs to have an intellectual partner with whom we can have verbal exchanges, have a dialogue, and try to discover better options. And, according to my experience, the best intellectual partner is no other than your spouse.

Everyone has adopted what may be called the adjustment culture – the businessman with his customers, every working man or woman with his or her boss. I think this is good, although the goal of this adjustment is only the money to be earned. But this adjustment culture is essential also between husband and wife. By adopting this adjustment culture in married life you can earn something that is far more important than money.

It is my personal experience that when you converse with your partner, it is bound to give rise to new ideas. In this sense the process of intellectual partnership leads to intellectual development. And, intellectual development is the greatest goal for every man and woman.

Man is an explanation-seeking animal. So when you talk about adjustment in married life, both the partners could ask, "Why adjustment?" So you have to give a good explanation, otherwise any talk of adjustment will not have the right impact upon them. They may agree with your sermon on adjustment, but they will not follow it in their practical life.

My experience is in the field of scholarship, I know that study is the basis of scholarship, but only book-reading is not enough to develop a high level of scholarship. This requires exchange and dialogue. This is the concept of those activities which are called seminars and conferences. But your spouse is an ever-ready intellectual partner. He or she is available at all times, day and night. Home-conferencing is far more beneficial than the formal conferencing which takes place in an auditorium. Discover this aspect of married life and any amount of adjustment will seem to be insignificant.

The Concept of a Better Tomorrow

Just as the night cannot prevent the day from following it, no untoward circumstances can ever deprive man of the hope of a better tomorrow.

The concept of a better tomorrow is ingrained in human nature. Every day man witnesses the fact that day follows night. And will always follow night. The same is true of life. In human life there is no full-stop. There are only commas until it reaches the final destination.

The concept of tomorrow is only relevant for human beings, not for animals. Humans always think by taking the future into consideration. No setback can take away this tomorrow-oriented concept. It is because of this concept that the struggles of human life are never given up as being futile. Just as the night cannot prevent the day from following it, no untoward circumstances can ever deprive man of the hope of a better tomorrow.

This tomorrow-based concept begins from individual life, covers national struggle, then goes on to the global hope of building a civilization. It is this continuity of hope which is man's most distinctive feature.

It is generally held that death puts a stop to this continuity. But, the reason to believe in the eternal continuity of life is: if this process continues up to death, then why not after death? Death only comes to the physical dimension of the human personality. The other dimension, that is, the mind, is an eternal phenomenon. It is quite certain that the mind-based personality continues to exist even after the apparent death of the physical aspect of human life.

Discover the Alternative

You must come out of being obsessive and then you will see that the world is full of alternatives.

If you are driving your car along the road and another car is speeding towards you from the opposite direction, you will promptly veer to one side and avoid the oncoming car. If both the cars approached each other head on, that would result in an accident. But if one car travels on one side of the road and the other on the other side, their onward journeys will continue in complete safety. In other words, both the cars, by taking the alternative route, avoid an accident.

Life is full of confrontations: at home, in society, in national and international life. At any time a crisis may develop, which can lead to a confrontation between two individuals or groups. In such a situation, the best thing to do is to discover an alternative. This is the simplest way to manage life's crises.

Taking the alternative road is a universal law of nature. For example, rainfall is a common natural phenomenon. Rain falls everywhere, both in the plains as well in the mountainous areas. In the plains rain comes in the form of a downpour, while in the mountains snowfalls are common. In the plains rivers are directly fed by rainfall, so that their copious supply of water can be used throughout the year. In the mountains there are no such large rivers. But here nature finds the alternative by preserving snow in the form of ice which gathers on the mountain peaks. This then continues to melt slowly throughout the year, thus providing the hilly areas with an adequate water supply.

If there should be a crisis in your life, you should search for an alternative to confronting it head on. If you think with a calm mind, you will always be able to find a peaceful alternative by which to manage the crisis situation.

For example, freedom was the goal of the Indian people during the British rule. At that time, Subhas Chandra Bose said: 'Give me blood, I will give you freedom.' But this formula failed to work. Bose and his army died before seeing a free India. Gandhiji realized that the violent method was not working, and so he found an alternative in terms of non-violence. This alternative proved successful and India won its freedom in 1947.

This principle is applicable to every walk of life. When you face a crisis, do not let your mind get disturbed, but instead try to find some alternative. This will guarantee you success.

If you are working in a company and feel that you are not being promoted, you plan to register a complaint. But if your complaint goes unheard, you should adopt the 'wait and see' alternative. Where the first formula failed, you will see that the second formula will work.

You may feel that your income is less and your expenditure is more. You want to increase your income but cannot find a way. Then do not despair, because here too you have an alternative. Instead of aiming to increase your income, you should reduce your expenditure. You will find that where the first formula didn't work, the second formula will easily work.

If you are in the habit of becoming angry in unpleasant situations, which leads to tension, then here also you have an alternative. That is, change your attitude by adopting the simple formula of taking things easy. You will see that soon your mind has become peaceful.

People frequently allow their lives to be governed by obsessions. It is because of this that they are unable to discover alternatives to the course they are following. You must come out of being obsessive and then you will see that the world is full of alternatives.

Don't Complain

Why the only practical solution to the problem of complaints is not to make them a subject of discussion and debate. Instead, you should think that the only way to solve them is to forget them, not to find out if they are true or false.

Complaining is a very deadly thing. It is the habit of complaining that is at the root of various social problems. When several people live together, it is but natural that they will have differences, which are often then allowed to turn into complaints against each other. These soon get transformed into enmity, abuse and a never-ending cycle of hatred.

The only solution to complaints is not to take them seriously. Instead, they should simply be forgotten. In the event of a complaint against someone, there's no need for you to investigate it or to remember it. Instead, you must forget it—and you should do this on a unilateral basis. It is natural for complaints to arise when living together with others. But the solution to the problem of complaints is not that you should go about trying to verify them in a bid to solve them.

In this world, it is simply impossible to stop complaints. The only practical thing that you can do in this regard is to not store in your mind any complaints you might have against others. This is the only solution to the problem. From the practical point of view, there is no other solution. If you want to live in this world with a positive mind, and also to leave this world with a positive mind, you really have no realistic option but this.

Complaints are always a serious matter. That is why the only practical solution to the problem of complaints is not to make them a subject of discussion and debate. Instead, you should think that the only way to solve them is to forget them, not to find out if they are true or false.

Experience suggests that investigations never put an end to complaints. In fact, they often only further complicate them. Given this, forgetting complaints is the only practical way to solve them.

VII

The Wisdom of Life

Obey that Impulse

❦

When you make an incorrect statement or talk about a matter that is not right, your conscience gives you a signal from within. And if you hear that signal, you can certainly avoid wrong thinking and wrong speech.

Everyone is born with a perfect nature. Nature is the best guide of every man and woman. One's nature gives the right direction on all occasions. This natural signal, when followed sedulously, is a guarantee of human success. For example, overeating is a common problem. It leads to obesity and all kinds of diseases. Yet, it is very simple to avoid overeating. A few minutes before reaching the stage of overeating, the stomach gives out a light signal. If you listen to that signal and stop eating there and then, you can prevent yourself from eating too much. This is the easiest way to save yourself from all kinds of unnatural diseases.

When you make an incorrect statement or talk about a matter that is not right, your conscience gives you a signal from within. And if you hear that signal, you can certainly avoid wrong thinking and wrong speech. And, there is no doubt that wrong thinking and speaking are the root causes of failure.

Suppose while engaging in some activity, it

appears after some time that you are not getting the expected results and that your step is proving to be counterproductive, then this kind of negative result is a signal. If you listen to this signal, objectively reassess your activities and redraft your plan of action, then such self-correction will certainly lead to success.

Then, there is a very important signal which teaches you by way of advice. Other people are like mirrors. You can fail to see the marks on your face, but a mirror doesn't fail to reflect them. The advice given by other people is just like the mirror's reflection. That is, others' objective advice is also a signal. Sincerely heed this signal and try to understand others' point of view. You will then readily reach the right conclusion. This will help you to correct your course of action and will finally help you to reach your goal.

If in the rainy season you go out without an umbrella, and midway it starts raining. In this case the rain is also a signal. It reminds you that you failed to take the precautionary measure of taking an umbrella. This is an example from nature. So is the case of human life. In human life, everyone always receives some signals, sometimes internally, and sometimes externally. The best way to ensure your success is simple—Listen to that signal, obey it and you will certainly reach your goal.

Suppose that you are a leader, you organize a street protest and are able to successfully gather a crowd. But when you lead that crowd, you discover that a disturbance has been caused in the flow of traffic, commercial activities have been disrupted, and very soon you find yourself in a situation of confrontation and bloodshed. This kind of negative result is also a signal. You have to rethink your plan and understand that your method was wrong. You have to recognize the truth of the well-known Gandhian saying, 'The end does not justify the means.'

There is a historical example of this principle. In 1920, the Indian National Congress under Mahatma Gandhi's leadership launched the Non-Cooperation Movement. It was understood that the satyagrahis would remain peaceful. In 1922, however, a mob of protestors became furious and killed some policemen in Chauri Chaura. Fearing a slide into violence and anarchy, Gandhiji immediately called for the struggle to be suspended.

Everyone is free to act according to his plan, with the only condition that one's activities will not result in a new problem. Problem-free activities are good, but problem-ful activities are equally bad.

Money: A Double-Edged Sword

It requires great wisdom and hard labour to acquire money.
It is very strange then that one chooses to be stupid when it
comes to spending that hard earned money.

Everyone knows how to earn money. But few people know how to spend it. This is the most common experience in every society, whether religious or secular. A wise person is one who discovers this fact and plans his life by taking a lesson from it.

Money is the greatest booster for a person, but at the same time, money may prove to be the greatest source of disaster for him. Initially, money is a source of strength. It is its use that makes it good or bad for a human being. People earn money by applying their wisdom, but when it comes to the use of money, people can be remarkably stupid.

Recently, I was invited by a friend to visit his farmhouse which had been built beside an important road. It was fitted out with all kinds of comforts and luxuries. But practically, it was like a white elephant. I said to the owner that this had been a serious wastage of money and that if he had built a school on this site, that would have been a much better use for his money.

If you spend your money for some constructive purpose, that is very good, but if you spend it on ostentation, then it is really bad. It requires great wisdom and hard labour to acquire money. It is very strange then that one chooses to be stupid when it comes to spending that hard earned money.

If you spend money for the betterment of society, it will enhance your goodwill and earn the respect of others. But if you lavish your money on your family or children, that will only be providing them with easy money, and easy money is the worst of all things, in terms of the consequences it has for them. It is good to have money, but if money makes you arrogant, then it is worse than poison. If, on the other hand, money makes you modest, then it is the greatest source of your personality development.

If you make money your sole concern in life, that means that you are underutilizing yourself. Money, of course, is a necessity, but its acquisition should not be your sole purpose in life.

There is a saying, 'In comparison do we understand'. If you compare money with learning, you can easily understand the difference between the two. Money is a risky form of capital, for you can lose it through an expected or unexpected event. But learning is a permanent asset. If you have an insatiable nature, apply it to learning, don't apply it to money, which is a dubious investment.

I know of a person who was born into an ordinary family, but who, in his later years, came by a lot of money and became rich. One of his friends complained that before he had become rich, he had been easily accessible to everyone, but that now it was very difficult to meet him. The wealthy person replied: *"Mere upar daulat ki bijli giri hai."* (The lightning of wealth has struck me). Externally, wealth seems to be a good thing, but internally it is otherwise. Every wealthy person lives under great stress.

Once I happened to meet a businessman who took me to see his godown. Although this godown seemed to be a junkyard, there a poor labourer was lying on the ground and having a very sound sleep. Seeing the labourer, the businessman remarked, "I envy him, because although I have a luxurious bed, I've never had this kind of sleep."

It's good to make money your servant, but it's bad to let money become your master.

U Turn - A Principle of Life

A wise man is one who can reassess himself, reset his priorities, re-plan his project, moulding himself according to changing circumstances.

Once I was travelling in a part of India with which my driver was unfamiliar. He made a wrong turn at one point but drove on for five miles before he realized he was on the wrong road. He had to stop the car then and make a U-turn, and soon we safely reached our destination.

This kind of U-turn is not only a part of road culture, it is a principle of life. Every person, every community, every nation needs at some point to make a U-turn. Failing this, an unbearable loss could be the result.

For example, the Tatas established a car factory in West Bengal to produce the Nano car in 2007. Very soon they discovered that West Bengal was not favourable for their industry, so they dismantled their factory and re-established it in Gujarat. Now Nano cars are successfully running in every city of India. This success was the direct result of adopting the U-turn policy.

The same is applicable to nations. One such example is the course adopted by the United Kingdom after the Second World War. The British leaders, especially those who were associated with the Fabian Society, felt that they were now unable to control India and other British colonies and proceeded to adopt a policy of decolonization. As we know, Churchill emerged as a hero in WWII, but he was defeated in the 1945 election. The reason for this being that a desire for post-war reform was widespread amongst the British population and that the man who had led Britain in war was not seen as the man to lead the nation in peace.

There are numerous examples in history of the success of those who adopted the policy of U-turn and the failure of those who did not.

In this world, nothing is certain, neither for individuals nor for nations. So every individual or group of people ought to adopt this policy. When they find that their journey is taking them down a blind alley, they need to revise their policy, they must reassess the whole matter, and if it appears that they were heading in the wrong direction, they should change course without any further ado.

India is also a good example of this kind of policy. After Independence, India adopted the socialist model for its economy, but the result was hardly encouraging. Then in 1991, India introduced a new policy in its economic planning. In 2013, Indian authorities brought about such great changes in economic policies as may be described as a paradigm shift.

The U-turn policy is a law of nature. No one is able to see the unseen. No one can foresee all that is going to happen in the future. This makes the journey of life a jump into uncertainty. A wise man is one who can reassess himself, reset his priorities, re-plan his project, moulding himself according to changing circumstances. Don't try to fight against realities. Simply accept them. When you cannot change the reality, change yourself.

Sometimes it appears that the U-turn policy will lead to some loss, but any such loss is the lesser evil, while going against reality is to opt for the greater evil. The U-turn policy is only another name for what may be called acceptance of reality and adjustment to the changing times.

The U-turn policy is the policy of the wise: it ensures success, while not adopting it is risking failure. Success and failure are both in your hands.

A Case of Break in History

If a person, by committing a mistake, loses this identity, he will lose his value in the eyes of others.

Rajat Gupta was born in 1948 in Calcutta. He lost his parents when he was a teenager. He was able to take this as a challenge, it only enhanced his incentive. After some years he moved to the USA, and after long effort rose to the position of managing director of the prestigious global consulting firm McKinsey & Company.

After a successful career in business he committed a serious mistake. In June 2012 a US jury convicted Mr. Gupta of conspiracy and securities fraud related to his passing on confidential information on Goldman Sachs. He received a two-year jail term and was ordered to pay a fine of $5 million from a US judge. Apparently, his career was finished on this date.

In his six-minute statement before being sentenced, Rajat Gupta said: "I have lost my reputation that I have built over a lifetime." Rajat Gupta was quite right in giving this statement. I would only change the wording. It is better to say that Rajat Gupta's case was a case of break in history. After committing this mistake, he lost his history, which is greater than anything else.

One can afford loss of money, but no one can afford loss of his or her history. Everyone, whether he works as a domestic help or enjoys a high position in an institution, creates a history for himself through his performance. It is this history that is the greatest asset of anyone. The world is a marketplace and everyone receives from this market just as much as he deserves, neither less nor more. It is one's history that determines the level of deservation. One's history is greater than bank balance or property or any other material gain. Others will judge you by your history. One should be very cautious in this regard.

According to a saying: 'If wealth is lost, nothing is lost. If health is lost, something is lost. But, if character is lost, everything is lost.' I would like to replace character with history in this saying, and say that everything that man loses has compensation, but if you lose your history then you cannot compensate it with anything.

People know of the loss of 'break in service' but they don't know of the loss of break in history, and perhaps Rajat Gupta was not an exception. One's history is one's identity. It includes honesty, integrity and reputation. These things make one's identity. If a person, by committing a mistake, loses this identity, he will lose his value in the eyes of others. This is break in history, and if due to some reason, one loses this historical identity he will lose his most precious asset. Such kind of a mistake can never be compensated for.

Apparently, there is no rescue for Mr. Gupta, but for others it is a great lesson. Those who are in employment are cautious about what is called 'break in service', but people must be cautious regarding break in history more than they are for break in service. Break in service is redeemable, but break in history is not. There is a line in Persian: *Man na kardam shuma hazar bekunaid* (You take it as a lesson and don't make the mistakes I made). Perhaps this is the best message that Rajat Gupta can give to others.

Learning from others' mistakes is the easiest way of not repeating that kind of mistake again. One can learn the formula of successful life before entering it. Although Rajat Gupta failed, he can say, 'I hope my failure gives others a tested secret of success.'

Life is a Tightrope Walk

Life is, indeed, like a tightrope walk. If you lean to one side, you are bound to fall. So save yourself from leaning to one side, and maintain a balance between the two sides. This is the only formula for a safe journey in life.

Life is like tightrope walking. Tightrope walking means maintaining your balance between two opposite positions, proceeding very cautiously so that you avoid either of two equally bad situations.

The word 'tightrope walk' was initially coined for an act of entertainment, that is, a tightrope is a tightly stretched wire or rope fixed high above the ground which someone walks across in order to entertain people. But the spirit of the tightrope walk, i.e. maintaining a balance between two opposites, is a great principle in real life.

You like sweet items but your doctor says that you are diabetic, so you have to avoid sweets. In this case you will try to find a balance between your desire and the doctor's advice. At home, you experience a disturbing situation, but when you are in your office, you feel that you have to deal with office affairs with a cool mind, so you try to find a balance between two contrary mental states. You are walking on the road, and some scooter driver hits you. Naturally, you become angry and you want to beat him up, but you think that if you turn violent, the police will arrest you and take you to jail, so you try to quell your anger and control your emotions. In your business, you have suffered some loss and have fallen into despair, but you think: 'I have lost the present, and if I become despairing, I will lose the future also.' So you control your emotions and try to find a balance between two opposite mental trends.

There are hundreds of such situations in our daily lives. We face them every day. No one is an exception. In most situations, two opposite states of mind vie with each other, and if we incline more towards one, we suffer with regard to the other.

Life is, indeed, like a tightrope walk. If you lean to one side, you are bound to fall. So save yourself from leaning to one side, and maintain a balance between the two sides. This is the only formula for a safe journey in life.

For example, a student who failed in an examination, falls into despair and frustration, and decides to commit suicide. Then he remembers the well-known saying: try, try, try again. He then starts rethinking his future plans, and says, 'If I have lost the first chance, there is every possibility that I will be able to avail of the second chance.' He therefore starts studying with renewed diligence, appears in the second examination and passes with good marks. This student was able to maintain a balance between two opposite choices and was saved.

According to the common dictionary, a tightrope walk is an item of entertainment. But there is another dictionary—the dictionary of wisdom. In this dictionary, tightrope walk means 'living with wisdom'. A dictionary of words can enhance your vocabulary, but a dictionary of wisdom gives you a chance to achieve success while remaining unaffected by the vicissitudes of life.

Everyone is full of desires, but the world outside of us is full of realities. You have to maintain a wise balance between your personal desires and external realities. This is the real art of life. This is an art which is required by everyone, be he a leader or a common man, a wealthy person or a poor man, an educated or an uneducated person.

Life is the same for all. Almost everyone is destined to face the same situations, so everyone would be well advised to adopt this very formula of tightrope walking.

Making Life Meaningful

The right formula of life is that which can give a person satisfaction till the end of life, and not just for some temporary period.

There is an English proverb, 'The end justifies the means'. Perhaps, there is another more relevant principle which may be expressed thus: 'The end justifies the beginning.' It is the end result that proves whether the beginning was right or wrong.

Many people have started their lives with great enthusiasm. But the latter period of their life has proved that their beginning was not the right one. Their case was a case of miscalculation, rather than one of right calculation. For example, the Greek emperor Alexander the Great (356 – 323 BC) was a very ambitious person. His goal was to conquer the world. But, his human limitations overcame him and he died at the age of 32 in Babylon, about 3,000 km away from his homeland. The same is true of Adolf Hitler (1889 – 1945) who, likewise an ambitious man, rose to the position of Chancellor of Germany. Then he decided to rule the whole of Europe, for which he initiated a war which escalated into the Second World War. Yet, Hitler could not fulfil his dream, and committed suicide at the age of 56 in a bunker.

There are thousands of such examples throughout history. Certain individual started out in life with high hopes, but failed to achieve their goal and died in a state of frustration. In the beginning they were hopeful, but in the end they died in a state of utter hopelessness.

'Right here, right now' is a formula of life that has gained popularity in the present age. This seems to be a beautiful formula. I know a number of persons, both men and women, who have adopted this principle. Although in the beginning they were very happy, in the latter period of their lives they felt that they had been unsuccessful in achieving their goals. Finally, they fell a prey to frustration and died of some fatal disease, and in a state where they had lost all their hopes and enthusiasm.

Happiness in the present is not the criterion of success. The right criterion is whether a person is able to maintain his happiness and sense of satisfaction right to the end of his life. The value of a tree is gauged by the fruit that it offers when it has reached the stage of full growth. Similarly, the right formula of life is that which can give a person satisfaction till the end of life, and not just for some temporary period.

A tree is known by its fruit, which is the final phase of the tree's life. Similarly, the pattern of human life will be judged on what it turns out to be in its final days. Never make the mistake of planning for life by taking only immediate gain into consideration. A person should always plan by keeping the future in mind. It is the future that counts and not the present.

An individual should first of all discover his own self and then plan accordingly for his life. People generally set their goals out of zeal, but this is certainly not a mature way of making decisions. The better way to decide one's goal is to understand the realities of life, and then act in accordance with them. Failure to do so is the main reason for people dying in frustration after having set out full of enthusiasm: when they set themselves goals, it was under the influence of emotions, without due consideration. Such a plan does not work for long. It is like a sandcastle which is destined in the long run to fall apart.

The Price of Being a Taker

~§§§~

The status of first class-citizen cannot be achieved through legislation. It can be achieved only by assuming the role of giver in society.

In the course of my several visits to the USA over a period of years, I have happened to meet Indians of both the Muslim and Hindu communities. I realized that senior members of both communities have a common concern: they fear that the future generation is rapidly losing the identity of its traditional culture. Indeed, I have seen that although families of both the communities have achieved substantial material progress, they are nevertheless unhappy. They feel strongly that their children will suffer a fate commonly known as cultural assimilation. I told the senior members of both the communities that their fear might be genuine but that their present efforts were not going to yield any positive results.

What is the real problem with these generations? It is that both the communities are living in the USA as takers and not as givers. Both the communities strive to earn American dollars but they don't try to figure as giver members of American society. In the course of a conversation, one senior Indian remarked that the present development of America was due mostly to the labours of the immigrants. I said, "No, although apparently immigrants seem to be working in the developmental activities of the USA, in actual fact the credit goes not to Mr. Immigrant but to Mr. Incentive."

It is a fact that these immigrants have failed to perform well in their own countries, whereas in the USA they are seen to be involved in almost all the activities of development and progress. The reason is that in the USA every success is based on merit, so these immigrants become heroes in achieving that success. By taking account of this fact, one can say that the credit goes to Mr. Incentive and not to Mr. Immigrant.

After independence, India's economy came under the control of the state – a system whereby everything depended upon state policy. That meant that there was no free competition, everything being decided by the state, with the individual entirely subjected to state policy. It must be conceded that a state controlled economy renders people incentive-less and incentive-less people work only as is laid down in rules and regulations and not according to their full and natural capacity.

Once, on a visit to the USA in 1893, Swami Vivekananda walked along a street in Chicago, clad, according to the swami custom, in just two lengths of untailored cloth. At that time in the USA, this form of attire was quite unfamiliar. On seeing this, a woman whispered to her husband, "I don't think that man is a gentleman." Overhearing this remark, Swami Vivekananda approached the lady and said politely:

"Excuse me, Madam, in your country it is the tailor who makes a man a gentleman, but in the country from which I come, it is character which makes a man a gentleman." I narrated this story to an American professor. He smiled and said, "In the past maybe this was the Indian culture but now character is an export item for Indians. It is not meant for domestic consumption." If the Indian community wants to save their next generation, they should try to make themselves a giver group of American society. If their next generation continues to be taker members of American society, no effort will ever save them from being assimilated in American culture.

Some Indians may complain that in the USA they are treated as second-class citizens. If so, it is not due to any kind of discriminatory legislation. And even if there were strong legislation upholding equal status for all, Indians would still inevitably become second-class citizens. The status of first class-citizen cannot be achieved through legislation. It can be achieved only by assuming the role of giver in society. There is a well-known saying, 'It is in giving that we receive.' This saying aptly applies to the present situation of the Indian community.

Individual, Nature and Society

~§§§~

Difference creates an intellectual challenge. Intellectual challenge leads to discussion, and discussion and dialogue result in all kinds of progress.

Man, according to his inborn qualities, is a complete human being. But at the same time he depends upon two foreign influences: nature and society. From one major point of view, man depends completely upon nature. Water, sunlight, oxygen, food, all parts of the life-support system, are supplied by nature. Man cannot afford to dissociate himself from these natural resources. Here dissociation would mean committing suicide.

The same is true of man's relationship with society. It is said that man is a social animal, not simply in the sense that man lives in a society but, more explicitly, that man completely depends upon society. From personality development to civilizational progress, everything depends on society. Here also dissociation from society would mean committing suicide.

Some people develop a kind of individualism. This kind of individualism may appear to be a beautiful idea but, in the practical sense, it is not advantageous. No individual can afford to live just for himself in this way.

This is like self-existence, and self-existence is purely an attribute of God.

No individual can separate himself from society. Every individual is a part of society and it would be ill-advised of anyone to go against it. But, if society is corrupt, then one can dissociate oneself from it on these grounds. But this aspect of social existence accounts for hardly one per cent; the other 99 per cent is not objectionable. Thus, we are seldom obliged to dissociate ourselves from society. If one's temperament is out of the ordinary, one must mould oneself according to society. It is not society's concern to change itself to suit an individual. Each individual must attune himself to the norms of society. No one can afford to indulge in individualism. The problem is that everyone is born as Mr. Different and Ms. Different. It is this birthright feature that creates the problem. When people try to live together in society, they feel again and again that they are living in a world of differences. Every difference is like a challenge. So living in a society means living with constant challenges. This perturbs people and they become individualists. But this kind of individualism is little more than escapism. It is a fact that escapism is not a workable option for anyone, be it a man or a woman. Then, difference is not an evil. In terms of results, it is a boon. It is a natural gift to mankind. There is a well-known saying that when everyone thinks alike, no one thinks very much. So difference means diversity. It means that man is not like a single tree in this world. He is part of a big garden. The difference in trees only enhances the beauty of the garden. Without this variety, the garden would be colourless. In fact, difference gives every human being great advantages. Difference activates people's minds, compelling them to think more and more. Difference creates an intellectual challenge. Intellectual challenge leads to discussion, and discussion and dialogue result in all kinds of progress. Individual living means living in a limited sphere and as such is a constant obstacle to future development. Individual living deprives one of interactive learning, greater experience, and the opportunity to learn lessons. It is like living in a cocoon. This kind of living is correct for the larva living in a cocoon but not for man. Man cannot afford to live in a cocoon. For the larva living in a cocoon, it is a life but, for man, it is no less than death. Social living means living through experiences, meeting challenges, learning lessons, teaching and learning. Society is like a living university. One who tries to go against society will commit social suicide. No one can afford to opt for either natural suicide or social suicide. Therefore, complaint is a futile exercise, whether against nature or against society. Adjustment is the only possible formula.

Avail of the Immediate Frame of Reference

If your school is a source of formal education for you, then your family is a source of informal education. And both are equally important.

Our life is full of connections through which we come to grips with the negative or positive aspects of life. So we have to be very circumspect about availing of the opportunities afforded by the natural connections or relationships which are formed in the course of our existence.

For example, you family is your first frame of reference. It is your family members with whom you spend your days and nights. You have various experiences with them, sometimes sweet and sometimes bitter. In this sense, your family is the most important part of your social environment.

You should avail of every kind of lesson that you receive from your family. If you find that certain happenings in your family are undesirable, you have to be tolerant on such occasions. You have to appreciate how even in your family circle the tenor of life cannot always be free of unwanted situations. If you find that at such times you cannot show any leniency, you are going to find life very difficult outside the family circle when you enter society at large and encounter all kinds of unpleasantness.

So, you have to accept that unpleasant experiences are an inescapable part of life. And you have to be capable of adopting a give-and-take attitude within the family circle as well as outside in society.

Your family is not just your family: it is also a source of training for you. In this sense, your family serves as the cradle for your future career. If your school is a source of formal education for you, then your family is a source of informal education. And both are equally important.

For example, if you have an unfortunate encounter with a family member, don't take it as an evil. Take it as a first, very necessary training lesson, because you are destined one day to go out of your home and live in society. And in society there will be many occasions on which you will have similar negative experiences. You must realize that your family is a blessing for you, for it is like a training centre that sends you out into society as a prepared or mature person. Indeed, your family is the mainspring of your future life.

Everyone knows that formal education is very important for his future. Without a good formal education, it is not possible to get a good job. I do agree with this point of view, but in terms of one's all-round existence, education is not the be-all and end-all of everything. For a better quality of life you need something more - and that is informal education. Everyone's family is the centre of informal education for him. To gain admission into this institution, you don't need to pay any kind of admission fee. It is destined by nature and by birth - a fact of life. You should therefore make certain to avail of whatever your family offers you in terms of informal education.

The family is a unit of society. In this sense, every family is like a mini-society. You have to try to train yourself in this mini-society so that you will be able to enjoy a better life in the larger society. One who fails to live a good life in his family circle will certainly fail to live a good life in society.

Adjustment, a principle of life, is what makes all social life run smoothly. If you enter social life without first having learned to make adjustments within the framework of the family, you will have only two options: either learn to make immediate adjustments or stoop to hypocrisy and then live in a never-ending state of tension.

The Greatest Good

One can achieve one's personal target only by taking into consideration what lies beyond oneself. That is the only realistic approach and is therefore the wisest approach.

What is the greatest good for a man or a woman? Justice is generally regarded as being the greatest good in human life. Theoretically, this would appear to be the right answer, but in any practical sense, it is adjustment that should be regarded as the greatest good.

To illustrate this point, I would like to cite the example of Pakistan and Japan. Pakistan had its inception as a separate country after the Second World War. More than sixty years after its establishment, Pakistan is commonly regarded as a failed state. Why? It is because Pakistan adopted a confrontational stance with its neighbouring country. Such an approach yielded nothing for Pakistan except further loss.

The opposite example can be seen in Japan. Japan also began a new phase in its history after the Second World War. There were serious issues between Japan and the U.S.A. But Japan adopted the formula of adjustment. The Japanese Emperor of that time, Hirohito, gave a clear-cut direction to his nation. He said in one of his broadcasts just after World War II: "We have to endure the unendurable, so that we may be able to reconstruct our nation in the post-World War period." And now it is generally accepted that the result of this policy has been miraculous, for now Japan has emerged as an economic super power in the present world.

The same holds true for individuals. A certain banker of my acquaintance, who was in a senior position in an international bank, had a heated exchange with his immediate superior. He was so upset by this incident that he resigned from his post. But what was the result? He is now unemployed and living in a state of frustration.

Another acquaintance of mine, who was also in a senior position in a bank, had a similar problem with a more senior executive and he wanted my advice. I told him my advice was based on a four-point formula: first, adjustment, second, adjustment, third adjustment, and, lastly again adjustment. He took my advice and now he is very happy with his job.

What is the difference between the concept of justice and the concept of adjustment? The difference is that obtaining justice, having to be effected on a bilateral basis, becomes a very difficult task, while adjustment, being a unilateral matter, can be instantly achieved. In the case of injustice, when some other party is behaving unfairly towards you, justice becomes a thorny issue between the two rival parties. In the quest for justice, demands and protests will naturally be made; a confrontation ensues and sometimes this even leads to violence. Frequently such action proves to be counter-productive.

The case of adjustment is completely different. In this case there is no rival, no other party. You are the only player. When you opt for adjustment, you instantly find the starting point; and if justice in practice leads to confrontation, adjustment always leads to peace.

There is a well-known saying: Politics is the art of the possible. This saying pertains not only to political affairs, but also to all the affairs of human life. This being so, the best way to proceed in all aspects of human existence is to adopt a realistic approach. You have to differentiate between which target is possible and which is not; between what is achievable and what is not.

All men and women have to strike a balance between their own desires and the external situation. Simply by running after one's own desires, one does not necessarily achieve one's goals. One must fully comprehend the external situation, the external circumstances and the external opportunities. One can achieve one's personal target only by taking into consideration what lies beyond oneself. That is the only realistic approach and is therefore the wisest approach

Adjustment–The Golden Rule

The only realistic option for you is to adjust with other people. Here, adjustment means refraining from reacting, not trying to change others, not becoming negative, and not imagining issues to be insurmountable, but rather managing the situation with aplomb.

Adjustment is a way of life. What is adjustment? To all intents and purposes, adjustment is a form of accommodating or palliative behaviour that you adopt – ostensibly towards someone else, while it is actually for your own benefit and your own peace of mind. Once equable adjustments have been made in undesirable situations, one may live in a state of mental equilibrium.

The problem is that, in accordance with the creation plan of God, our world is a world of differences. Every human being is either Mr. Different or Ms. Different. Moreover, all human beings have the freedom of choice to behave in whichever way they want. This being so, everyone must live perforce in a jungle of differences. And it has to be conceded that the creation plan is immutable. Then, what to do in such circumstances?

The only realistic option for you is to adjust with other people. Here, adjustment means refraining from reacting, not trying to change others, not becoming negative, and not imagining issues to be insurmountable, but rather managing the situation with aplomb.

In every situation you have two options: either to adjust with others or remain at loggerheads with them. If you decide not to make any adjustments, that will only aggravate your problems. You will go on living in a state of tension, feel mentally disturbed and will waste your time and energy. But, if you opt for adjustment, you will be able instantly to relax mentally and will be able to save yourself from all kinds of negativity.

Adjustment gives you a chance to proceed with your own affairs. While the policy of being unaccommodating is bound to interfere with the smooth running of your life, either temporarily or permanently.

Adjustment does not mean adopting a submissive attitude. It rather shows wisdom. It is the same principle which everyone follows when they are on the street. On the street, there is traffic moving in opposite directions. So, everyone opts for the keep-right or keep-left policy, in accordance with the traffic rules of their country. This is a way of adjustment on the roads. If you refuse to follow these traffic rules, you are certain to face a disastrous situation, perhaps even death. Adjustment is based on a natural formula: 'Save yourself'. When you are not in the position to change others, change yourself. It is this behaviour that is called adjustment.

According to the law of nature, settlement is the best way of life. When you face any kind of difference with another, rather than get into a confrontational situation, go for adjustment. This is best for you in terms of the result. By adopting this formula, you will reach your goal without any delay. Be practical and do not waste your time and energy. Tread the path of adjustment, and ensure your success.

Planning based on Remnant

The best formula in life is not to concern oneself with what has been lost, but by wise planning, to avail of what is still extant. Sooner or later, you will emerge as a super-achiever.

The German statesman Otto von Bismarck (1815 – 1898) once rightly observed that politics is the art of the possible. This aphorism can be usefully extended to include planning. Planning should be done on the basis of whatever is available to you. This means to plan on the basis of what remains. Such planning can be termed as 'planning based on remnant'.

In chalking out a course of action, people are generally obsessed with the concept of totality. They want to have things in totality and are reluctant to accept the fulfilment of their goals in any partial way. But thinking along these lines goes against the law of nature. The realistic formula in this regard is that if the total is not achievable, one should be content with achieving just a part.

There are nations in many parts of the world which

were eager to achieve things in totality, but failed in their ambition – even after a struggle lasting a hundred years. The following Hindi maxim applies to their case: *Aadhi chhod ke sajji dhave, aadhi rahe na sajji pave* (One who runs after the whole, leaving behind the part, loses both the part and the whole). This is why, although these nations launched their initiatives with great enthusiasm, they ended up as failed states. They could neither achieve what they had set out to do, nor were they able to retain what they already possessed.

A contrary example is that of the respective achievements of Japan and Germany. After the Second World War, both nations lost areas of land they had possessed before the onset of the war. Germany lost to the Soviet Union the eastern part of its country, the total area of which, including part of Berlin, was 108,333 km². A similar case is that of Japan, which surrendered the Okinawa Islands, with an area of 1,206 km², to the United States.

However, both countries made plans for their future economic development by first setting aside what they had lost. The result was miraculous: Germany, led by its first post-war Chancellor, Konrad Adenauer, emerged as the industrial leader of Europe. Similarly, Japan, under the wise leadership of Emperor Hirohito, rose to be the economic superpower of Asia.

This is the miracle of planning based on remnant or planning based on the remaining part of a whole, unlike planning which entails the pursuit of an erstwhile whole. The best formula in life is not to concern oneself with what has been lost, but by wise planning, to avail of what is still extant. Sooner or later, you will emerge as a super-achiever. This holds true for both nations and individuals.

Another good example of the above principle is to be found in the history of Singapore. Previously part of Malaysia, Singapore was expelled from the Federation of Malaysia in 1965 and became an independent state. Under the leadership of its former Prime Minister Lee Kuan Yew, Singapore likewise adopted the policy of planning based on remnant. Although Malaysia is more than 400 times greater than Singapore in area, today, in development, the latter is far ahead of it.

All individuals and nations have certain ambitions which they seek to fulfil. Wise planning for the fulfilment of a goal requires adjustment between two things: personal ambition and available resources. The secret of truly successful planning lies in the correct weighing up of one's personal ambitions vis-à-vis the available resources. No one can change the course taken by the external world. No one is the master of nature. We have only one option: to find a way of making a realistic adjustment between our ambitions and the resources available in the real world.

The Age of Competition

Human life always has its ups and downs, but none if this can totally obstruct a person's life journey. In all such situations, the law of nature will prevail.

In times gone by, favouritism was the order of the day. But, in the present day, competition is the decisive factor in how life progresses. This shift in has been basically due to the advent of democracy. That is because the culture of democracy is based on merit rather than on favouritism. If you prove to be competent to do your job, you will be rewarded, otherwise not. The concept of vested interests being the sole telling factor was eliminated, in theory, after the establishment of democracy.

The present-day culture of competition has given rise to a new social principle with maxims such as 'Compete or Perish' and 'Merit-based Progress'. In this highly competitive scenario, some people have emphasized that the idea that a competition based system has produced two different classes – a privileged class and a deprived class. While the privileged class are bound to achieve success, the deprived class will be doomed to lead a life of penury. Activists in this field constantly try to improve the condition of those unfortunate enough to be unable to compete. But such action has ultimately proved to be negative in terms of its results, for their particular conception of this dichotomy as being unjust was wrong.

According to the law of nature, if an individual finds himself in a deprived state, it is not a full stop for him; invariably, there are commas all along his future path. And his very sense of deprivation gives him the incentive to improve his lot in life. One who is said to have 'perished' does not in reality perish; instead he stands up with a new motivation to establish himself so thoroughly in his chosen sphere that no one will have grounds to belittle or dismiss him. A class made up of such incentivized individuals will ultimately come into being, leaving their state of deprivation far behind them. It is they then who will prevail in society.

There are many historical examples of how motivational factors account for personal progress. For instance, the American business magnate and investor, Bill Gates, said while sharing his experiences, "I failed in some subjects in an exam, but my friend passed in all of them. Now he is an engineer in the organization and I am the owner of that organization." In this statement, an important fact was left undisclosed. This was that when Bill Gates saw that he had lagged behind in the competition, he felt strongly motivated – according to human nature – to prepare himself better than before. And then he forged ahead.

People generally take things at their face value and remain ignorant of how nature is at work in the background. For example, if you have a tree in your garden and you cut off one of its branches, you will very soon find that a new branch has grown back at the same spot. This is the law of nature, which is applicable to human life also, with this addition – one can take away your first chance but no one has the power to stop you from taking a second chance. Therefore, the formula of compete or perish is not the be-all and end-all of existence. It is simply an ultimatum meant to spur people on to outdo others so that they may succeed in life. If a person has failed in the first instance, he does not necessarily perish, for everyone has the potential to avail of second chances and regain what was lost in the first instance.

Human life always has its ups and downs, but none if this can totally obstruct a person's life journey. In all such situations, the law of nature will prevail.

Now or Never

You should think that every day is the last day for you, so you have to decide what to do in the very first instant, otherwise you will not be able to do anything.

I once happened to meet a youth who was intelligent and well educated but who, for some reason, had fallen into the bad habits of smoking and drinking. I advised him to give up these habits. I said: "These habits are ruining your health, and are also slowing your intellectual development. From all points of view, this is a disaster." I advised him to treat getting rid of these habits as an emergency. After a pause, he replied: "I'll do it." I said: "No, you should say, 'I have done it.'"

In life the principle that works is 'now or never'. We don't have any time to lose. Saying 'I will do it' is a kind of luxury that we cannot afford. We have not only to take quick decisions, but we must also act upon them at once. You should think that every day is the last day for you, so you have to decide what to do in the very first instant, otherwise you will not be able to do anything. Time is running out fast. Remember the old saying, 'Time and tide wait for no man.'

I pointed out to the young man that the mind, with its various windows, has enormous capacity. These windows normally open up only in emergencies when a man has to take an urgent decision. For example, if you are suddenly faced with a cobra, you will retreat with great speed. The reason is that the fear of the cobra activates your mind and the result is that some of the windows of your mind, which had remained closed, are immediately thrown open.

Every human mind has this potential, but generally people utilize this capacity of the mind only in moments of extremity. But, a wise man is one who heeds the maxim, 'There is no time like the present' and opens up the windows of his mind even in normal circumstances in order to utilize the full capacity of his brain for positive planning. Human beings and animals are both activated by fear. But what differentiates a human being from an animal is that he has the ability to draw upon his latent potential without having to be activated by fear.

Demonstration versus Result

There are two ways of doing things: one is demonstration-oriented and the other is result-oriented. A task that has a demonstrative impact very soon becomes popular. It creates news, gathers crowds and enjoys great public acclaim.

However, this kind of activity is lacking in substance. It may generate news, but it ultimately yields no positive result. People who work along these lines always perform their tasks in a high-profile manner. And while they do gain something in terms of personal interest, they fail to offer anything constructive to the society of which they are a part.

The second way of working is by engaging oneself in an activity that has no demonstrative side to it. Those who do so necessarily work by keeping a low profile and, of course, seldom acquire fame. Their work may go unnoticed by people at large and may be left unreported in history. But, these are the people who are the best of mankind. They give to others without taking anything for themselves and, in so doing, they establish valuable traditions that benefit the coming generations.

The demonstrative method of work, by proceeding on a short-term basis, aims at instant profit. According to the law of nature, any work that aims at earning immediate gain cannot possibly yield anything fruitful. On the contrary, since the result-oriented method is concerned with producing results, those who make this their target, plan out their work on a long-term basis. In this world, it is solely by working in this way that concrete results can be produced.

The Unintended Consequences of One's Actions

It is a wise man who takes into consideration all the relevant factors before drawing up his plan of action and then takes an objectively well-thought out step.

US President Barack Obama blamed former President George W. Bush for the rapid rise of Islamic State terrorists. He said in an interview with VICE News (March 17, 2015) that the emergence of this terrorist group was a consequence of the war launched by Bush in Iraq. "ISIL is a direct outgrowth of Al Qaeda in Iraq that grew out of our invasion, which is an example of unintended consequences, which is why we should generally aim before we shoot."

During the tenure of former President Bush, America attacked Iraq with great military might on March 19, 2003. One and a half years before the attack, when there was news that the US might invade Iraq, I gave prior warning in an interview to The Times of India, (September 16, 2001) that the U.S. aggression would be counter-productive. And later events were to bear out my prediction.

There are few human beings, whether belonging to the political field or not, who have not taken such steps as have been counterproductive in their outcome. That is, the action taken lead to a negative result, which had not been anticipated. This is true not only of the United States, but is perhaps the story of many countries and individuals in positions of power throughout history.

One of the greatest human weaknesses is the tendency for people to overestimate their own capacities. Because of this, they take such steps as are unlikely to lead to the fulfilment of their expectations. It is a matter of record that human history is regularly punctuated by stories of defeat or Pyrrhic victories. Perhaps, there has never been any victory which could be called an out and out victory.

The fact is that of the different kinds of socio-political and religious factors that are of significance in this world, there are some which work in our favour and others which do not. There is the frequent recurrence of the phenomenon of 'unintended consequences' or 'undesirable results' because people are intent on fulfilling their ambitions, without taking into account the external factors which may go against their plans.

It is a wise man who takes into consideration all the relevant factors before drawing up his plan of action and then takes an objectively well-thought out step. If the individual fails to proceed in this way, he shall have to bear with unintended and unanticipated consequences. This principle holds true for both superpowers and countries of a lesser world stature.

Misadventure Never Pays

Confidence is good, but overconfidence is quite the reverse. Being adventurous may be good, but risk-taking can be disastrous.

On December 24, 2014, due to dense fog on the Agra-Noida route, a speeding truck on the Yamuna Expressway hit a car from behind. Several other vehicles coming from behind rammed into each other, creating a massive pile-up. In this accident, two people died and 23 were injured. Deputy Superintendent of Police Arvind Kumar said: "What appears to have led to the accident was a combination of over-speeding and near zero visibility due to fog."

But it was not a combination of two factors. It was rather the outcome of a single factor – overconfidence. When there was fog, the drivers should have taken the precaution of not speeding up their vehicles. But, because they were overconfident, they took the unnecessary risk of over-speeding. The result was quite expected, that is, their journey ended in a serious accident, described by the traffic police as a 'mega crash'.

Confidence is good, but overconfidence is quite the reverse. Being adventurous may be good, but risk-taking can be disastrous. This is the important lesson to be learnt from this incident.

Be of Use to Yourself and Others while Still in Your Prime

Everyone must realize that he or she is subject to the law of nature. People can build their future only by following the law of nature. If we deny this law, we shall have no place in this world.

According to biological studies, every human being has four phases in his or her life. Everyone, without exception, is subject to this law of nature. The first is that of childhood, lasting from birth to about ten years of age. During this period, one's basic personality is developed. The second is the phase of adolescence. This is from ten to twenty-five years of age. During this time, a person attains maturity, both at the physical and mental levels. The third is the period of maximum strength, that is, from twenty-five to thirty-five years of age. Old age is the last phase, that of biological degeneration. The process of ageing begins after thirty-five years of age, and continues throughout the rest of one's life.

According to this biological definition, everyone has ten really good years in his life. During this period, the individual enjoys full strength and energy – the greatest natural gifts for every human being – and right throughout his life reaps the benefits of the physical and intellectual powers that he develops for himself. This is the age during which one can accomplish great things.

Everyone must realize that he or she is subject to the law of nature. People can build their future only by following the law of nature. If we deny this law, we shall have no place in this world.

It is the first duty of every individual to acknowledge this fact and understand that winning in this matter is winning forever, and losing in this matter is losing forever.

Self-Confidence

Self-confidence is a sign that you are still alive, and lack of it is a sign of death. But self-confidence has a minus-point, which can sometimes completely destroy someone. This negative-point is what is called over-confidence.

Self-confidence is an important attribute. You need to trust yourself. You need to have the necessary determination to do the task you have set for yourself. You need to have the confidence to plan your course of action, without hesitation and keeping in mind the available opportunities. You need to be able to discover what opportunities exist and act accordingly. All these are related to self-confidence. You need self-confidence to be successful in any and every sphere of life.

Self-confidence is a sign that you are still alive, and lack of it is a sign of death. But self-confidence has a minus-point, which can sometimes completely destroy someone. This negative-point is what is called over-confidence.

If a little stream runs past your house and you leap across it to the other side, it shows that you have self-confidence. But if instead of a stream, it is a wide river and you want to jump across it and reach the other shore, you won't be successful, of course. You will fall into the river and be drowned.

In this world, all of us exist between two dimensions—our selves, on the one hand, and external conditions, on the other. In other words, for any effort to succeed, your role is 50%. The remaining 50% depends on the external conditions.

In this regard, then, what you need to do is that before you take any practical step you should consider both aspects. If you only look at what you want or like and ignore the external conditions, your plan is bound to fail. And then you will start complaining about others, even though you yourself, and not somebody else, are the cause of your failure.

A Dangerous Attribute

If you fail to immediately correct a wrong way of behaving, it is very possible that you will develop a taste for this behaviour.

Very often it happens that something people try out turns, if they don't control it, into a habit. If the habit is not stopped, it turns into an addiction. And an addiction very often becomes so deeply engrained that people reach the point of no return, when it becomes practically impossible to cure them of it. This is the case with every bad habit and addiction.

Given how quickly habits can turn into seemingly incurable addictions, it is very necessary to repent for mistakes as soon as we might make them. At that very moment, you should introspect, acknowledge your mistake and change your way of behaving. You should not postpone it to tomorrow to make amends for your mistakes. You must make amends not just today, but immediately, right away.

If you fail to immediately correct a wrong way of behaving, it is very possible that you will develop a taste for this behaviour. And then, it may become a habit and later even an incurable addiction

Dates on a Calendar

Every new day that dawns brings with it many opportunities. These opportunities do not loudly announce themselves. Rather, they speak very silently. It is for us to recognize them and to use them in a properly-planned manner.

Someone has rightly said, 'A day you have lived fully was your day. All other days are simply dates on your calendar.'

There are two ways of leading your life. One is to simply pass your time, and the other is to avail of your time. If you live just to pass time, you are simply wasting your life. But if you spend your days meaningfully, you are truly living. You are making proper use of this amazing blessing that is called life.

Every new day that dawns brings with it many opportunities. These opportunities do not loudly announce themselves. Rather, they speak very silently. It is for us to recognize them and to use them in a properly-planned manner.

You need to be able to skilfully discern the opportunities that come your way every new day. You need to able to recognize which opportunities are truly for you and which are not. You should be able to appreciate how the opportunities that are indeed for you can be availed of in a peaceful way.

You need to be able to know the best and most realistic way of employing these opportunities, and also the limits within which you must remain while doing so. Furthermore, you should be aware that in using them you do not transgress into someone else's territory.

There is another very important thing you need to remember while setting about using the many opportunities that come your way every day. And that is that you are not alone in this world. Just as you want to go ahead with making your life, there are vast numbers of other people who are impelled with the very same purpose. If you want to succeed in your life, it is very important for you not to come into conflict with others. You need to be able to navigate your life without clashing with them.

Just as you have some interests, others, too, have their own interests. A successful person carefully avoids clashing with other people's interests and sails ahead to attain the purpose of her or his life.

The Last Word

Spirituality is not a mysterious term. It is only another name for positive thinking. Positive thinking means living in positivity in spite of all kinds of negative experiences. This is the key to spirituality. Any man or woman who wants to live as a spiritual person must adopt this formula, that is, the art of conversion: converting negativity into positivity. Spirituality is not a natural gift: it is an acquired attribute.

Spirituality makes you tension-free and gives you a peaceful mind on a permanent basis. Spirituality in itself is a non-material quality, yet it is the basis of all kind of success, including material success. If you want to live as a successful person and die as a successful person, then you have to learn the art of spiritual living. Spirituality makes a man a superman and a woman a superwoman. Spirituality enables you to unfold the hidden treasures of your nature. Spirituality is the secret of super-achievement in this world.